Prospects for Socialism in America

Jack Barnes, Mary-Alice Waters,
Tony Thomas, Barry Sheppard,
and Betsey Stone

Edited with an introduction by
Jack Barnes and Mary-Alice Waters

PATHFINDER PRESS, INC.   NEW YORK

PATHFINDER PRESS, Inc.
410 West Street, New York, N.Y. 10014

Contents

Introduction

The political structure and life of the United States, as described by the schools, the press, and the elected politicians, has several prominent traits that are treated as virtually unchangeable. The political "mainstream" is composed of the Republican and Democratic two-party system. For good or ill, competent or incompetent, honest or corrupt, the best hope for representative government is said to reside somewhere in the political spectrum that exists inside the two dominant parties— the Republicans supposedly representing "big business" and "small farmers"; the Democrats, "small business" and "big labor." Outside of the mainstream there is only the fringe, advocating simplistic, utopian, or even dangerous panaceas that will never seriously influence the majority of the American people.

This political cliché endures because of a single undeniable fact: the century-long monopoly of political power by the Republican and Democratic parties. For the rest, the platitudes that the government is only a reflection of the governed and has the same interests and outlook are a smug rationalization by those who now hold power for upholding the interests of private property.

Though the real lines of cleavage in American society are not revealed in elections, they run sharp and deep. The divisions between worker and employer; poor and rich; Blacks, Chicanos, other minorities and the racists; women and their detractors, cut across the superficial distinction between Democrat and Republican. These oppositions are a surer gauge of where American capitalism is headed, and what options are realistic and which unrealistic. On this more profound level of relations between the classes, races, nationalities, and sexes, the "mainstream" bipartisan policies of the ruling elite can more and more clearly be seen to represent not a consensus of the majority of the governed, but the privileged interests of a rich and powerful—but tiny—capitalist minority.

At the polls the Republicans and Democrats continue to divide up most of the votes from a disgusted and declining percentage of the electorate. But these are mainly votes of habit, not of confidence and conviction. They are cast under the impact of press and broadcast media monopolized by defenders of the status quo that deny equal coverage to or even basic information about the socialist alternative.

A Harris poll released in March 1976 showed that 63 percent of those questioned felt that "most people with power try to take advantage of people such as myself." This is almost double the 33 percent who agreed with this statement in 1971. Some 77 percent felt that "the rich get richer and the poor get poorer," when only 45 percent thought this was true in a 1966 poll. And 61 percent believed that "the people running the country don't really care what happens to me." This is well over twice the 26 percent who felt this way ten years ago.

The March 25, 1976, *Los Angeles Times* offered this gloomy—for them—comment on the findings:

"Up to now, the main source of disaffection has been the existing leadership of major public and private institutions rather than the system under which Americans live. How high this level of disenchantment can go before faith in the system crumbles is a question that should be of the deepest concern to those at the power centers of this society."

This deepening crisis of confidence among growing numbers of working people in the justice or even competence of the present social order is an essentially new feature of twentieth-century American politics. A no less important development is the drive by the capitalist class and its political parties and institutions to shift the burdens of an economy in decline more and more onto the shoulders of the workers—with the unorganized, the poor, the Black, the female, the unemployed, and the old getting hit the hardest. This drive went into high gear with the government's publicly announced goal of "zapping labor" during the Nixon-Connally wage freeze of 1971. It accelerated during the 1974-75 depression. Its aim is to force down real wages and cut back social services in order to improve the profitability and competitiveness of U.S. corporations in a period of worldwide capitalist stagnation, recession, and sharpening rivalries. Its first effects have begun to provoke angry responses from those most affected—more bitter strikes, demonstrations, and protests—and this is only the harbinger of things to come.

We are entering a period fundamentally different from the conservative and stable 1950s and early 1960s, which reflected the long post-World War II economic boom that has now come to an end. Unable to count on the expanding markets and steady growth of the past, the corporate rich are stepping up an offensive against the labor movement and the oppressed national minorities to redivide the national income for their own benefit. But they are compelled to wage this offensive under conditions of growing distrust in their representatives and deepening disbelief in the good will or impartiality of their government. This is strikingly illustrated in small incidents that have become almost commonplace today but would have been unthinkable a decade ago.

In March 1976, William Colby, who had just been relieved as director of the Central Intelligence Agency, began a national speaking tour in defense of the CIA. At Cornell University and at Southern Illinois University, he was compelled to debate Syd Stapleton, national secretary of the Political Rights Defense Fund and a leader of the Socialist Workers Party. There was more than a little irony in the confrontation. The former head of the powerful CIA had to debate as an equal the representative of a revolutionary socialist party that the CIA had spied on and tried for decades to destroy!

Colby, speaking for what he called "the mainstream," was greatly upset about the flood of information about the secret machinations of his agency falling into the hands of the people in whose interests the CIA claims to act. The government has proceeded throughout its history as though it had the unquestioned *right* to shroud in secrecy all of its "intelligence" and policy-making actions. "We're in the process," Colby said at Cornell on March 8, "of working out a new definition of what has to be kept secret and what has to be made public in this free society of ours." And he was jeered by the audience. Stapleton was applauded when he replied:

"It's becoming clearer and clearer that the American government is not a protector of democracy, but an *enemy* of democracy; not a defender of the rights listed in the U.S. Constitution, but an *opponent* of those rights; not a force against violence, terrorism, and assassination, but a *source* of violence on an international scale."

Such radical rejection of the status quo is not limited to the campuses or centered there. In the course of the depression of 1974-75, with its rampant inflation and unemployment, mammoth cutbacks and layoffs, shortages and breakdowns, a qualitative turning point was reached in the consciousness of masses of people. Discontent today is focused on the desegregation battles in Boston and Detroit, among the city workers being stripped of their jobs and pensions in New York and a score of other cities, among working mothers in San Francisco and elsewhere fighting for child-care centers, among the Chicano farm workers of California, and in the steel and auto plants of the Midwest.

This book has its origins in discussions in the leadership and among the members of the Socialist Workers Party over 1975. Once the character of the ruling class offensive was analyzed and the evidence assembled to gauge the scope of discontent, these discussions sought to grapple with this central problem. How could the situation be turned around so that the working class and its allies could effectively fight back? Around what demands and what organizational forms could the burgeoning potential for mass action be realized? Through what steps could working people be mobilized, overcome the divisions in their ranks, and compel the government and the employers to retreat? How can the defensive actions undertaken today go over to the offensive tomorrow? And ultimately, how can the oppressed achieve the only long-term guarantee of their political and economic rights— the creation of a workers' government in the United States— before its present capitalist regime leads us further in a descent toward human degradation, ecological destruction, or nuclear conflagration?

The results of these discussions are a series of proposals that the authors and the Socialist Workers Party wish to advance for consideration and further discussion by all those who have a stake in the fight for political democracy, economic rights, and socialism.

Several basic themes run throughout this book. One of the most important was first suggested by the exiled Russian revolutionist Leon Trotsky in discussions on the American situation with leaders of the SWP in 1938. He said that the American working class would never be able to shake off its conservatism and contend with the capitalist rulers for power until it had learned to "think socially and act politically." American capitalism has skillfully fostered divisions within the working class and between workers and their natural allies along national, racial, and sex lines. These cannot be overcome so long as the principal organizations of the working class, the trade unions, view their role as limited strictly to the issues of job conditions and wages of the members of their unions. It is necessary to think *socially*.

This means seeing that no individual solutions, advancements, or escapes are possible for the great majority of working people. Only by thinking socially, by looking beyond the level of one's own job prospects or the issues facing a single union, by supporting and defending the rights of Blacks, Chicanos, Puerto Ricans, and women outside the unions as well as inside, can a bond of mutual respect and trust be forged that can bring together all the oppressed and exploited in the fight against capitalist misrule. This goes beyond trade union consciousness and is the essence of real class consciousness. That is not only being *against* domination by the employing rich, but being *for* and identifying with the interests of the oppressed and exploited in their totality.

At the same time working people can never win lasting gains so long as they abstain from politics in their own name. It is in the political arena that laws are passed and enforced, that the selection of administrators takes place, that classes build and test their organized strength. Today the United States remains the only highly industrialized country in the world so politically backward that the great majority of the workers have no mass political party that even pretends to represent them. They vote for the hand-picked agents of the rich and the superrich who control the Republican and Democratic parties. To think politically means to construct a mass workers' party in opposition to the existing capitalist two-party system. It is foolish to strike against the bosses in the factories and offices one day, and demonstrate against their antiminority and antiwoman actions the next, and then turn around and vote their political representatives into office.

Beyond this central theme—think socially and act politically—there are others that try to define the context determining the aims and possibilities of the contending forces. First, the economic crisis of American capitalism, which underlies its anti-working-class offensive, is rooted in a deteriorating international situation for world capitalism. Its sources can be found in the exhaustion of the motor forces of the long postwar boom, and in the revival of German and Japanese market rivalry with the U.S., the accumulated inflationary pressures of the gigantic war budget which have eroded the position of the dollar as the world trading currency, and the rise of the colonial revolution which has soured prospects for investment and stable imperialist profits in Asia, Africa, and Latin America. The world crisis, beginning with the oil shocks of late 1973, has in turn devastated the economies of the semicolonial countries. Billions of people, from India to Chile, from Zaïre to South Korea, face the most terrible prospects in their history.

In answer to this challenge, Washington has nothing to offer but the threat of military force and the advice to keep the "communists" out of government. But the problems of the world's people are not military problems. They are social and economic: poverty, exploitation, lack of industry, lack of jobs, lack of control over their lives. All Washington has to offer is the installation and support of right-wing military dictatorships, from Argentina and Brazil to the Philippines and Iran.

A second feature of the world crisis of capitalism is the way it is hammering the imperialist metropolises as well as the semicolonial countries. The specter of socialist revolution haunts Portugal and Spain and is in the offing for Italy, France, and Britain. In part, this rise of revolutionary ferment in Europe has been caused by the United States itself through its trade and tariff pressures and competitive devaluations of the dollar from 1971 onwards. In seeking to export the crisis, American capitalism has helped to deeply shake the stability of its capitalist allies. Washington has no effective foreign policy that can shore up the fortunes of capitalism as a world system. It only lashes out to crush opposition, to make somebody else pay.

The third aspect of the crisis of American capitalism is the spread of unrest and radicalization to the United States. This is shattering a long-standing ideological prop of this country's rulers: the claim that class conflict is a feature of the Old World, while the New World, at least the upper portion of the Northern hemisphere, has escaped such problems through its egalitarian and democratic origins and institutions. The great lesson of today is that the United States is not immune to the class struggle.

Its ruling class is driving ahead to diminish the expectations of working people, to push back women, Blacks, Chicanos, and Puerto Ricans from the few gains they have made, to restrict democratic rights accepted by long tradition, to gain acceptance for long-term unemployment at drastically higher levels than in the past, to bring into question the right of unions to protect the workers who belong to them, to ravage the environment, and to sharply curtail or eliminate a whole range of even minimal social services such as health care, child care, welfare, decent public transport, training programs, expenditures on public education, and assured retirement, that had come to be looked on as rights of citizenship. And it tries to put over all this as "necessary belt tightening" while maintaining as untouchable the $100-billion-plus war budget!

One of the most insidious sides of the ruling class offensive is the use of the capitalist monopoly over hiring and firing and the allocation of city, state, and federal funds to foster racism and sexism in an effort to deepen divisions among working people and their allies. Employed workers are incited against "welfare cheats," the privately employed against "boondoggling" municipal workers, taxpayers against the recipients of social services, the unemployed and nationally oppressed against better-paid skilled workers.

On the political level, while there is still no mass labor party or Black or Chicano party that can directly take on the Republicans and Democrats, the ruling class faces the deepest loss of public confidence in modern history. The Harris poll cited earlier found that 68 percent of those questioned feel that "the people in Washington, D.C., are out of touch with the rest of the country." This sharply limits the options of the dominant parties. No candidate of the ruling parties today inspires confidence or enthusiasm or even belief.

Growing numbers of Americans are convinced that the government lies to them, that it keeps its doings secret because it is a corrupt agency of the corporate rich. A major issue in the fight to mobilize opposition to the system is now, and will be more in the future, the right to *know*. Working people want to know how much money there really is in the corporate treasuries and in the city, state, and federal budgets. They want to know what plans are being made behind their backs for new aggressions that can lead to further Vietnams. They want to know what the multitudes of bloated police agencies, from the FBI to the CIA, are doing with their secret snooping into the private lives of American citizens and their efforts to disrupt and destroy political opponents. They will not accept Colby's "new definition of what has to be kept secret."

The Socialist Workers Party has sought to survey these interrelated elements of the unfolding crisis and project a strategy that can protect and enlarge the gains made by workers, the oppressed national minorities, and women during the 1960s, a strategy that can keep the unions from being taken on one at a time by the employers and broken up. This means approaching the layoffs, cutbacks, inflation, the antibusing mobs in Boston, as part of a single problem that requires a united response by the people who create the wealth of this country.

One of the central aims of such a strategy must be to transform as many of the unions as possible into a revitalized, popular labor movement that sees struggle against, not collaboration with, the boss as its guideline, and that sees the movements of other sectors of the oppressed and exploited as allies. This calls for unconditional support to the rights of the most oppressed. That is what the hundreds of political candidates of the SWP have been saying, and it is the fear of widespread acceptance of this program that motivates the persistent and massive efforts by the FBI and other government agencies to harass, bug, and burglarize the SWP.

The party has challenged this illegal use of police power head-on by filing a $27 million damage suit against the federal government. The suit, sponsored by the Political Rights Defense Fund, has led to the disclosure of thousands of pages of previously secret FBI documents that show a decades-long campaign of wiretaps, efforts to have SWP members fired from their jobs or evicted from their apartments, and the fabrication of false charges to try to split the civil rights and antiwar movements, in which the SWP has played an active part.

The FBI and the policy makers who stand behind it in the White House, on Capitol Hill, and in the corporate boardrooms imagined that they could get away with their police-state tactics because they see history through the eyes of the ruling class. For them the working people are a despised and manipulated substratum of society, beneath the level of consciousness. The vocal and organized representatives of the working class are seen—or more accurately, they are portrayed—as "outside agitators" and dangerous fanatics; to silence them any means is justified. This includes the outright assassination of any representative of the oppressed who wins a mass following, such as Malcolm X and Martin Luther King.

Up to now our history has largely been written as seen through the eyes of the rich and white. People are more and more beginning to look at where we have come from through the eyes of working people, of Blacks, Chicanos, and Puerto Ricans, of women. This tells a very different story. Many of the heroes of today's schoolbooks will be tomorrow's villains, just as the U.S.

cavalry in the Westerns looks different after Vietnam and after the rise of the American Indian Movement.

The government's justification for its conspiracy of violence and lies against unions, Blacks, and socialists is that their demands are making the country ungovernable. Why should this be? Capitalism cannot grant the most elementary rights and needs of the great majority of the working population. All it can do is try to shut them up and push them down. The country *is* ungovernable under capitalism—except, in the long run, as a police state. This is the most compelling proof that the rulers of today have no right to govern; their interests are unreconcilable with those of the mass of the American people.

*   *   *

The Socialist Workers Party is totally unlike the Democrats and Republicans. Its members are mainly working people, and it is controlled by its members, not by outside monied interests. Its highest body is the convention of rank-and-file delegates held every two years or less—not caucuses of lawyers, ad men, and financiers. The convention elects the party leadership, but even more important, it first arrives at definite policies through democratic discussion which are then adopted by majority vote of the delegates and which the leadership is bound to carry out.

This principled and democratic proletarian form of organization conforms to a worthy tradition in the international working-class movement, despite the corruption of these methods by the Social Democratic parliamentarians and by Stalinism in the Soviet Union. The Socialist Workers Party was founded in 1938 by the American supporters of Leon Trotsky and the wing of the international communist movement that he represented, which fought to preserve and extend the internationalist, revolutionary, and democratic essence of Marxism against the Stalin dictatorship.

The SWP was then and remains now a component part of the world working class party founded by Trotsky, the Fourth International, although because of reactionary legislation in this country it is not permitted to hold formal membership in international organizations.

The main document in this book, "Prospects for Socialist in America," was drafted by the SWP leadership in May 1975 to help focus the attention of the party membership on the changes taking place in American politics around the new radicalization of the working class. It was first submitted to a meeting of the party's National Committee, where it was discussed and many suggestions were made by activists in different areas of the mass movement for improvements based on their own experiences. From there it went to the members for discussion over a three-month period, leading up to a party convention in August 1975 where further suggestions were made before it was adopted by the delegates.

This main political resolution takes up in part the relationship between the movements of the oppressed nationalities and the labor movement. Since it was felt that this key question required more concrete and extended treatment, a second resolution, "The Fight for Black Liberation: The Current Stage and Its Tasks," was also adopted by the convention. The other articles in this book are reports to the National Committee and to the convention on these resolutions, which examine in richer detail the complexities of the period we are now entering. Two of the articles, those by Barry Sheppard and by Betsey Stone, were reports to the membership on what socialists, and particularly the SWP itself, could do in the coming months to help strengthen resistance to the bosses' rollback and union-busting efforts, racist campaigns, and attacks on women's rights.

These resolutions and reports are not the whole of the SWP's current program and outlook. In preparation for the party's next convention, scheduled for the late summer of 1976, Catarino Garza has presented to the members a resolution of the National Committee on the struggles of Puerto Ricans in the United States, and Olga Rodríguez has presented a separate National Committee resolution on the Chicano movement. These will be published in the fall of 1976 after the members have had their opportunity to read, discuss, and amend them.

On an ongoing basis, the SWP's views of current developments can be found in the socialist newsweekly, the *Militant*. This was the newspaper that first broke the story of the FBI Counterintelligence Program (COINTELPRO), the disruption campaign aimed at the left as a whole and especially at the SWP. Also of interest to readers of this book is the weekly world newsmagazine *Intercontinental Press,* which reflects the views of the Fourth International.

Many of the ideas expressed here have been developed over time by the SWP and by the world Marxist movement. "Prospects for Socialism in America" owes much to a previous document, "The World Political Situation and the Immediate Tasks of the Fourth International," which was adopted by the SWP in January 1974. It can be found in the book *Dynamics of World Revolution Today* (New York: Pathfinder Press, 1974).

The thinking of the SWP on women's liberation is summed up in its 1971 resolution "Towards a Mass Feminist Movement," which is reprinted in the book *Feminism and Socialism* (Pathfinder, 1972).

Two other books under the Pathfinder Press imprint contain recent documents of the SWP and articles by some of its spokespeople on the new rise of feminism, the general student radicalization of the 1960s, and the prospects at the beginning of the economic downturn for building a mass socialist movement. These are *Towards an American Socialist Revolution* (1971) and *A Revolutionary Strategy for the 70s* (1972).

Also of great value in the work ahead to transform the unions into instruments of revolutionary struggle is the four-volume work by Farrell Dobbs, former SWP national secretary, on the Minneapolis Teamsters movement of the 1930s, when that union was under revolutionary leadership and fought for the interests of the oppressed. These are published by Monad Press under the titles *Teamster Rebellion, Teamster Power,* and *Teamster Politics.* A fourth volume, *Teamster Bureaucracy,* is scheduled for publication in 1977.

*   *   *

When the reports in this book were made, the SWP was on the threshold of a major turn in the focus and character of its work. Among other tasks, Barry Sheppard and Betsey Stone discuss the need to establish more and smaller branches in new neighborhoods and new cities to more deeply involve the party in the communities and the struggles of the oppressed and exploited. Much of this has been accomplished in recent months. Today SWP branches are located in most of the cities that were mentioned in the reports as still lacking the beginnings of a socialist organization.

The SWP's approach to its own growth is far different from that of the capitalist parties. The Republicans and Democrats who solicit the votes of the people on election day would like them to shut up and keep quiet the other 364 days of the year. The

SWP, on the contrary, places the highest value on the daily involvement of every individual in its ranks and believes that the contribution of each member to the fight makes a difference. Part of the fight for a socialist society and part of the guarantee that it will genuinely place power in the hands of working people is to involve all members of the workers' and socialist movement in making the decisions they are carrying out, in drawing on their creativity, and learning from one another.

If, when you finish the book, you find you agree with the goals it outlines and are convinced that the methods suggested to achieve them are realistic, then you should join with the rest of us to help bring them about. The Socialist Workers Party is *your* party.

Jack Barnes
Mary-Alice Waters
April 20, 1976

Prospects for Socialism in America

This is the main political resolution adopted by the Twenty-seventh National Convention of the Socialist Workers Party, held in Ohio, August 17-21, 1975. The first draft of this resolution was approved by the SWP National Committee at its May 1975 plenum and submitted to the membership for discussion and amendment under the title "The Decline of American Capitalism: Prospects for a Socialist Revolution."

The effects of the combined social and economic shocks of the last half-decade, coming on top of the changes in attitudes wrought by the movements of social protest and the radicalization of the 1960s and 1970s, have brought us to the threshold of a new period in the transformation of the political consciousness of the American working class.

A different stage in the process of radicalization is opening; new types of struggles are coming onto the agenda.

This resolution examines on a world scale the roots and the various components of the crisis of American capitalism. These are compared and contrasted both to the post-World War II period of capitalist economic boom and political reaction, and to the depression and labor radicalization of the 1930s. The goal is to explain the dilemma faced by the ruling class, the structural and ideological changes taking place in the American working class and among its allies, and the revolutionary perspective inherent in the radicalization of the working class that is just beginning to unfold.

I. GROWING CONTRADICTIONS OF WORLD IMPERIALISM

In the three decades since World War II, recessions have occurred in each of the major capitalist powers. Each of these separate slumps, however, was cushioned by the fact that industrialization, productivity, employment, and trade continued to run their expansionary course in at least several other capitalist countries. The current Americaň depression is not only the longest and deepest of the six U.S. postwar slumps; more important, it is a component part of the first *world* recession since 1937-38, simultaneously affecting all the major capitalist economies.

This recession on a world scale is a product of the increasing exhaustion of many of the motor forces that fed the quarter-century world capitalist boom—for instance, the reconstruction of European and Japanese industry, the massive growth of the automobile and related industries in the 1950s and 1960s, the mechanization, automation, and computerization of whole new branches of industry.

The expansionary stimulants of deficit financing and massive credit growth, used to help bring capitalist economies out of slumps in the last quarter of a century, have turned into perilous measures. Government engineered inflation is less effective and more dangerous than ever before as a means of bringing capitalist economies out of a recession. It can threaten to soar out of control even in the midst of a depression.

The war in Indochina brought clearly into the open the shift in the world relationship of class forces against imperialism. It demonstrated the new limits imposed on the *use* of American imperialism's massive military machine. The imperialist giant today finds itself increasingly hobbled not only by the nuclear power of the Soviet Union, but by the absence of semicolonial allies and clients with solid popular support in their own countries, by the drain on U.S. capital that propping up dictatorial regimes entails, and by political opposition from the American people.

The defeat in Southeast Asia was a setback of historic proportions for U.S. capitalism.

Meanwhile, in Europe, the powerful working-class offensives registered in the May 1968 prerevolutionary upsurge in France and the "creeping May" in Italy in the autumn of 1969 demonstrated the growing trend toward broad *social* crises in the heart of the imperialist powers of Europe. This trend has been reconfirmed by the revolutionary ferment that exploded in Portugal in the spring of 1974.

From being an allied reserve, offering military, political, and economic support for embattled American imperialism vis-à-vis the colonial revolution and the workers' states, sectors of European capital are becoming an additional source of weakness.

As the oil crisis, the prelude to the 1974-75 depression, demonstrated anew, American imperialism remains by far the single most powerful force in the world capitalist arena. Its economic output alone is as great as all the other major capitalist powers put together.

Furthermore, the competitive pressures of the unfolding social and economic crisis eliminated all pretense that the European Common Market countries would establish a single currency and state structure as a counterweight to U.S. imperialism and an effective challenge to its hegemony.

However, all these events of the end of the 1960s and beginning of the 1970s coincided not only with the end of the long wave of the post-World War II capitalist economic expansion; they also reflected a major decline in the productivity edge American capitalism had over its most powerful competitors.

The edge in labor productivity had enabled the dollar to play its role as the world currency, exporting inflation and allowing modest but real wage increases for American labor. It had also enabled U.S. imperialism to make massive investments and military expenditures abroad simultaneously. The peaking of the postwar international capitalist boom in the 1968-71 period thus signaled the opening of a period of increasing interimperialist competition and conflict, of further shifts in the relationships among the imperialist powers, and of a new long wave of economic stagnation and explosive inflation.

Before the nuclear arms age, such shifts in the relationship of forces would have precipitated an interimperialist war for the redivision of the shrinking world market, as in 1914 and 1939. But the qualitative military superiority of American capitalism within the imperialist camp and the deterrent presence of the Soviet nuclear arsenal have radically altered the framework in which these classical interimperialist contradictions have to be resolved.

The policy of détente, too, is based on a mutual recognition of these new economic and military relationships of forces. While Moscow counts on economic aid from the capitalists to boost Soviet industrial and technological capacities, American imperialism, through a tacit political understanding, is assured of assistance from the Soviet bureaucracy in the form of counterrevolutionary intervention against the independent actions of the world working class. The Stalinist parties around the world are called upon to collaborate in this task. This *quid pro quo* constitutes the essence of the policy of détente and is brought to bear in every new revolutionary upsurge of the oppressed.

The convergence of these factors has precipitated a major crisis of world capitalist leadership.

II. CRISIS OF PERSPECTIVE OF THE AMERICAN RULING CLASS

The American ruling class that was so confident and arrogant from 1945 on is now floundering in search of a new world strategy. This is reflected in the pessimism expressed by the bourgeois statesmen and commentators as they seek to assess the prospects of American imperialism from a broader historical perspective. To them the collapse of the "American century"— which they were so sure of thirty years ago—evokes visions of declining empires and a coming "dark age." They see the world as careening toward a new "era of scarcity," or suggest decades of zero economic growth as the only alternative to the destruction of the life-supporting capacity of the earth's environment. They "philosophically" weigh the probability that "democracy" cannot be maintained much longer if inflation and social unrest continue.

Such pessimism stems from a recognition of the shift in the world relationship of class forces to the disadvantage of capitalism, the shift in relative weight among the imperialist rivals themselves, and the scope of the problems generated today by a decaying world capitalist order.

This crisis of leadership and orientation is not confined to the American bourgeoisie. Despite the relative decline of the American dollar and Washington's power, there is no other capitalist power, not even the strongest, Germany or Japan, capable of stepping in and replacing Wall Street's hegemony.

However much the lesser capitalist powers may chafe under U.S. domination, they cannot free themselves from dependence upon Washington. Singly or collectively, they cannot afford, nor are they able, to police the world. Yet they cannot afford not to have it policed.

These are the sources of the disarray in the American and world bourgeois leaderships and the increasing divisions among them. As these divisions become intensified, they lead to further loss of confidence among the ruling classes in their own ability to rule. These conflicts, and the crisis of capitalist leadership, deepen the general malaise in the population.

Under these circumstances the *real* perspectives that continued capitalist rule present to the American workers are cuts in the standard of living, new military adventures, and curtailment of democracy.

1. The ruling class will seek to boost profit rates by squeezing even more out of the American workers. This means holding down real wages, whittling away working conditions, lowering the standard of living, and slashing social welfare programs. It means seeking to increase divisions among the workers through the use of racism and sexism especially, and trying to prevent the development of international working class solidarity.

It also means cutting down on the social legacy to be bequeathed to future generations—the natural environment, schools, hospitals, housing, organization of the cities, and the entire productive system. And it means increasing social dislocation—crime, alcoholism, drug addiction, mounting social and psychological pressures, and deepening alienation. This is the quality of life capitalism has in store for the great majority.

In its struggle against the relative advance of German and Japanese capital, the American bourgeoisie calls on the masses to be "realistic" and accept the doleful fact that American capitalism cannot sustain the relatively high and growing standard of living the working class has come to *expect* as a *right*. The capitalists call upon the workers to sacrifice to make up for "excessive" wage increases and consumption of social services, and to lower their expectations in order to "keep America strong."

2. The threat of military adventures, and along with them the possibility of nuclear annihilation, will continue. Rivalries among the imperialist powers will sharpen as they compete for markets and raw materials. There will be increased efforts to impose American imperialist needs and perspectives on the masses of the colonial and semicolonial world with the inevitable resistance this will generate.

Washington will continue to come up against the limits of the Stalinists' capacity to control the outbursts of class struggle on a world scale. Since détente was proclaimed, events in Greece, Cyprus, Portugal, the Arab East, and Indochina have amply shown how impossible it is for Moscow and Peking to prevent the masses from disrupting the status quo.

At every opportunity, the ruling class will push as far as it can, testing the limits on the use of its massive military power and nuclear blackmail, trying to see how much of an edge it can get through threat of military action. The danger of miscalculation is always inherent in this bellicose probing.

3. The ruling class will seek to curtail the democratic rights of the American workers, to undercut their ability to learn the truth about the actions and activities of the big corporations and the government, to hamper them from entering the political arena in an independent manner. They will strive to drive back both the social gains and the new rights won by the oppressed minorities and women in recent years.

Driving down the living standard of the masses of American workers, maintaining American economic positions abroad by deploying U.S. military might, curtailing the rights and liberties won by the American people on the job and in society as a whole—these are the realities America's imperialist rulers hold out for the coming period.

III. CHANGING CONSCIOUSNESS OF THE WORKING CLASS

Black struggle

A mounting skepticism toward what was vaguely seen as "the American system" began in the 1960s. It took the form of a *moral* questioning by young people as they came to see "the system's" refusal or incapacity to meet the just demands being made by Black people. Little Rock, the sit-ins, Mississippi and Selma, then Watts, Detroit, and Newark became symbols of the social injustice and inequality pervading America. Bourgeois democracy was not based on liberty and equality for all as the schools taught.

From the Black struggle and all it revealed about the racist inequalities of American democracy, this questioning spread to other benighted outlooks and institutions upholding capitalism and upheld by it—religion, the "work ethic," unequal education, anticommunism, the "organization man" and hierarchical authority, marriage, and the family.

A new stage was opened by the Vietnam War as outrage over the aims and methods of American imperialism became a mass phenomenon reaching beyond the campus and the youth. The resulting radicalization extended to new arenas of struggle and challenged more of class society's sacred cows. Other oppressed nationalities, soldiers, women, gays, prisoners, the elderly, began to vocally and actively demand their full human rights.

Legacy of Vietnam

The experience of the Vietnam War produced a profound change in the attitude of masses of American workers.

The strength of what the bourgeois pundits call the "new isolationism" constitutes the heritage of the overwhelming opposition of the American people to the government's intervention in Indochina, and their skepticism toward Washington's military adventures.

The American people have been sensitized to threats to use American military power. The credibility gap makes it more difficult to stage provocations like the Tonkin Gulf incident.

"Revisionist" reassessments of Washington's role and designs in the origins of the cold war, the Korean War, and even World War II are gaining a wider audience.

There is more awareness that increasing escalation of the military budget brings something besides jobs for those employed in the war industries—it brings death, destruction, senseless maiming and killing, and misery to the world, to American GIs, and to workers' families here at home.

Among the radicalizing effects of the Vietnam War and the antiwar movement was the dawning realization that war, war preparations, and the accumulated burden of the costs for past wars are central parts of the rulers' "answer" to world capitalist competition and its periodic crises.

Impact of Watergate

In the last half decade an alteration has also occurred in the American workers' understanding of the reality of American democracy.

The working of American "democracy" abroad has been revealed in Vietnam and Chile, in Cuba and the former Belgian Congo, as a part of the real story has been unearthed from the records of the Pentagon, the CIA, the State Department, the White House, and Congress. But even more than the foreign operations, it was the extensive violations of democratic rights at home that were profoundly shocking to so many Americans as Watergate unraveled and the domestic crimes of the CIA, the FBI, and the Internal Revenue Service were exposed.

As the Watergate scandal unfolded, American workers began to see this spectacle not as an isolated case of crooked politicians being caught, but as proof of a general mode of operation that constituted a threat to fundamental democratic rights. These methods were initiated, carried on, and covered up by a ruling class determined to halt and eventually roll back the social and economic gains made in recent years by the working class and its allies. The real targets of the Watergate methods—as revealed by the Huston plan, Cointelpro documents, the Ellsberg case, the murder of the Chicago Black Panther leaders—were the Blacks, the Chicanos, the women, the youth, the prisoners, the antiwar GIs, the undocumented immigrant workers. The Watergate methods were part of the "law and order" response by the ruling class to the spread of the very idea that working people have a right to a say over war, a right to basic human necessities, and a right to fight for these things.

More Americans came to suspect that references to "national security" were intended to hide the real actions and motivations of the rulers. The "credibility gap" that began with Vietnam and escalated to unprecedented proportions with Watergate represents in reality a crisis of political confidence in the government, the beginning of a crisis of legitimacy. For the first time since the 1930s tens of millions of American working people not only disbelieve what the rulers tell them but question the goals and values of the ruling class.

Changing social values

Significant and progressive shifts in cultural patterns and values have already taken place in broad layers of the population, even though some of these have been expressed in escapist and subjective responses.

These shifts are reflected in such developments as the rise of the gay liberation movement, the independence displayed by juries in political cases, the politicalization and mood of rebellion in the prisons, the readiness to reveal secrets that led to exposures of such scandals as the Pentagon papers, and the Cointelpro revelations.

Social norms and relationships are being newly examined from the standpoint of the historically oppressed or exploited. The critical reappraisals testify to a loosening of the bonds of bourgeois ideology and its conservative assumptions.

Modern means of communication, especially television, have played an unprecedented role in the rapid spread of news, ideas, and action, making more vivid the realities of wars and crises, and spreading innovative trends.

The actions connected with the radicalization of the 1960s took place by and large outside the framework of organized labor. This absence of the organized power of the working class was the strongest limitation upon the development of the radicalization.

But by the beginning of the 1970s the young workers especially were beginning to be significantly affected. They responded not so much as producers or unionists but as young people sensitive to the injustices of society.

Between the wage-freeze offensive of August 1971 and the economic depression of 1974-75, the workers began to discover that, in addition to being morally questionable, the system as a whole was just not giving them what they expected and needed. They reacted against the strong doses of wage controls, speedup, food shortages, the energy crisis, cutbacks in social welfare, double-digit inflation, double-digit unemployment in some sectors of industry and layers of the population, and large-scale layoffs.

Today growing numbers of American workers sense that they are faced not with just a temporary economic depression, as serious as that may be, but with a more enduring *social* crisis that is worldwide. It is not simply that they hear such admissions from prominent figures on television; the working class can see the evidence all around. They can see it in the decline in education, public facilities, health care, and housing, and in the growing pollution of the environment.

They are beginning to sense that the economic problems they face are much greater than before, that the prolonged period of relative prosperity has definitely come to an end; and while the period now opening may have its ups, the ups won't be high or lasting and the downs will be really deep and long.

The forebodings of the workers are accurate. We face a period in which stagnation will predominate over boom and in which the employers will seek to tighten their control over job conditions, speed of the line, health and safety conditions, the organization of the work.

Combinations of breakdowns and shortages, slumps and inflation, speedup and degradation of labor, new wars—that is what American capitalism promises for the future.

Fed by unrest over the current depression, the greatest collapse in public confidence since the Hoover administration has accelerated the crisis in leadership faced by America's rulers.

Reform and revolution

The only program capable of blocking eventual radicalization of the unions would be massive social reform—that is, large-scale concessions in the form of job-creating public works programs, unemployment benefits, housing, medical care, education, protection against inflation, and similar reforms.

While the ruling class is capable of making concessions and may even at some point initiate a number of highly publicized projects as part of a new "New Deal," social reforms of the scope that could meet today's expectations are beyond their reach. That course would necessitate the stabilization of the world capitalist economy, renewal of its expansionary course, and a vast strengthening of America's dominant position.

Three major obstacles block a perspective of reform so far-reaching as to assure an extended period of social and political stability.

First, the international evolution of the class struggle itself will touch off new explosive convulsions throughout the world. An imperialist foreign policy able to block further advances of social revolution is beyond Washington's reach. It was the transformation of the "New Deal" into the "War Deal" that rescued the capitalist economy from the crisis of the 1930s and defused the radicalization of those years. Any attempt to emulate that course today would spark massive political opposition.

Second, the state of the international capitalist economy following the end of the long boom precludes social and economic concessions to the working class on a scale sufficient to close their minds to radical ideas. The more likely perspective is continued convulsive developments in the world capitalist economy, sharp fluctuations, unexpected breakdowns, renewed inflation and shortages, with some of the satellite regimes skirting bankruptcy. A new massive increase in the already bloated war budget of the Pentagon, far from helping to resolve the crisis as it did at the end of the 1930s, would rapidly set off another round of rampant inflation, triggering new social struggles by the American people.

Third, American capitalism's real economic perspectives will make it increasingly difficult for the ruling class even to maintain concessions and advances already won, let alone meet the heightened expectations of the oppressed and exploited.

There will be no willing patriotic sacrifices for some supposedly higher "national interest." While appeals to racist and sexist attitudes to offset the radicalization will evoke a response in some sectors of the working class, they will be qualitatively less effective than before and will stiffen the resistance of their victims.

The United States is not heading back to the prolonged prosperity, reaction, and quiescence of the 1950s and early 1960s. The road ahead is one of increasing class consciousness, class struggle, and class polarization, leading from radicalization toward a revolutionary situation, regardless of the oscillations along the way.

The world crisis of capitalism does not favor extensive and effective long-term capitalist *reform* in the United States but development of the prerequisites for a *revolution*.

IV. CHANGING CHARACTER AND COMPOSITION OF THE WORKING CLASS

Contrary to the widely trumpeted myth of bourgeois sociology, class differences did not vanish during the postwar boom nor was the American proletariat dissolved into a generally comfortable new petty bourgeoisie. In fact, the opposite occurred.

Wealth and economic control have become concentrated in the hands of a smaller and smaller percentage of the population. At the same time, the extensive industrialization, automation, and monopolization of factory, farm, and office in the 1950s and 1960s led to a massive increase in the size of the American working class, both in absolute terms and in relation to other classes.

Spurred on by the needs of monopoly capital in a period of accelerated expansion, these changes of the last three decades have produced major alterations in the composition and placement of the class:

• Agricultural industrialization and mechanization drove millions of farm families off the land while simultaneously increasing the key role played by the agricultural proletariat on the farms.

• Industrialization of the South brought about the proletarianization of the majority of the Southern population.

• These two processes, together with the large-scale Northern migration of the Black population, produced a rapid proletarianization of Afro-Americans.

• Chicano and Puerto Rican labor entered the urban work force, as well as the agricultural proletariat, in large numbers.

Like Blacks, the Chicano and Puerto Rican people have become more urbanized than the white population.

• The expansionary boom brought millions of women into the labor market.

• The growing utilization of "part-time" workers absorbed additional large numbers of women as well as youth into the work force. Alongside this extensive proletarianization of the population, there have been important changes produced by the automation and monopolization of American industry in the placement, disposition, and character of American labor.

• The percentage of workers employed as craftsmen, operatives, and laborers, what government statistics call "blue collar workers," has fallen.

• As in all advanced capitalist countries, there have been sharp increases in the service sector of the economy, the percentage of clerical workers, and the number of public employees working for the various departments of the federal, state, county, and municipal governments (none of whom the ruling class statisticians call "blue collar workers").

• The mechanization of many trades has eroded the skill levels and standing of a growing number of crafts. For example, in the building trades, the skills of masons, carpenters, and painters are less needed as prefabricated construction increases.

• The "industrialization" and automation of a large amount of white collar office and sales work, and even what is referred to as "intellectual labor," has created a new reservoir of proletarianized and alienated labor.

This monopolization and industrialization, extending up and down the line from farms and mines, processing and transportation, to storage and distribution, has sharply reduced the classical petty-bourgeois dreams and illusions of even skilled sectors of the American workers. Proletarianization has altered the workers' concepts of themselves in comparison with earlier generations. American workers think of themselves nowadays more as permanent workers than as potential independent producers. Fewer believe they will one day be able to have a shop, farm, or small business of their own, assuring them an independent livelihood. They are more interested in wresting some degree of control over the machinery, work decisions, and health and safety environment they are subjected to, than in aspiring to own a small business or escaping back to the land.

At the same time, while they do not expect to be able to rise above their own social class, they believe their children are *entitled* to a better education and a better life than they had. With fewer traditional petty-bourgeois illusions than any previous generation of American workers, they nonetheless feel they have a *right* to what are considered "middle class" standards of living. These encompass a guaranteed income, rising as productivity increases; expanding medical and retirement guarantees; adequate transportation; a decent and continuing education; peace; and a healthy environment for their children. They believe that the American economy, if run correctly, can produce this standard of living for all. These convictions are a revolutionizing—not a conservatizing—factor.

The changes in the composition of the working class and in the mass organizations of the workers, the unions, deserve a closer look.

Blacks

The Black population is today more proletarianized and more urbanized than the white. A significantly higher percentage of Black women are in the labor force than white women.

A higher percentage of Blacks than ever before are engaged in basic industry, especially auto, steel, and transportation. Through affirmative action suits and quotas they have made gains in jobs, upgrading, pay, and job security.

Blacks comprise about 22 percent of all workers employed in manufacturing and in construction. At the same time Blacks make up a disproportionately large percentage of the lower-paid service jobs and lower rungs of public employment. About 27 percent of all employed Blacks are service workers.

The unionization of Black workers reflects this employment pattern. In the United Automobile Workers, the Steelworkers, American Federation of State, County, and Municipal Employees, Letter Carriers, and Postal Clerks, Blacks comprise about 20 percent of the union membership. In many locals it is significantly higher. In the Longshoremen the percentage rises to nearly half.

The unions today are the organizations having the largest Black membership in the country. In auto the percentage of Black union-local officials is higher than the percentage of Blacks in the industry, and many locals are run largely by Blacks. The Coalition of Black Trade Unionists is an initial reflection of this development.

The rapid expansion of the service and public employee sectors of the economy; the proletarianization of Black and female labor; the significant concentration of Blacks and women in these sectors; and the fact that these are also the most rapidly growing sectors of union organization are all interrelated phenomena.

Women

The increase in the percentage of women in the work force has been one of the biggest changes brought about by American capital in the postwar period.

In 1930 women constituted only 20 percent of the work force, and less than 25 percent of all women of working age were employed. By 1945, largely because of the needs of the war industry, women constituted 30 percent of the work force, and more than a third of all women of working age were employed. But by 1972 women constituted 37 percent of the work force, and 44 percent of all women were employed.

While the decade following World War II saw a small decline in the number of women in industry and employment, reversing some of the gains established during the war years, by 1955 the curve of employment began to climb again. The last twenty years have seen a steady rise in female employment. During the boom of the 1960s two-thirds of all new jobs created were taken by women. This rate of increase in female employment occurred because of the rapid rate of expansion of the economy as a whole.

The highest percentage of working women, while classified by the government as "white collar," went into the fastest growing sectors of the working class—office workers, service employees, sales, public workers, and teachers.

Toward the end of the postwar boom, through the enforcement of quotas and affirmative action suits, women even began to win a slightly larger percentage of jobs in basic industry.

Forty percent of all working women are either the sole or major wage earners in their households. At the same time, working wives are the single largest source of the "affluence" of many American working class families.

The growing integration of women into the work force has brought with it a heightening of class consciousness among women. As they increasingly see themselves as long-term and permanent members of the work force and are recognized as such by others, the need to protect their jobs and working conditions by joining unions and bringing their militancy to bear in the labor movement becomes more obvious and urgent. This is part of the process that has given rise to formations such as women's committees in the unions and the Coalition of Labor Union Women.

Youth

The American working class in the 1970s is younger than at any time since the 1930s. In 1960 only 16 percent of the work force was under twenty-five years of age. Today it is more than 23 percent.

The rise in the formal educational level of the working class as a whole is especially marked in this generation of young workers, male and female, who spent more time in school before permanently entering the labor market. Today more than 27 percent of the labor force has completed one or more years of college education, up from only 16 percent twenty years ago.

This means that more of the American workers coming into industry are subjected to the social, cultural, and ideological influences affecting their generation as a whole for a longer period before their assimilation into the work force.

The young workers of the present generation are different in another sense. They are a completely fresh and undefeated layer that does not bear the scars or the memory of the Great Depression, the witch-hunt, and the cold war. They are imbued with the more militant attitudes of the developing radicalization. Since they came into the labor force when there was close to steady work for all adult members of the household who wished to be employed, they expect more as their rightful due.

It is the young workers who have reacted most militantly to the speedup and deterioration of working conditions in the last half-decade. And they look least to the ossified union bureaucracies to protect their interests. They have been the initiators of several waves of wildcat strikes and local actions. Their deep alienation is often expressed through sabotage on the line, high turnover rates, and absenteeism.

In the decade of the late 1960s and early 1970s the young workers often tended to be hostile to the unions or indifferent to them, not identifying with them as *their* organizations. But, as the struggles with the employing class intensify, the problem of either transforming the unions into instruments of struggle against the bosses or facing massive defeats is beginning to appear in a new light.

Trade unions

At the beginning of the radicalization of the 1930s barely 5 percent of the working class was unionized. Those who were organized were trapped in the antiquated structures of craft unions led by a conservative bureaucracy that stood in the way of building fighting organizations of the working class.

Labor's giant step in the 1930s and 1940s, the organization of basic industry and the establishment of industrial union shops in auto, steel, rubber, and elsewhere, transformed the character of the American labor movement. In a few short years it became one of the most powerfully organized working classes in the world.

By the end of the 1930s close to 16 percent of the labor force was unionized. By the end of the war it had risen to more than 23 percent, and the percentage continued to rise until 1953 when it peaked at 25.5 percent.

The ossification of the union leaderships over the last two decades, their failure to fight to maintain working conditions, to organize the unorganized, to combat antilabor legislation, and to mobilize the unions in behalf of progressive social struggles, and their political subordination to the needs of the employers' two-party system, have led to a stagnation and decline in union membership since then. Today roughly 23 percent of the labor force is unionized.

Among the more striking defaults of the union bureaucrats has been the absence of any sizable advances in unionizing the South, parallel to the growing industrialization and urbanization of that region.

Similarly, they have shown brutal indifference to—and in the case of the Teamster bureaucracy even helped lead the attack against—the fight to unionize farm labor.

Big inroads have been made by the construction bosses against the craft unions. Mechanization and prefabrication in the construction industry, coupled with the reactionary white-job-trust mentality of the bureaucracies of the skilled trades, led to stagnation and a decline in membership among the skilled craft unions and the undermining of union-shop conditions. The weakening of such unions is now being registered in the mechanization of the building trades like painting and carpentry, and automation of the printing trades. Industrial conditions are tearing down the craft-union structure along with its accompanying business-unionism mentality and customs.

But expecting the big boom to last forever, the union bureaucracies set themselves up, not as the leadership of a class with a historic mission in society, but as representatives and defenders of the benefits enjoyed by a small layer of the most privileged white male workers.

V. RADICALIZATION AND MOBILIZATION OF THE ALLIES OF THE PROLETARIAT

The failure of the union bureaucracies to fight for the elementary needs of the masses of workers they represent has already led to the first revolts against some of their most corrupt sectors. The overturn of the Boyle machine in the United Mine Workers, the establishment of the right of the miners to vote on their contracts, and the growing social consciousness of the miners have given a glimpse of the initiatives to be expected from the powerful industrial proletariat.

The large-scale, rapid unionization of public employees in the last decade, including the unionization of millions of teachers and others who formerly considered themselves "middle-class professionals," has brought significant new forces into the labor movement.

For public employees, every struggle comes up against a series of obstacles. Antistrike and antilabor laws are used against them. They are weakened by the lack of broad labor unity mobilized in their support. They are crippled by the past failures of their leaderships to support the struggles of the oppressed communities. And they must confront not only the government as boss, but the Democratic and Republican parties to whom the unions have been subordinated by the misleadership of American labor.

Public employees are today the main target of the ruling-class offensive to drive down wages, working conditions, social welfare, and social services, and to weaken and demoralize American labor. They are more vulnerable to attack than the powerfully organized industrial workers, who create the profits for America's rulers. Successful efforts by the public workers to fight back and overcome these obstacles could provide an example and constitute a turning point for the entire American working class.

But this will require a new kind of leadership, new consciousness, and new methods of struggle. The transformation of

American labor into a class-conscious social and political force will be heralded both by massive social struggles outside the unions and by the rise of a class-struggle left wing in the union movement. Such a formation will strive to provide leadership for all types of social struggles by the oppressed. It will chart a political course of class independence for the unions, breaking millions of workers and their allies away from the two-party system of the bourgeoisie and its agents.

Even in a country like the United States where the workers comprise the vast majority of the population, the working class cannot succeed in wresting power from the capitalist rulers and beginning the socialist reconstruction of society without strong support from its allies. At the same time, these allies—the oppressed minorities, women, small farmers, craftsmen, and proprietors, the GIs, the student youth—all have a life-and-death stake in the socialist revolution.

The traditional allies of the workers have been primarily the small independent producers, craftsmen, and proprietors, both urban and rural. This still held true during the radicalization of the 1930s when the farm population was about 30 percent of the total. However, the large-scale changes wrought since then in the structure of industry, agriculture, and the labor force through the growth and further monopolization of American capital have radically reduced the size and altered the configuration of these classical petty-bourgeois strata.

The composition and character of the allies of the proletariat have undergone significant changes as the structure and composition of the proletariat itself have altered dramatically. But these changes in no way lessen the importance of understanding the independent needs and struggles of these allies or of winning them to the side of the socialist revolution. To the contrary, clear and concrete answers must be given to their demands if the revolutionary workers are to mobilize full striking power against the forces of capital. In so doing, they will eliminate the central obstacle before the coming American revolution—that is, the divisions within the working class.

The oppressed nationalities
and national minorities

The oppressed nationalities and national minorities have a dual character. They constitute a growing percentage of the working class itself and at the same time they are the most important allies of the working class. In this respect they differ from the oppressed layers of the petty bourgeoisie, and all other allies except the women. To see only one side of this duality, and to ignore the other, would be a fatal error for a revolutionary party.

Oppressed nationalities and national minorities are exploited as proletarians. This exploitation is intensified by their pariah status since they are at the same time oppressed as distinct peoples. The struggle against this twofold oppression is one of the central driving forces of the coming American revolution. It is closely intertwined with all the problems and issues facing the American working class.

Their importance as allies of the proletariat stems from several factors:

National oppression and the racism used to justify it are rooted in the historical development of American capitalism, in the uncompleted tasks of the second American revolution (the Civil War, which emancipated Afro-Americans from slavery but failed to lead to full equality), and in the rise of imperialism with its self-justifying racist ideology.

National oppression is used by the ruling class to divide the working class, to buy off leaders and privileged strata, thus weakening both the class consciousness and political independence of the workers, and bolstering capitalist rule. With or without legal sanction, a major component of the industrial reserve army has been kept in a pariah status.

The overwhelmingly proletarian composition and superexploitation of the oppressed nationalities and national minorities mean that they will be the most consistent and cohesive of all allies of the working class in its struggles. More and more they will furnish leadership in the fight to transform the labor movement into a fighting social movement, using its power to back the struggles of all the oppressed.

Blacks

The most important changes in the Black population have already been noted:

• The postwar mechanization of Southern agriculture.

• The urbanization and proletarianization of the Black population in the South.

• The massive Northern migration of the Black population.

• The big influx into basic industry during and after World War II.

• The increase in the number of years Black youth spend in school and the percentage that receive high school diplomas and some post-high school education.

The period since 1945 has also seen a historic advance in the struggle for Black liberation.

"Jim Crow Must Go"

In the postwar years American imperialism drove to expand its domination in Asia, Africa, and Latin America. To do so it needed a new, less racist image. In addition, the changes taking place in the economic structure of Southern society created the need for new forms of social control. The more alert representatives of the American ruling class began to recognize that Jim Crow, the Southern system of legal segregation maintained through legal and extralegal terror, had ceased to be the most effective means of perpetuating the second-class status of the Black proletariat.

Under pressure from growing mass resentment, the U.S. armed forces were formally desegregated during the Korean War, and then in 1954 the Supreme Court declared school segregation unconstitutional.

But it was only the decade-long direct-action struggles, mobilizing millions of Blacks and their supporters, that downed Jim Crow. Their power and determination played a decisive role in altering Black consciousness and self-confidence. This was reflected in the rise of Black power and Black nationalist sentiments; in the popularity of Malcolm X; in the upsurges of other oppressed minorities and social groupings; in the moral questioning that has so deeply motivated the youth radicalization; and in the modification of the opinions of masses of white workers.

The effects of the mass struggle to end segregation, followed by the powerful rise of Black nationalist sentiment, were subsequently seen in the vanguard role played by Black GIs in opposition to the Vietnam War.

The high point in the "civil rights period" of the new rise of the Black struggle came with the battle of Birmingham and the march on Washington in 1963, the passage of the 1964 Civil Rights Act and the 1965 Voting Rights Act, and the Selma, Alabama, confrontation. The impact of the masses in action was even grotesquely echoed in Lyndon Johnson's "We shall overcome" speech before the Congress.

The ghettos explode

Rebellions in the Black communities, beginning in New York in 1964, spreading to Watts in 1965, and Newark and Detroit in 1967, and culminating in the 1968 nationwide outbreaks after the death of Martin Luther King, ushered in a new stage of struggle in which Black nationalist ideas spread rapidly. These spontaneous upsurges, along with intensified struggles by Black students and other sectors of the Black community, forced more concessions from the ruling class and brought forward new leaders who became targets of stepped-up government repression.

Riding the crest of the postwar boom, the ruling class co-opted a layer of the leaders or potential leaders of the rising Black radicalization by granting them economic, political, and social concessions.

The percentage of Black enrollment in the country's colleges and universities tripled in a five-year period at the end of the 1960s and beginning of the 1970s. "Great Society" dollars were poured into poverty program funds, a good part of which went into salaries of "aspiring leaders," Black and white.

The face of the Democratic Party also underwent a significant change. The threat posed by the unconditional opposition of Malcolm X to the Democratic Party and the first halting steps toward independent Black political action, such as the Michigan Freedom Now Party and the Lowndes County Freedom Organization, was adroitly countered. From the Mississippi Freedom Democratic Party to the election of Black mayors in a half-dozen major industrial cities, to the emergence of the Congressional Black Caucus, and the election of more than 1,100 Black officials in the deep South—where less than a decade ago the masses of Blacks were barred even from voting—the lure of "working within the (two-party) system" attracted the overwhelming majority of a generation of potential Black leaders.

The following features should be added to the picture of the crisis of leadership of the Black movement:

1. The total default of the organized labor movement, whose class-collaborationist leadership was unable to rise above its own narrow concern of maintaining its privileged position and refused to mobilize the power of the labor movement in support of the Black struggle.

2. The calculated policy of the powers that be of eliminating any potential individual leaders—such as Martin Luther King,

who inspired the Black masses to struggle, or Malcolm X, who was beginning to urge Black people tôward independent political action against capitalist oppression.

3. The failure to effectively meet government harassment and murder of a layer of leaders in the generation of the 1960s. Groups like the Black Panthers, whose ultraleftism turned them away from any mass perspective, were left defenseless before the government's cold-blooded use of agents provocateurs and terror.

4. The numerical weakness of the revolutionary Marxists, which prevented them from providing a revolutionary leadership except in the realm of program and socialist perspectives.

But despite this crisis, the rise of Black nationalism and the massive ghetto explosions brought about a historic advance in the self-confidence of Blacks and their image of themselves as a people. The upsurges also changed the way white Americans viewed Afro-Americans. Despite the lack of adequate leadership of the Black movement, its power won numerous concessions and registered advances throughout the decade of the 1960s. This has been symbolized in the at least token participation of Blacks at every level of society and culture, from TV commercials to sports, from elected union posts to the Supreme Court. In the late 1960s even the income differential between Black and white workers narrowed by a tiny, though perceptible, amount. Blacks began fighting for preferential quotas, training, and upgrading in industry and the educational system, as necessary and irreplaceable steps along the road to real equality.

The counteroffensive

But the costs of the Vietnam War and the increasing economic crunch brought an end to the Johnson period of concessions and buy-offs as a tactical expedient in coping with rising Black militancy. The Nixon-Connally 1971 wage controls and economic offensive followed recognition that the new economic realities and world relationship of forces not only precluded continuing increases in real wages and social services, but meant that many concessions already won would have to be reversed. Further progress toward equality became more and more incompatible with maintaining competitive superiority in the world market.

The Black population did not share in the brief economic upturn of 1971-72. From the high point of Black median incomes equaling 61 percent of white median incomes in 1969, the ratio fell to 58 percent in 1973. Black unemployment *rose* steadily from 6.4 percent in 1969 to 10 percent in 1972.

The 1972-73 Nixon policy of rollback in virtually every area of social expenditures—housing, education, transportation, child care, welfare, etc.—was part of the drive to take back the gains won by the radicalization of the 1960s. These cutbacks, aimed at the working class as a whole, hit Blacks and other oppressed nationalities and minorities the hardest. But instead of reversing the radicalization, the cutbacks helped, along with the antiwar movement, to create the opposition that spurred forward the Watergate crisis and the downfall of Nixon.

These are the present battle lines in relation to Black liberation and the labor movement. While the ruling class is forced to try to reverse the drive toward real equality, the Black movement must press forward with demands for immediate government enforcement of concessions already won and for preferential treatment. Especially in a period of economic stagnation, the racist counteroffensive in education, housing, jobs, and other areas puts the Black leadership and the labor movement to a decisive test.

Chicanos

The late 1960s and early 1970s saw an upsurge of Chicano nationalism. As with Afro-Americans, the new militancy was rooted in the major economic and social changes within the Chicano population that took place during and after World War II—a significant urbanization and proletarianization of the Chicano population and a large influx of Mexican workers to provide inexpensive labor for the expanding agribusiness in the Southwest.

The ascending Chicano movement in the 1960s was influenced by the advances of the Black civil rights movement and the rise of Black nationalism, the colonial revolution, and the student radicalization.

Later the growing opposition to the Vietnam War plus the disproportionately high Chicano casualty rates helped fuel the militancy. The Chicano movement, led by a layer of radical Chicano leaders who were less affected by ultraleftism than those in the Black movement, organized sizable actions against the war.

Starting in the mid-1960s, the focal point of the Chicano movement became the broad campaign developed in support of attempts to organize the Southwest and West Coast migrant farm labor employed by the most advanced monopoly agribusiness in the world. Radical students were rapidly drawn into support activities.

From the beginning *la causa* was conceived not only as a union organizing drive, but as a broad social movement in the interests of all Chicano people. As such, it was—and remains—in marked contrast to the prevailing character of the rest of the labor movement.

While Chicano nationalism partly took its inspiration from the Black movement, several important differences should be noted:

1. While statistics vary, as much as half of the Chicano population may consider Spanish to be their first language. The right to use their own language in school, at work, on the ballot, and in all aspects of life is one of the central demands of the Chicano struggle.

This is closely tied to the struggles of Chicano students who face, in addition to inferior educational facilities, a denial of the right to study and learn in their own language, resulting in an even higher rate of functional illiteracy than among Blacks. Language and related cultural oppression were major factors in precipitating the massive Chicano high school student "blow-outs" in Los Angeles, Denver, and several Texas cities in the 1960s.

2. Eighty percent of the Chicano population is located in a well-defined geographical area of the country, and is linked by history, culture, and language to both Mexico and the United States.

3. A racist and xenophobic offensive against foreign labor and particularly "illegals," who are easiest to victimize, is one of the central campaigns of the ruling exploiters in every economic crisis. International labor solidarity is fundamental to unifying and defending the working class, its gains, and its organizations. The right to move freely back and forth across the border, the right to work in the United States when and where a worker chooses, without fear of harassment because of lack of work papers or immigration documents, is one of the demands at the very heart of the Chicano struggle. This claim puts the labor movement to a severe test, one that the AFL-CIO officialdom has flunked miserably up to now.

Because the bulk of Chicano workers are concentrated in basic industry, and comprise a significant proportion of the members of the trade unions in the Southwest, they can play a major role in fighting to reverse the reactionary prodeportation policy of the AFL-CIO leadership.

The Farm Workers

The farm worker organizing drives in California, Texas, and elsewhere face tremendous obstacles. A factory in the fields is more difficult to organize than a factory within four walls. The increasingly seasonal and migrant character of the labor force compounds the difficulties. Farm workers also face some of the most powerful monopolies in the world, whose interests are protected by the federal, state, and local governments. The strikebreaking role of the Teamster bureaucracy and the foot-dragging indifference of the AFL-CIO bureaucracy have created additional problems.

Yet despite these enormous difficulties, the United Farm Workers union organizing drive in California has scored some significant victories. In the elections that followed the August 1975 passage of the California Agricultural Labor Relations Act, the UFW came out ahead despite coercion, intimidation, and widespread rigging. This testifies to the viability of *la causa* and its deep roots among the field workers.

The UFW has also been strengthened by the position it now takes on the undocumented Mexican workers. Recognizing that its earlier demand for deportation of so-called illegal aliens was hurting the farm workers' struggle, the UFW leadership has been working to win the votes of the undocumented workers and fighting grower-Teamster efforts to victimize them.

Although a minority of the Chicano labor force is employed as agricultural workers, the fierce exploitation and brutal oppression they suffer will continue to generate renewed struggles. Efforts to mobilize the Chicano community and other allies in support of *la causa* will continue to be a focal point for the entire Chicano movement.

Experience is showing that it will take a determined, independent mass movement to force the growers to terms—even after union elections are won—and to extend the organizing drive to other sections of agriculture. The question of political orientation and the need for independence from the liberal Democrats, or any other capitalist politicians, is sharply posed.

In recent years the Democratic Party has increased its efforts to hold onto the Chicano vote. This has resulted in the election of

Chicanos to two state governorships for the first time. While most influential figures in the Chicano community have remained tied to the Democratic Party, the response to various attempts by Raza Unida Party formations to move in the direction of mass independent political action has confirmed that when presented with a viable alternative, significant numbers of Chicanos can be broken from the Democratic machine.

La Raza Unida

The Chicano movement has stepped ahead of the Black movement on this important front. The various attempts to construct Raza Unida parties—with their strengths and weaknesses—are some of the most advanced initiatives yet made in the direction of political action independent of the two capitalist parties.

A key test for the Raza Unida parties came in the 1972 presidential elections. At the first "National Convention of Raza Unida Parties" in El Paso, Texas, in September 1972 it was clear that a big majority of party activists favored maintaining independence from both the Democrats and Republicans.

The real test came in the actual campaign. The Texas party ran its most ambitious statewide election campaign and, despite programmatic limitations, it was clearly independent of and in opposition to the Democratic Party. In Colorado the Raza Unida Party also ran a clearly independent campaign, although on a smaller scale than the Texas party.

Although there are excellent opportunities for developing a powerful mass Raza Unida Party movement, the growth of the parties remains limited and uneven.

The clearest indication of this unevenness is the smallness of the Raza Unida groupings in Southern California, where there is a Chicano population of more than one million in Los Angeles County alone. Moreover, the Los Angeles Chicanos have repeatedly displayed their combativity, and several independent election campaigns have demonstrated significant support for independent political action. Yet no leadership has emerged capable of organizing that support and consolidating even the nucleus of an independent party.

The Texas Raza Unida Party is the strongest, having enjoyed a growth in organizational and political influence over a period of several years. While even the Texas Raza Unida Party has achieved only a small part of its potential, its survival and progress offer testimony to the viability of the concept of an independent Chicano party.

The challenge that confronts these independent Chicano political formations is to win the Chicano masses away from the Democratic Party and to the banner of the Raza Unida parties. This can only be done by combining electoral actions with a program of immediate, democratic, and transitional demands around which the Chicano masses can be brought into struggle for their needs and aspirations. In the process of fighting around such a program, Chicanos will gain confidence in their own power and inspire other victims of capitalist injustice, winning them over as allies of the Chicano movement. Such an accomplishment would be a powerful example for emulation by Black organizations and trade unions.

Puerto Ricans in the United States

Some of the biggest changes in any of the oppressed national minorities since the radicalization of the 1930s have been among the Puerto Ricans. Because of the massive emigration from the island since World War II, 40 percent of all Puerto Ricans now live in the United States, with the largest number in New York City.

The superexploitation of the Puerto Rican colony by U.S. imperialism imposes conditions much worse than those on the mainland even in prosperous times. Prices are higher than in the United States, wages are one-third to one-half those on the mainland, and unemployment is three to four times higher. During a depression, this superexploitation has a catastrophic impact on the Puerto Rican working masses.

The Puerto Rican minority in the United States is concentrated in the hardest, lowest paid, and least organized jobs in industry. However, in some public employee unions such as the hospital employees and service workers, Puerto Ricans make up a considerable part of the membership, and they are a significant and growing percentage of the garment workers on the East Coast. There are also between 50,000 and 100,000 Puerto Rican seasonal farm workers, most of whom are employed on the truck farms and in the tobacco fields of the East Coast.

The struggles of Puerto Ricans living in the United States are primarily directed against the racist discrimination they suffer and toward bettering their living and working conditions. In this sense they are distinct from the struggles in Puerto Rico. But the connections between Puerto Ricans living in the United States and in Puerto Rico also serve to link them with the struggle for independence in Puerto Rico and to the colonial revolution in general.

The Puerto Rican minority has been deeply affected by the Black struggle and has close contact with it because of the proximity of the Black and Puerto Rican populations in the ghettos and because there is a significant percentage of Black Puerto Ricans. However, the ruling class has tried to find ways, especially through the use of poverty funds, to pit Puerto Ricans and Blacks against each other and prevent them from uniting in struggle.

In a few cities in the Midwest, particularly Chicago, Puerto Rican and Chicano communities exist side by side. Struggles of mutual interest include those against discrimination on the basis of language and against the general racist abuses directed at people of Latino heritage, and the organization and mobilization of migrant farm laborers.

The right to bilingual education, bilingual civil service exams, bilingual ballots; the right to Spanish-speaking personnel in public facilities like hospitals and libraries; and the right to be able to conduct legal proceedings in Spanish are fundamental democratic rights around which significant battles are being fought. The struggle for Puerto Rican, Black, and Chinese community control over the schools in District One in New York City stands as one of the most advanced struggles of this type.

As with the Black and Chicano movements, the ruling class has sought to draw the Puerto Rican radicalization into the two-party system to prevent it from taking an independent route. Herman Badillo's election as the first Puerto Rican in Congress, representing the Bronx, is a case in point.

Native Americans

Their size, location, and place in industry do not give Native Americans the same social weight as Blacks, Chicanos, or Puerto Ricans. But their moral weight is immense. They stand as a living reminder of the real 400-year history of American capitalist expansion and its attendant degradation. They testify to the fact that class society could advance only on the basis of extermination of collectivist, egalitarian forms of social organization, and subsequent misery and crushing oppression of Native Americans.

The nationalist cultural awakening of the Native Americans

and the growing militancy of their struggles against the abysmal conditions into which they have been driven has added another important element to the upsurge of the oppressed national minorities.

The coldly calculated victimization of the leadership of the American Indian Movement as part of a government plan to destroy it as an organization shows that the ruling class ascribes a political importance to Native American struggles beyond their social weight. Their demands for political and cultural autonomy, for respect of treaty rights, and for restoration of lands stolen from them are a component part of the coming American socialist revolution; and the granting of these demands will be one of the responsibilities of the coming workers' government.

Other oppressed national minorities

Chinese-Americans, Filipinos, Japanese-Americans, Dominicans, Haitians, Arabs, and other oppressed national minorities each have their own particular history of emigration, oppression, and superexploitation. American imperialism's white racist ideology has provided justification for discrimination against them as pariah sections of the industrial reserve army.

Lacking a social and political weight comparable to the Afro-Americans, Chicanos, or Puerto Ricans, these national minorities are neither as large in size nor as extensively employed in basic industry. Nevertheless, the radicalization and accompanying nationalist awakening have already increased the militancy of these groups against their oppression as racial minorities.

The emergence of Asian-Americans Against the Vietnam War; the role of Chinese parents in the District One struggle for community control in New York; Asian-American student struggles in California; Chinese struggles against discriminatory hiring policies in the construction industry and against police brutality; the role of Filipinos in the California farm workers' organizing drive; the actions of Dominicans and Haitians against the deportation of undocumented workers and political exiles; and the demonstrations of Arab auto workers are all signs of this development.

Even national or racial groupings that are not oppressed national minorities or nationalities in the United States suffer from the pervasive racism and xenophobia intensified by the ruling class in periods of social crisis. Anti-Semitism aimed at Jews is the clearest example.

Women

Women constitute both a growing percentage of the working class and an increasingly important ally of the working class. Women are not a minority. They constitute more than one-half the population and are not restricted to any geographical area, social stratum, or occupation. Like the American population as a whole, they are increasingly proletarian in composition.

Sexism is also one of the main ideological tools by which the ruling class keeps the working class divided, weakening class consciousness and unity, and reinforcing reactionary religious and obscurantist ideology.

Widespread acceptance of the idea that "woman's place is in the home" is used to promote the myth that women do not seek employment out of necessity but out of choice. The consignment of women to the home keeps a reservoir of extra labor available and reduces the social costs and consequences of large numbers of periodically unemployed women.

The oppression of all women as a sex, like national oppression, creates a pariah section of the industrial reserve army, a labor pool whose superexploitation generates high rates of surplus value, helps drive down the wage level of all workers, and weakens the labor movement.

The oppression of women as a sex does not stem from the particular needs of capitalism alone. Its historic origins go back to the dawn of class society. Sexism is the necessary ideological underpinning of the maintenance of the family as an institution of class rule. The family is a primary mechanism for inculcating authoritarian, hierarchical attitudes into each new generation. It is the institution to which the rulers abdicate social responsibility and care for the young, the old, the sick, and the unemployed, and to which they shift the burden of economic crisis and breakdown—a burden felt especially keenly by the working class.

The struggle for women's liberation poses the problem of the total reorganization of society from its smallest repressive unit (the family) to its largest (the state). The liberation of women demands a thoroughgoing reorganization of society's productive and reproductive institutions in order to maximize social welfare and bring about a truly human existence for all.

The search for solutions to the issues raised by women's liberation is one of the driving forces of the coming American revolution. The ability of the workers' vanguard to provide clear and concrete answers to the questions posed by capitalism's oppression of women and to fight for their realization will be decisive in mobilizing the forces necessary to overturn capitalism.

Women's liberation movement

A women's liberation movement emerged in the late 1960s with a political character and social depth vastly different from the forms through which women participated in the last working class radicalization, in the 1930s. Three processes—developing over the postwar decades—led to this resurgence.

• The large-scale integration of women into the labor force and the significant rise in general educational level that accompanied this process.

• The growing realization among millions of people that the development of the productive and technical capacities of industry and science has now made possible unlimited abundance and the socialization of "women's work" if society is rationally organized and planned.

• The challenge to bourgeois social and moral norms, a consequence of the broad radicalization, made it possible for significant numbers of women to develop as organizers and political leaders.

All of these conditions converged at the end of the 1960s when the antiwar movement and student radicalization were at their height. Many of the initial organizers of the women's groups came out of these movements. The rapid spread of the movement, its deep reverberations through all layers of society, penetrating into the organized labor movement, attested to the ripeness of the conditions that bred it.

Because of women's distribution throughout society, and the radical character of the questions posed, the rise of the women's liberation movement has already deeply affected mass consciousness and every aspect of culture in the broadest sense of the term. Literature, TV, movies, and other avenues have felt its impact. There is a tendency to challenge all values and mores and to review all aspects of existence, every facet of society by looking at them through women's eyes.

The most basic assumptions of class society about women are being carefully scrutinized and rejected by millions of women and men. The ferment over the woman question today recalls the radicalization of the Debsian pre-World War I period, or even the pre-Civil War radicalization, where the specific question of women's role in society was also a distinct component of the general social ferment—although on a much more restricted practical and theoretical basis. The vanguard role of women in other social movements is also parallel.

Struggles by women directed toward their emancipation are among the clearest indicators of the depth of the current *social* crisis and radicalization. The fact that these struggles began to emerge *before* the effects of a major economic crisis were felt confirms this all the more emphatically.

Progress and reaction

The large increase in the percentage of employed women, in the number of women who are heads of households, and in the unionization of working women, combined with the rise of the women's liberation movement, has created a difficult problem for the ruling class. The acceptability of the use of women as reserve labor—the vast majority of women who drop out of the labor market in hard times are not even counted as unemployed—has been diminished.

As with the oppressed nationalities, the road toward true equality and equal opportunity for women lies through preferential treatment—quotas and affirmative action in industry, education, politics, and society—to correct the inequality of opportunity established by centuries of discrimination.

Thus, the attempt by the ruling class to wipe out the gains that oppressed national minorities and women made through preferential hiring and upgrading victories is an important part of the political and economic counteroffensive mounted by the Democrats and Republicans. And the resistance of women to being shoved out of work on the basis of last hired, first fired is growing. There has been rising opposition among women to having seniority rights broken by maternity leave, being denied access to apprenticeship programs for skilled or "heavy" jobs, receiving unequal pay, or being denied the right to participate in bargaining units because of "part-time" classifications.

The radicalization of women and the examples of direct action by others in the last decade have made housewives react with anger and frustration to the economic squeeze on their budgets and have led them to be more inclined to try to do something about it themselves. The 1973 meat boycott and the popularity of consumer investigations like those of Ralph Nader are harbingers of the protests to come.

The challenge to the bourgeois social order represented by the rise of the women's liberation movement means that the gains won by women have become a major target of reaction, second only to the Black movement. In Boston the antibusing drive, the attempt to reverse the right to abortion, and the anti-ERA demonstrations have provided an instructive example of the combination of targets selected in the country as a whole by the most rabid reactionary forces.

The right to abortion and constitutional and legislative guarantees of equal rights for women, as obvious as they may seem to some, represent a challenge to class society and its entire ideological superstructure. The protectors of the bourgeois order know this. They will continue to try to chip away at all such gains.

Many of the initial participants in the women's liberation movement rapidly faced a crisis of perspectives. Some were won to revolutionary Marxism. Others went in the direction of ultra-leftism or forms of personal escapism. Still more were drawn into the two-party game of capitalist politics, where the ruling class was again quick to create openings for leaders of the movement.

Like the withdrawal of troops from Vietnam and abolition of the draft, the Supreme Court decision to legalize early abortions was part of the ruling class's general attempt to defuse the radicalization and eliminate some of the issues that had become focal points for mass mobilizations.

But the abortion victory, as with other democratic concessions to women, can not eliminate the roots of the oppression of women or defuse their struggle for long. On the contrary, while such gains may lead to temporary lulls or downturns in mass action, over time they only serve to generate new demands and to create more favorable conditions for building an independent mass feminist movement capable of mobilizing women in struggle against their oppression.

Small farmers

The mobilization of the traditional petty-bourgeois allies of the working class in the United States poses problems far different from those in countries where the working class is a minority and surrounded by large numbers of independent producers, including a massive peasantry.

The extensive monopolization and mechanization of American agriculture in the decades since World War II; the vertical growth of many of these monopolies, giving them control of everything from the land, seeds, fertilizer, and farm machinery to harvesting, processing, packaging, distribution, and giant retail outlets;

the generation of a sizable agricultural proletariat that has a significant "nonwhite" composition and is overwhelmingly seasonal and migrant; the transformation of many farmers' cooperative associations into big businesses or subsidiaries of the largest commercial banks; the internationalization of the agricultural monopolies, which play an important role in American imperialism's foreign policy—all this has been one of the biggest economic "revolutions" of the last quarter-century.

The elimination of the less productive small farmers who cannot compete with finance capital's collectivization, mechanization, and monopolization of food production continues. At the end of World War II, 17.5 percent of the population lived on the land. By 1960 this had fallen to 8.7 percent. Today it stands at 4.5 percent and continues to drop. During the same period farm output per hour of labor increased 600 percent. Agribusiness is now the sector of American imperialism with the greatest relative productivity edge over all foreign competitors.

The results of this gigantic explosion in agricultural productivity help highlight the disproportion between the productive capacity of American labor and the limitations and distortions of production and distribution brought about by the capitalist market and national boundaries. The glaring contrast of vast personal wealth for some while millions go hungry or die of famine has become one of the generators of the coming upheavals in both the United States and other countries.

While farm dwellers today constitute a small percentage of the total population, their importance is greater than their numbers would indicate. Disruption of the relationship between agriculture and industry directly affects the quantity, quality, and cost of the food, fibers, and other farm products the working class must buy. Soaring food prices, threatened shortages, as well as militant actions taken by small farmers to dramatize *their* plight, have brought this home to American workers in the last few years.

The Democratic and Republican politicians do their utmost to exacerbate conflicts between the farmer and worker, to set each against the other in order to maintain the dominance of capital over both. If the workers' vanguard proves capable of pointing to and fighting for solutions to the problems faced by the small farmers, it will be able to win them to labor's side. Thus, the real antagonism—that between the small working farmer, the agricultural worker, and the urban proletariat on one side, and the interests of monopoly capitalism, including the giant agribusinesses on the other—will be understood and will emerge as one of the important elements in the coming American revolution.

The "middle class"

While the monopolization of American capital has diminished the relative importance of the petty bourgeoisie, it has not eliminated it. In fact, monopolization continually breeds a petty bourgeoisie that occupies the cracks and crevices of production, distribution, and services, where they play an essential role. Some sectors of the petty bourgeoisie—those offering specialized services and technical skills—even increase in significance relative to the population as a whole and relative to their own past weight.

The exact configuration of the middle classes must always be examined concretely since it varies greatly from one country to another and often from one area to another inside a country.

For example, in the United States the independent owner-operator truckers—whose job action in early 1974 attracted national attention to the way they were being squeezed by soaring oil prices—play an important role in distribution. But, unlike France, the small independent baker is a marginal phenomenon.

It is also necessary to examine the spectrum of professionals, technicians, and others situated between wage labor and the bourgeoisie.

At one end, sizable numbers of teachers, technicians, service employees, government employees, etc., are really for the most part skilled or semiskilled, usually salaried, workers. They have no perspective of ever being able to make their living other than by selling their labor power to industry or the government. Their goal, in good times or bad, is not to open their own little school or laboratory somewhere. Growing numbers are willing to consider the idea that the solution to the social and economic squeeze they feel is to organize as part of the union movement and fight collectively—using labor's methods of struggle—to better their condition. The ruling class does its utmost to perpetuate the illusion that they are really "professionals" who belong to the "middle class," not the working class. In reality, however, the distinction between a teacher, or a lower salaried technician, or a municipal employee, and a woman or man on the assembly line at Chrysler is a distinction within the working class itself between skilled, semiskilled, and unskilled, between wage and salaried workers.

To an intermediate category belong the modern small masters, the independent truckers being one example. The small masters are a broad and variegated category, hybrids between capitalist and laborer. Included are those who have accumulated enough capital to begin to hire others to work along with them, those who are on the verge of becoming capitalists. Also included are those who simply own their own tools, even if they are expensive tools, hire no labor, and with each turn of the business cycle find themselves much closer to joining the unemployment lines as "fellow workers."

At the other end of the spectrum of professionals and technicians are the well-heeled doctors, engineers, and lawyers, many of whom are self-employed and whose skills are remunerated by the ruling class at a rate enabling them to live at a standard qualitatively above even the most skilled workers. They are able to make sizable investments, assuring them security in old age. This layer as a whole consciously identifies with the employing class, its political command, and its ideology.

However, even these professionals, especially the younger ones, are not immune to the changes in social values and mores, as actions like resident doctors' strikes in New York and New Orleans indicate. Beginning to react against capitalism's archaic and inhuman organization of medicine as a priestcraft, utilizing labor's methods of struggle, the young doctors are advancing demands that are quite comprehensible to the masses of workers (eighty-hour week; no more than forty-eight hours on duty at a stretch, etc.). The more radical young members of such professions can move sharply to the left under the hammer blows of a growing social crisis.

Allies and foes

Leaders of the working class also have to distinguish between occupations required to maintain the present *relations of production,* and those needed to maintain and expand the *forces of production.*

Among the former are those whose function is to increase the rate of exploitation (time-and-motion experts, foremen), those whose role is related to the state's repressive apparatus (cops, parole officers, certain social workers), and other social parasites (lawyers, advertising specialists, insurance agents).

Among the latter are many skilled individuals such as technicians, engineers, and statisticians.

History shows that while the vast majority of the former remain enemies of the movements of the workers and their allies, many of the latter can be attracted to a revitalized class-struggle workers' movement and are needed in the tasks of establishing workers' control of industry and planned production of the economy.

It is also important to examine carefully the character of protest actions often dubbed "middle class" by the media, that are taken under the pressures of capitalist crisis. Many are not petty-bourgeois actions as such, that is, actions aimed at winning demands that concern and interest the petty bourgeoisie as a specific social class (like the silver standard crusade among the small farmers of the 1880s and 1890s or the fight backed by small merchants to maintain "fair pricing" laws).

While large numbers of middle-class women were involved in and helped spark the meat boycott, for example, this was an action including and appealing to masses of workers as *consumers*, and certainly was not a petty-bourgeois movement.

Interest in and support to consumer protest and environmental protection movements, and muckraking exposés like those initiated by Ralph Nader and his associates are not the concern solely of the petty bourgeoisie and a thin layer of the most privileged workers. The availability and cost of credit for housing, cars, and durable consumer goods; the quality, operating costs, and safety of these goods; and the profiteering in utility rates, medical expenses, transportation costs, pension funds, the oil shortage, and similar items directly affect the great majority of the American working people.

The impact of protests around such problems is limited at present by the absence of a class-struggle labor leadership capable of linking up with them, associating the power of labor with them, and generalizing and leading them in a class-struggle direction. Nevertheless, these protests are bound to increase as the social crisis deepens, and the labor movement will find it more and more difficult to abstain from playing an active role in them. It will be increasingly obliged to participate not as part of the Democratic Party machine or through government agencies but as the independent and unifying organizer of the working people as a whole.

Students

Under the impact of a virtual technological revolution, the changes in the needs of American industry since World War II have meant vast alterations in the size and character of the student population since the 1930s. As potential allies of the proletariat, college students occupy a place different from the one they held earlier in the century, when they were predominantly bourgeois and petty-bourgeois careerists attending college to better prepare themselves to take on their responsibilities within the bourgeois world.

Today more than 75 percent of teen-age youth in the United States graduate from high school, and of those well over 50 percent go on to some college institution. The average number of years spent in school is one of the biggest differences between today's youth and the generation of their parents. In 1940 the average youth leaving school had not completed the ninth grade. Today the figure is 12.3 grades.

Another trend toward increasing education is illustrated in New York City, where open enrollment victories, won in the big student struggles at the end of the 1960s, more than tripled the number of Black and Puerto Rican college students.

Each student is of course deeply marked by his or her class origins. The family unit in which they are raised gives a child his or her first class identity, outlook, and expectations. Students are affected by the attitudes of the social class to which they belong, or to which they believe their education will lead them. But students as a social grouping *per se* have no direct specific relationship to production. In terms of their role in the economic structure, students do not function as workers, capitalists, or petty bourgeoisie. They are preparing to assume one of these economic roles. The majority of students today are on their way to becoming wage or salaried workers of some kind; and they anticipate a future in which they will be able to live only by offering their labor power for sale.

Thanks to the vast increase in the number of students, the percentage of workers with some college education is up; the percentage of college students who will become wage and salaried workers is up; the percentage who are working on jobs while going to college is up. The relative homogenization of social and ideological values of youth is increased by the length of time they spend together in high schools and college institutions.

While there can be a decline in the percentage of students as a proportion of the population because of conjunctural factors—especially economic downturns—there will be no fundamental reversal of the trend or the changes that have already taken place. The overall requirements of capitalist production and accumulation preclude this.

Students and political action

Given the large concentrations of students, their social composition, intellectual stimuli, the antiauthoritarian attitude of many youth, and the relative freedom of student life, the majority of students can be highly sensitive to social and political issues. In large numbers they can be radicalized by and respond to major developments in the class struggle on a national and international scale. The concerns of the majority of students are part of this larger picture, and almost invariably related to it. The tendency of the majority of them today is to ally themselves with progressive social struggles taking place at home and abroad whose goals and values they can understand and appreciate.

The new political importance and potential of students, resulting from the massive post-World War II expansion of the educational system, was admirably demonstrated by the key role the student movement played in developing and maintaining a mass opposition to the imperialist war in Vietnam. This experience drove home the permanent importance of systematic political work among students, organized through a revolutionary socialist youth organization.

The "red university" strategy, on which the Trotskyist youth organization, the Young Socialist Alliance, has been built, is not a narrow "student power" orientation, but an overall strategy intended to help turn the universities into organizing centers at the service of the working class and its allies—including the students—in their struggles. They are bases from which to win large numbers of campus youth to Trotskyism and to the revolutionary workers movement.

In the period since the signing of the Paris peace accords and the withdrawal of U.S. combat personnel from Vietnam there has been a downturn in the intensity of student political activities. But it would be a mistake to confuse a period of relative quiescence with either a basic turn to the right or a long phase of political apathy on the campuses.

The campuses have become permanent centers of dissatisfaction and protest. Many students are losing confidence in the capitalist system and the institutions and future of American bourgeois democracy. But as throughout the rest of society, the coming crises will have a *polarizing* effect on the campuses. This polarization will turn the campuses into an important battle-ground of competition for political cadres between the reactionary right and radical left, as well as among the various working-class tendencies. There will be no return to the long political quiescence of the late 1940s and 1950s.

The GIs

The ranks of the armed forces must also be counted as one of the most important allies of the working class. Young, over-whelmingly working class in composition, and with a high percentage drawn from the oppressed nationalities, the soldiers today are deeply affected by all the changes taking place in their generation and their class. Because of their assigned role as cannon fodder for the interests of private property and imperial-ist oppression and aggrandizement at home and around the world, their attitudes are of great importance.

Unlike World War II when there was general—if at bottom reluctant—support for the "war against fascism," the Vietnam War from the very beginning generated profound suspicion concerning the motives and goals of the rulers, and growing opposition among GIs to being used in Washington's schemes to police the world.

The antiwar radicalization and deepening disaffection within the army itself—reflecting the attitudes prevalent in the rest of American society—was one of the important factors that blocked U.S. imperialism from pursuing the war of aggression in Vietnam. The emergence of the antiwar GI as a conspicuous and widely popular figure marked a change in thinking of historic import.

The American army, owing to its composition and to today's political climate, is less and less suited to play its assigned role as a world police force. The American imperialists know full well that they must have such an instrument because planes, bombs, and the dragooned troops of a puppet regime are often not sufficient, as Vietnam has again demonstrated. But Washington does not have too many options. The legacy of the Vietnam War and the accompanying radicalization outside and inside the army is one of the new minus factors the ruling class must include in its calculations.

Every social protest movement—women's liberation, the radicalization of the national minorities, gay liberation, etc.—was reflected inside the armed forces.

The radicalization within the army itself inevitably focuses on the struggle to defend and extend the democratic rights of the soldiers. The concept of the citizen soldier as one who gives up none of his elementary freedoms and rights upon entering the armed forces is deeply embedded in American history from the time of the militia forces of the Revolutionary War to the present. Such concepts, which originated 200 years ago in the popular support for the political goals of the militia forces, are anathema to a military caste formed in the Prussian pattern. But they are so closely associated with the fundamental rights the American people believe to be theirs that the ruling class has not dared to risk a head-on confrontation on this matter during a period of rising mass antiwar sentiment.

The ruling class's decision to eliminate the draft in hopes of creating a more reliable instrument for implementing its imperialist aims creates two new problems for them. First, the rising percentage of Black troops in the combat divisions leads to a composition of this repressive force that makes it less reliable for use against the colonial revolution or in the suppression of ghetto uprisings and labor battles at home. Second, modern wars cannot be fought without conscription; and attempts to reintroduce the draft in the future, as the ruling class will be obliged to do in new imperialist aggressions, will inevitably call forth a quicker and greater antidraft sentiment than appeared during the Vietnam War.

VI. THE REAL COURSE OF AMERICAN BOURGEOIS DEMOCRACY

Bourgeois democracy in America has had an uninterrupted 200-year history. During that time, extensions of democratic rights—beginning with white male property owners—have been gradually won despite reactionary attempts to reverse the process. The gains were made at great cost. To win even elementary rights for nonproperty owners, nonwhites, workers, Blacks, women, and youth, a second revolution and civil war and immense efforts in the class struggle over a prolonged period were required.

But these gains in rights are only one aspect of bourgeois

democracy in America. As a form of class rule that only rich capitalist ruling classes can afford, American democracy has always rested on brutal force and crushing exploitation. First and foremost was slavery. There were also other forms of forced servitude, the expropriation and virtual extermination of the Native American population, the conquest and incorporation of half of Mexico, the superexploitation of immigrant labor, spoliation of vast natural resources, and the advance into the Caribbean, Latin America, and the Philippines.

As American imperialism emerged in the late nineteenth century, the continuation of bourgeois democracy in America increasingly required the massive superexploitation of other countries, the vast international "slave holdings" of American capitalism.

The economic crisis of the world capitalist system in the 1930s ended the prosperity and ate into the reserves on which dollar democracy rested. Democracy in the weaker imperialist countries (Italy, Germany, Spain, Portugal) went under first. If the capitalists instead of the workers were to have the last say, the political future of the United States was foreshadowed in the march of reaction and fascism in Europe.

Cold war to Vietnam

Post-World War II democracy in America was based on the uncontested domination of U.S. imperialism, which had vanquished its rivals (both "Axis" and "Allies") and brought whole new sections of the world under its yoke. Much of the former empires of the British, Dutch, French, Italian, German, Belgian, and Japanese ruling classes fell. U.S. imperialism took over the colonial slaves of its competitors. To keep them in bondage, financial, political, and military support—American foreign "aid"—were extended to the most brutally repressive and totalitarian "independent" regimes throughout the former colonial world.

The advances of the socialist revolution following World War II were countered with the institutionalization of the cold war at home. The reactionary domestic political climate was intended to support a world anticommunist "rollback" strategy.

The first phase of the cold war involved utilizing the monopoly of the atomic bomb to put heavy pressure on the Soviet Union. In preparation for war, careful attention was paid to the home front. Efforts were intensified to whip the liberals into line behind the cold war and to strike at the militancy and independence of the CIO. By the end of the 1940s the witch-hunt had largely succeeded in housebreaking the CIO bureaucracy and intimidating the ranks of labor. With the "loss of China," the cold war was deepened in the United States. A protracted period of conservatism and labor quiescence set in.

McCarthyism, which was the extension of the cold-war antilabor policies and loyalty purges initiated by Truman, had an incipient fascist logic of its own that eventually proved counterproductive to the ruling class. The reactionary Wisconsin demagogue had his wings clipped. But it was only the world capitalist boom of the 1950s and 1960s that provided the economic base for eliminating, for the time being, any serious threat of a fascist advance within the United States. In the post-Korean War period the "normal" methods of bourgeois-democratic rule proved adequate.

The qualitative disparity between the economic, financial, and military power of the United States and that of its competitors insured American imperialism's dominance. There seemed to be no limits—military, economic, or political—to Washington's arrogant actions as world cop, although the military stalemate in Korea, and the less than fervent patriotic sacrifices of labor in that intervention on the mainland of Asia, gave warning signals of what was to come.

The rulers were convinced they could provide sufficient quantities of both guns and butter. They believed they could both militarily crush resistance to imperialism abroad and make wage concessions at home ample enough to assure social peace. The capitalist economy, touted to be free of depressions, brought a feeling of relative security to broad layers of the working class to whom the Great Depression was still a vivid personal memory. It also fashioned a "silent generation" of youth in the 1950s. For that entire decade the only significant social struggle was that of Black people, who fought largely on their own, unsupported by the labor movement or other powerful forces.

The decisive turning point came in the second half of the 1960s, following Johnson's decision in 1965 to escalate armed intervention in Vietnam. Primed earlier by the small "ban the bomb" movement and the Cuban revolution, and spurred on by the Black struggle and the student radicalization, Johnson's escalation gave rise to an unprecedented antiwar movement and radicalization. For the first time in American history an imperialist war became the catalyst for mass political opposition to the policies of the regime.

The Vietnam radicalization originated in a growing appreciation of the hypocrisy of the claim that the White House was establishing democracy abroad. The forced evacuation of villages and the My Lais of the Kennedy-Johnson years, the napalming of children, the Nixon-Kissinger carpet bombings, the Tiger Cages, the invasion of Cambodia—these crimes stirred mounting revulsion from 1965 through Nixon's second inaugural in 1973.

Democracy's true face

This sentiment was accompanied by the growing conviction that there must be some connection between the actions of American imperialism abroad and the methods applied against domestic critics. The police assaults on the Black civil rights fighters in the South, the habitual police brutality against the inhabitants of the Black ghettos in the North and South, the murderous suppression of the ghetto rebellions, the police rampage against the demonstrators at the 1968 Democratic Party convention in Chicago, capped by the Kent State and Jackson State massacres during the May 1970 Cambodian invasion, drove home the point that the real face of American democracy was something quite different from the pleasant countenance millions of Americans had been taught to revere.

Underneath the formal liberties and democratic guarantees, the real decisions were made in secret by a tiny minority with brutal disregard for the needs, interests, or rights of the majority.

President after president from Truman to Nixon pretended to speak in candid terms to the American people, only to be exposed as liars and self-serving hypocrites. The demagogic double-talk of capitalist politics became clearer.

All this developed before there was widespread knowledge, or even suspicion, of the degree of secret government infiltration, surveillance, provocation, and disruption of the Black, antiwar, and radical movements. It was unthinkable to the majority of the American people that such practices were applied not only to the "radical" or "minority" social protest movements but to the labor movement and even the "loyal opposition" within the two-party system.

When such things began to come to light in the Watergate affair, a chain reaction was set off that has not ended. The

Watergate experience marked the opening of a stage in which people are more perceptive and critical in judging the nature of the institutions of bourgeois democracy, the nature of the executive powers, the system of checks and balances, the role of Congress, secret diplomacy, etc.

The Watergate revelations about the application of imperialist policies abroad were new and shocking to millions. But most significant was their deeper impact in altering public consciousness: the feeling became widespread that foreign and domestic policy may be but two sides of the same coin.

Imperial arrogance, contempt for human values, unspeakable brutality, disregard for the fundamental democratic rights the American masses believe in, police-state methods of political spying, provocation, and assassination—these are not only the policies of American capitalism abroad; they are the practices of American capitalism at home.

The single most important ideological gain of the initial radicalization was a loss of confidence in the veracity of the capitalist leaders of the United States. This has been reinforced by the Watergate crisis and the attempted cover-ups, along with the offshoot exposes concerning the FBI, CIA, IRS, and secret diplomacy. They have deepened popular doubt about the rulers' intention to administer a government or to decide domestic and foreign policy in the *interests* of the broad majority.

The confidence of the American working people in their own ability to see things as they are, and their feeling that there is no remedy but to take action in *their own interests* have grown as their trust in the "elected officials" has diminished.

The radicalization of the last decade can be measured in the escalation of the struggle for fundamental freedoms. This includes legal and democratic rights, but goes beyond them. Motivating the struggle is a basic stand in favor of what Malcolm X called *human rights*.

This concept of inalienable human rights has motivated all the social movements of the 1960s and early 1970s—struggles by Blacks, women, prisoners, soldiers, veterans, farm workers, mine workers, "illegal" residents, gays, and the aged.

Concurrent with the growing determination to extend and redefine basic freedoms and to prevent acquired rights from being eroded, millions of Americans sense that American capitalism is heading in an antidemocratic direction.

Such forebodings are well founded. The four classical conditions for the maintenance of imperialist democracy—sustained economic prosperity, a satisfied or docile working class, contentment among major sectors of the petty bourgeoisie and other potential allies of the working class, and a successful foreign policy—all are being eroded.

VII. LABOR'S STRATEGIC LINE OF MARCH

The Marxist model for constructing a revolutionary program in the imperialist epoch is the founding document of the Fourth International, the world party of socialist revolution, founded by Leon Trotsky in 1938. The program is entitled *The Death Agony of Capitalism and the Tasks of the Fourth International.*

This "Transitional Program," as it has come to be known, was adopted by the Socialist Workers Party and presented for discussion and approval to the founding congress of the Fourth International at a time when world capitalism had been undergoing a deep economic and social crisis for nearly a decade. The new economic downturn of 1937 had further deepened political polarization in America. Both fascist currents and labor party sentiments were on the rise in this country. The New Deal was becoming the "War Deal" as the clouds of World War II gathered rapidly, threatening unheard-of slaughter and destruction.

Neither the Stalinized Communist Party nor the Social Democrats, nor the assorted ultraleft, sectarian, and centrist groupings were capable of presenting a program adequate to the needs of the masses searching for a way out of the crisis. In Trotsky's estimation, solidly planting the Fourth International on a correct programmatic foundation was a key requirement.

Today's situation offers some important parallels, both in the objective situation and in the tasks facing revolutionists. After almost a quarter-century of expansionary development, world capitalism has entered a period of economic stagnation—with the threat of debilitating inflation, shortages, famine, unemployment, bank failures, business crashes, world depression, sudden political shifts, and severe crises. Cyclical economic crises in each country tend to be deeper and more synchronized internationally.

This will inevitably lead to a sharpening of the American class struggle in all its forms and to deepening class polarization. While the tempo of this polarization cannot be predicted, its general features are clear. Millions of workers will search for the road to independent political action and will more and more turn to class-struggle methods. On the other hand, rightist demagogues and fascist movements pretending to offer "radical" solutions to the capitalist crises will come forward as candidates for power.

The sharpening of interimperialist competition and conflict, the pressure for a redivision of markets on a world scale, the persistent tendency toward wars directed at halting the colonial revolution—with China and the Soviet Union as the ultimate targets—are all on the agenda. And any military adventure by the White House carries with it the threat of escalating into a nuclear showdown.

The confusion and disorientation generated by the Stalinists, Social Democrats, and the new assortment of ultralefts, centrists, and opportunists demonstrate that the need for clarity on program and perspectives remains decisive.

As in 1938, we can see unfolding on a world scale a prerevolutionary period of education, organization, and agitation. After a long period of relative quiescence, the workers in the advanced capitalist countries, beginning with the weaker of the European imperialist powers, are once again beginning to move. Sections of the masses more and more tend to enter into action, and are open to revolutionary alternatives, as they seek a way out of the impasse.

Method of the revolutionary program

In the United States, as elsewhere, the revolutionists constitute a relatively small nucleus grappling with two central problems:

•How to help the masses, through their own experiences of struggle, to cross the bridge from general dissatisfaction and demands that stem from their immediate problems, to revolutionary socialist solutions.

•How, in this process, to gather fresh forces and train the cadres who, in the course of their experiences in the class struggle, can build a mass revolutionary party capable of leading millions of working people to victory.

The key to the solution of these problems is the correct and flexible utilization of the method of the Transitional Program, giving clear and timely answers to the problems faced by the working class and its allies in their struggles.

The conversion of the current radicalization into a revolutionary situation will be determined by mass forces beyond our control.

In this situation we must strive to use whatever time we have to win members and gain experience in the class struggle. We must strive to reduce whatever relative advantage the Stalinists or Social Democratic currents have over us in size and position in sectors of the labor movement, organizations of the oppressed nationalities, and other sectors of the mass movement.

Several points must be borne in mind in relation to the method of our program, the transitional method:

• We begin from the *objective* contradictions of the capitalist system and the direction in which these are moving. On that basis we derive our demands, and we formulate them in terms that are, as much as possible, understandable to the masses at their given level of consciousness and readiness for action.

• We do not begin by demanding that the masses understand what "the system" is or that they reject any particular aspects of it. Instead we chart a course, raise demands, and propose actions aimed at shifting the burden of all the inequities and breakdowns of capitalism from the shoulders of the working people onto the employers and their government, where it properly belongs.

• We champion the progressive demands and support the struggles of all sectors of the oppressed, regardless of the origin and level of these actions.

• We recognize the pervasiveness of the deep divisions within the American working class bred by imperialism and class society, and we press for revolutionary unity based on support for the demands of the most oppressed. We press the working class to give clear and concrete answers to the problems faced by its allies. And we unconditionally reject any concept that the oppressed should "wait" for the labor movement to support them before entering into their own struggles.

• We raise demands that challenge the "rights" of capitalist property and prerogatives claimed by the government to control the lives of the working masses and the wealth they create. We do not stop with the necessary struggle to defend and extend all democratic rights. We carry the fight for democracy into the organization of the economy and the process of making decisions over the standard of living of the working class. This is the dynamic leading to control by the workers over the institutions and policies that determine the character of their work and life, the dynamic of direct democracy through councils or committees of action, and the dynamic leading to a workers' government.

• Our method is one of class-struggle action leading to deeper and clearer class consciousness. We promote the utilization of proletarian methods of struggle where the workers can make their weight count advantageously in direct mass actions in the streets and in the workplaces. In this perspective united-front-type tactics are central. Our goal of mass independent political action by the working class precludes any subordination to the needs of bourgeois parties, figures, or institutions. It necessitates the workers building their own political instrument, a mass party of the working class capable of leading their struggles to their revolutionary conclusion, the establishment of a workers' government.

Think socially; act politically

To meet this revolutionary perspective the American workers will have to learn to think socially and act politically. They must see the big social and political questions facing *all* the exploited and oppressed of the United States as issues of direct concern to them. They must stop placing their hopes in "individual solutions" to capitalism's blows and begin moving toward collective political action independent of the employers and their Democratic and Republican hirelings.

Defensive struggles against the bosses and their government will generate the nuclei for a class-struggle wing in the unions. Striving to defend themselves against the squeeze on jobs, real income, social welfare, and on-the-job conditions, the workers will come into direct confrontation with the entrenched labor bureaucracy and its class-collaborationist perspective. A class-struggle left wing will begin along these lines—a wing that stands for the transformation of the unions into instruments of revolutionary struggle whose independent power will be used on every level in the interests of the whole working class, organized and unorganized, and its allies.

Labor's next giant step will be to break the stranglehold of the bourgeois two-party system to which it is tied and through which it vainly tries to find solutions to capitalism's breakdowns. With a labor party based on the organized power of the unions, all the interrelated social, political, and economic interests of labor and its allies can be encompassed and fought for. This will reinforce the independent mobilizations of all sectors of the oppressed and help aim their force at the common enemy. And the workers can effectively counter the efforts of the rulers to diffuse and co-opt independent struggles of the masses by using their two-party monopoly.

The precise slogans and demands that will be raised, and the order in which they will appear, will depend on the development of the crises faced by American imperialism and the intensity of the pressures generated by the spontaneous struggles of the oppressed and exploited. But it is along this line of march that the politicalization of American labor will take place. The role of independent political action will begin- to become clear to millions, placing on the agenda the decisive question of which class shall govern—the workers or the employers.

Against the imperialist war machine

The task of hobbling and disarming the American imperialist world cops with their vast arsenal of nuclear weapons is a special responsibility of the American workers. No other force can do the job. The survival of humanity rests on their ability to accomplish this task in time. We demand immediate, unilateral, unconditional nuclear disarmament of U.S. imperialism.

The enormous size of Wall Street's war budget is difficult to grasp. The billions in resources consumed by the war budget must be reallocated to help meet the basic needs of the workers and their allies. The first step in that direction should be a 100 percent tax on all profits made from armaments production. Take the profits out of war.

We reject the insidious lie that the workers have no choice but to rely on massive "defense" industry contracts or else suffer large-scale unemployment. The war industry plants must be nationalized and put under the control of workers' committees charged with retooling for the production of useful goods.

The U.S. military machine is the key piece in all the imperialist alliances. Our call is: out now—an end to NATO, an end to all the imperialist pacts. Support and link up with the struggles by workers and youth in other countries against NATO. End all the military and diplomatic alliances that are directed against the colonial masses and the workers' states. Hands off the workers' struggles unfolding in the imperialist countries—no intervention, open or secret, in Portugal.

Labor should insist on the dissolution of all special paramilitary or "advisory" bodies set up to police situations where the use of U.S. troops would be embarrassing to Washington but which often serve as a preliminary step for open aggression. Get out of the Mideast. End the military and CIA police training programs around the world.

No support to reactionary butcher regimes, the puppets of imperialism. End all the fake "food for peace" programs and other so-called humanitarian props to these regimes around the globe.

International solidarity

The American workers have a special responsibility toward the colonial revolution because of U.S. imperialism's role as the foremost slave master in the world. The slogan expressing our fundamental line is: HANDS OFF! No intervention anywhere. The half-million GIs stationed abroad must be brought home now.

We pay special attention to the fight against racism, xenophobia, and all forms of chauvinism, which are a powerful ideological prop of imperialist foreign policy and supply implicit justification for colonial aggression. In this respect the fight against racism at home is closely linked with the fight against imperialist aggression abroad.

In the spirit of international class solidarity we champion the rights of foreign students and workers in the United States and uphold their freedom to travel, immigrate, study, work, live, and engage in political activity wherever they wish.

It is the youth, especially its most oppressed and exploited sections, who are called upon to fight imperialism's wars. In the long run the Pentagon cannot raise an army large enough to meet Wall Street's needs without conscription. Opposition to counterrevolutionary wars is at the heart of our opposition to the capitalist draft.

We take the offensive in regard to democracy within the armed forces. Soldiers have the right to know and to discuss the true aims of the government, to form political associations, to publish their own leaflets and papers.

We fight for the right of the citizen-soldier to exercise every democratic right guaranteed to other Americans, including the right to run for office.

Old enough to be squeezed into the "volunteer" army—old enough to vote and hold office.

End secret diplomacy and backstage deals. Publish all secret international correspondence. The people have a right to know all commitments made by the government.

Take the war-making powers out of the hands of Congress. Let the people vote directly on war.

In defense of the working class

The starting point of workers' struggles is the defense of their standard of living and conditions of work.

In a society based on exploitation, a decent job is the most fundamental right of every worker.

In a depression, the first requisite in addition to unemployment insurance is a massive program of public works. Another called-for emergency measure is reduction of the workweek, with no reduction in take-home pay, in order to spread the work among those who need jobs.

The trade unions and other mass organizations of the workers and oppressed must take responsibility for organizing workers with jobs, those without jobs, and those with only "part-time" jobs. They should prevent the employers from creating a pariah category of unemployed whom the employed do not regard as fellow workers. Those out of work must be viewed as part of "us," not as "them."

To protect themselves against inflation, which is a permanent scourge today, the working class needs a sliding scale of wages—an escalator clause—with prompt and full compensation for every rise in the cost of living. A consumer price index drawn up under the supervision of the workers and consumers—not the bosses—is required. Escalator clauses must cover all social welfare payments, such as unemployment benefits and Social Security.

The workers and their families will have to fight to keep social welfare programs from being eliminated and to bring them up to adequate standards. During periods of unemployment, health insurance coverage should be maintained by the government. Mortgages and installment payments on homes, cars, appliances, and furnishings should likewise be underwritten by the government. Child-care facilities must be kept open and expanded.

Unemployment compensation should be at full union scale, and with no time limit.

The threat of being laid off and denied an income because of the bosses' control over hiring and firing is the source of all pernicious "job discipline." The bosses must be prevented from using rising unemployment to reverse gains the working class has won and to divide the working class.

The seniority system won through previous battles by the workers' movement is one tool in limiting the bosses from picking and choosing whom they will fire at will, starting with the most militant workers. It, like the hiring hall and closed shop, established a degree of workers' control over hiring and firing. In a similar way the workers will have to prevent the bosses' use of "last hired, first fired" to reverse the gains recently made through preferential hiring and affirmative action quotas. Layoffs cannot be allowed to reduce the proportions of minority and women workers.

The trade union movement should also firmly reject all attempts by the monopolists to solve their own profit problems at the expense of workers abroad. Protectionist measures professedly aimed at "keeping jobs in the United States" have the central object of permitting U.S. corporations to charge higher prices and reap greater profits in the face of foreign competition. They are no less inflationary than the devaluation of the dollar, which deprives workers of the possibility of purchasing less expensive foreign-made goods. Protectionism, tariffs, devaluations, are all aimed at workers in the last analysis, whether here or abroad.

Workers' control on the job

On the job the workers must protect themselves from the attempts of the bosses to make them pay for the capitalists' growing problems by extracting a higher rate of surplus value through speedup, automation, and chipping away at health and safety standards.

Struggles will grow for protection against speedup and layoffs, for safety and health conditions, regulation of and veto power over work rules, and health codes to protect workers against industrial hazards—asbestos fibers, coal dust, and chemical or radiation poisoning.

The workers must have veto power on questions of safety. They should insist that production be shut down at once on demand of the workers and at no loss in pay whenever safety of personnel is at stake. All safety controls and the speed of the production line must be set by the workers themselves. Acceptable levels of chemical pollution, control over purification of waste products, and similar standards must be established by the workers after full access to technical information and consultation with experts of their own choice.

Workers' committees must be empowered to decide directly, in consultation with citizens' committees responsible to the community, on projects to establish plants or use industrial processes that may adversely affect the environment of cities and regions. Such decisions have to be made on the basis of full and accurate information about the ecological and health effects involved, and with no concern for profits such as motivates the lobbyists and government representatives of big business. Only labor can fight to put science to work as the liberator of humanity, not its destroyer.

Just as they must reject the false dilemma of having to choose between unemployment or making instruments of mass murder, workers must reject the lies of the bosses that they cannot afford to stay in business unless pollution controls are lifted and safety standards lowered. The workers and the community cannot afford pollution, shutdowns, or bosses who put profits above all other consideration. Any plant closed down by such bosses must be nationalized and reopened under the control of workers' committees with complete access to all the financial and technical information required for retooling or meeting the requisite standards on pollution and safety.

Open the books

"Open the books for inspection by the workers" is a necessary provision to protect the public against the shortages, sudden breakdowns, and rampant inflation endemic in the decline of capitalism and to counter any claims of the bosses that they cannot satisfy the needs of the workers, either as employees or consumers.

The claimed "right to business secrecy" is used by the employers' bankers and their politicians in a drive to cut back on wages, working conditions, and public services in every city, county, state, and federal jurisdiction they control through their two-party system. When monopolies like the utilities, the postal service, the agribusinesses, the railroads, and the aerospace industries cry "bankruptcy," charge exorbitant rates or prices, or refuse services to those who cannot pay, they should be nationalized and run under control of the workers and worker-consumer committees.

In order to make their decisions on a sound basis, the workers' committees will have to proceed in cooperation with similar committees throughout their industry on a national scale, and other industries in their region. The facts must be shared nationally and internationally, and the public kept fully informed.

To acquire the needed information and resources of credit and planning, the entire banking system—now the accounting and credit system of the capitalist class—will have to be expropriated and opened up to the committees of workers and placed under their control as well. Only by winning that struggle can the workers begin planning and organizing the economy so as to prevent breakdowns, chaos, and the lowering of the standard of living of the entire working class and its allies. And along this line of march, beginning with individual industry and sectors, the expropriation of the bourgeoisie will be posed.

Even partial steps along this course, imposed by a rising mass movement that is rapidly gaining in social and political consciousness and led by a growing class-struggle wing of organized labor, will meet with stiff resistance from the bosses. To them it is a sacrosanct prerogative to run their business as they see fit—to keep the details of their operations secret from those they exploit, to throw thousands onto the unemployment lines, to charge extortionate prices, to move "their" factories to where the workers are less organized and less experienced in fighting for their rights, to slash the educational system and social services the workers have fought for, to destroy the earth's ecosystem if this will assure high profits today, to use legislatures and "public" agencies to advance their schemes to make a fast buck.

An increase in class polarization will go hand in hand with deepening class struggle. Fascism, along with war, was the ultimate "solution" imposed by the ruling class to the last world capitalist crisis.

To protect their struggles and gains against murderous attacks by goons, cops, and fascist bands, the workers will have to organize and train their own forces and use them in the most effective way. Starting with defense of picket lines and the right to strike, the protection of their demonstrations or those of their allies, and proceeding to workers' defense guards, workers' militias, and the requisite arming of the working class, the working masses will learn from their own experiences what measures to take. The lessons of history, incorporated into the general strategy of the workers' movement, will prove invaluable on this life-and-death question.

Human rights, not property rights

The strong belief of the American people that they are entitled to basic democratic rights has a progressive dynamic. As the capitalist system declines, bourgeois democracy does not gain in vigor but grows progressively weaker. This will lead to struggles that tend to go beyond the limitations of bourgeois democracy and strengthen the radicalization and politicalization of the American working class. Thus a fundamental responsibility of socialist workers and a feature of their program is to defend and strive to extend democratic rights against every attempt by reaction to encroach upon them or to roll them back.

The workers must fight to protect themselves against the bosses' attacks upon the right to organize; the right to strike, including the right to strike against the government; the right to vote on contracts; the right to settle all issues in a dispute without any government interference or government meddling in union affairs. Above all the workers must fight against wage controls proposed or imposed by the government under whatever name or guise.

The workers have everything to gain from taking the offensive whenever possible in behalf of those social and economic rights that they more and more consider their due—decent housing, decent jobs, education, transportation, health, Social Security, freedom from government harassment, etc. In the course of struggle they will learn the necessity of fighting to extend human rights for all the allies of the proletariat. Every such gain reinforces the strength and unity of the working class as a whole.

The struggle to maintain rights already won and to extend them to new areas—economic rights, social rights, rights on the job, rights to a direct say on issues of war and peace—has marked every aspect of the radicalization. This is exemplified in the struggles for abortion rights and the Equal Rights Amendment; the eighteen-year-old vote; civil rights for less than "legal" age high school students; human rights for soldiers, veterans, gays, the elderly, and children; full human rights for all prisoners; language rights; rights of noncitizens.

Still other rights have been redefined in the course of struggle—attempts to impose prior-restraint laws on publications have been fought with some success, literary and artistic censorship restricted, and capital punishment curtailed.

There is growing recognition of the right to preferential treatment—quotas, affirmative action in industry, education, politics, and society—to correct the inequality of opportunity established by centuries of discrimination because of race, nationality, or sex. Millions of working people see that without this there can be no true equality or equal opportunity for those historically oppressed and discriminated against by class society.

None of these advances have been won without hard struggle, and each gain has to be defended against attempts to dilute or reverse it.

The vision of the social and economic rights people should have is being considerably widened. They include the idea that every human being has a right to enough food, to decent housing, medical care, education, and well-made products; that tenants and urban residents have rights; and even that future generations have rights—the right to an environment capable of healthfully sustaining human life.

The fight to extend democratic rights into industry means establishing various forms of direct democracy. It necessitates finding ways and means for the workers and their allies themselves to make the fundamental decisions that affect their lives instead of letting the bosses and their political representatives do that for them. It means establishing broad united action committees through which the workers and their allies can fight to impose their solutions to economic and social problems, both at the workplace and in society as a whole.

The right to know

As demands for *personal* privacy have increased, so have demands to *limit government and industry's* "rights" to secrecy. Not only is there a feeling that our lives are our own business but that "their" business is our business, too.

The exposures of government lies and duplicity in domestic and foreign policy have led to greater acceptance of the idea that the people have a right to *know* what the government is up to, what deals have been made behind closed doors, what commitments contrary to the interests of average working Americans have been made. Such mechanisms of direct democracy as referendums on major policy issues like the war, child care, and environmental questions have become increasingly popular, as the assumed prerogatives of the bourgeoisie to rule through institutions elected under their rules are challenged.

We persistently struggle to extend the frontiers of what the workers consider to be their inalienable economic, social, and political rights that no government has the right to take away from them.

And in all these efforts we advocate proletarian methods of struggle based on the mobilization of the collective strength of the workers and their allies independent of the needs or desires of the rulers and their institutions.

VIII. THE REVOLUTIONARY PARTY

The breakdowns and cyclical fluctuations of the American economy are rooted in the contradictions of world capitalist production and trade. The very ascent of American capitalism to world supremacy has paved the way for a cataclysmic explosion on its home grounds.

In America, a country that has never been carpet-bombed, invaded, occupied, or made to pay war indemnities, capitalism for all its achievements has not been able to assure liberty, justice, and a decent standard of living for all of its people. As the mightiest and wealthiest capitalist power celebrates the 200th birthday of its revolutionary origin, growing numbers of Americans are beginning to ask, "If not here, then where?" If capitalism can't make good in the United States, maybe something is decidedly wrong.

The end of the long postwar boom, and the rise of unrest and social struggles in the United States, once again call attention to the fact that the victory of the European socialist revolution is not a necessary prerequisite for the development of a revolutionary situation in the United States.

Just as the first workers' and peasants' revolution could succeed in Russia, where the operation of the law of uneven and combined development thrust the most backward of the major capitalist countries in Europe to the forefront of the world revolution, so those same laws can produce severe shocks in the coming period within the heartland of the most advanced imperialist power.

But even the most devastating breakdowns of American capitalism cannot automatically produce a victory for the socialist revolution. As Lenin pointed out, there is no absolutely hopeless situation for capitalism. However deep the crisis, if enough commodities can be destroyed or devalued through war, depression, and bankruptcy, and the standard of living of the working class can be driven low enough, capitalism can recover for the moment.

While powerful *world* forces are laying powder kegs under American imperialism, only forces *inside* the United States can take power away from the American capitalists and disarm them. In the nuclear age this is more decisive for humanity's salvation than ever before; the alternative is the eclipse of civilization or a worldwide scientifically planned economy.

Various developments in the United States can leap ahead of those in other parts of the world in a rather brief period. In the last decades this happened with the rise of the struggles of oppressed nationalities, the antiwar movement, the youth radicalization, the women's liberation movement, and similar struggles for human rights. At the same time the advanced decay of American capitalism poses problems to these movements that cannot be solved short of a socialist revolution. And at a certain point revolutionary trends within the American working class can develop at a truly American speed and tempo.

Questions of perspective, program, and party building cannot be postponed with the expectation that they will be resolved by the colossal objective forces of a revolutionary upsurge. On the contrary, even a small propaganda nucleus that intends to become a mass party must be armed with a clear revolutionary perspective that puts the construction of the revolutionary party in first place.

The Social Democrats and Stalinists

There has been a striking change since the 1930s in the relationship of forces between the revolutionary party, the Socialist Workers Party, and its reformist socialist opponents on the left.

The American Social Democracy retains a base in the labor bureaucracy, where its influence is stronger than its small and fragmented organizations would indicate. The role of the Social Democracy is circumscribed by its perspective of trying to improve capitalism through petty reforms and its political orientation of participating in the Democratic Party in the prayerful hope of its "realignment." But we can anticipate that Social Democratic formations will play a more active and open role in the coming period.

Within the Social Democratic framework differences exist between the reactionary, racist, anticommunist, diehard conservatives of the Meany-Shanker-Rustin wing and the anticommunist, liberal reformers of the Harrington-Gotbaum-Reuther wing. The two wings differ over the tactical course to be followed inside the Democratic Party machine. The differences involve such questions as how to manipulate the weight of the labor movement in order to win some concessions and how to teach the labor bureaucrats to adapt more adroitly to radically changing expectations and attitudes.

Deepening social crises and rising class struggles will lead to further differentiations and splits within the Social Democratic circles, with some moving further to the right and some important forces moving to the left as centrist currents.

Decline of American Stalinism

The shift in the relation of forces on the left is most strikingly registered in respect to the Stalinists. In 1945 the Communist Party claimed 100,000 members. They dominated several major industrial unions and had a periphery of hundreds of thousands of fellow travelers, intellectuals, Black sympathizers, and so on.

American Stalinism began losing its leading position in the American left from that point on. Their wartime line of speedup and a no-strike pledge, their postwar line of support for the perspective of American-Soviet maintenance of the status quo and of class peace, yielded its first fruits when the ruling class turned against their wartime servitors in the cold-war witch-hunt. The Stalinists looked around for popular support and found they had none. The only permanent factor in their policies—subordination of the class struggle in the United States to the diplomatic needs of Moscow—won a bitter reward from the workers they had misled.

The crushing of the Hungarian revolution and Khrushchev's admission of some of Stalin's crimes further weakened the CP. The inability of the Stalinists to launch a viable youth organization and to recruit broadly out of the radicalization of the 1960s while the Trotskyist movement was making steady gains further altered the relationship of forces in our favor.

Unlike the situation in the 1930s the relative strength of the Socialist Workers Party puts us in position to challenge them for leadership in the struggles of the working class and its allies. But it is important to underline that the pro-Moscow Communist Party remains our single most important and strongest opponent on the left.

The pro-Peking Stalinists have neither the cadres, periphery, nor material base of the pro-Moscow party. They are divided into numerous groupings with deep differences, especially on domestic politics. But the Chinese revolution, which they claim to represent, gives them an international banner that attracts a following, often among youth inclined to ultraleftism. In the climate of deepening radicalization they are growing. For some time to come, our party will be competing with the various Maoist currents for cadres and influence among the radical youth and oppressed nationalities. It is important to note that the ultraleft mood that arose in the late 1960s was worldwide. It has not yet run its course.

The Socialist Workers Party

The two-party system of American capitalism remains the greatest shock absorber of social protest. The single biggest anomaly in the American political scene is the absence of a political party of the working class and the lack of a tradition of independent working-class political organizations in the American labor movement. To transcend this political backwardness remains the single greatest leap to be taken in the politicalization of the American working class.

There is, of course, an advantageous side to the political inexperience of the American working class. The class-struggle minded socialist workers confront no powerful traditional reformist party to which the working class remains stubbornly loyal. The workers are not weighed down with the conservatizing force of the class-collaborationist political routinism ingrained in the European proletariat by the mass Social Democratic and Stalinist parties. Although the American union bureaucracy is far stronger than in the 1930s and acts as a formidable surrogate for a mass reformist party, it is less of an obstacle to socialist revolution than the reformist workers' parties in the advanced capitalist countries of Europe.

The political education of the American working class does not necessarily have to pass through a reformist labor party or come under the domination of Stalinist or Social Democratic misleadership. Explosive developments, propelling events at extraordinary speed, could bring about a rapid transition to revolutionary class consciousness. A mass revolutionary socialist party could emerge during such a revolutionary upsurge—but only if its cadres are prepared beforehand with a clear perspective and program and only if they are conscious that *a revolutionary party is the historical key to victory.*

As Trotsky explained in the Transitional Program, "The building of national revolutionary parties as sections of the Fourth International is the central task of the transitional epoch."

Central task of our epoch

The Socialist Workers Party is internationalist to its core. Not only are world developments shaping the coming struggles at home, but the American workers' enemies are the exploiters on a world scale. The perspective of the *Communist Manifesto*— "Workers of the world, unite"—remains our fundamental goal. While reactionary legislation precludes formal affiliation to the Fourth International, the Socialist Workers Party, since its founding, has been an integral political component of the world party of socialist revolution.

At the heart of the Socialist Workers Party's revolutionary program and internationalist perspective is its proletarian orientation. Only a party that has deep roots in the working class, that is composed primarily of workers, and enjoys the respect and confidence of the workers, can lead the American working class and its allies to power.

The proletarian orientation means concerted, systematic work to root the party in all sectors of the mass movement and to recruit the most capable fighters to the party. It means participation in labor organizations, in industry and among the unemployed, in the organizations of the oppressed minorities, in the struggles for women's liberation, and in the student movement. Over the last eighteen years the Young Socialist Alliance, the Trotskyist youth organization, has established itself as *the* revolutionary socialist organization in the student movement.

Our proletarian orientation means functioning as a homogeneous campaign party capable of choosing realistic objectives and concentrating our striking power and resources with maximum effectiveness. It means professionalizing our work and adjusting ourselves to the demands and direction of the mass movement in order to help lead that movement forward.

The need to integrate the party into all aspects of the mass movement shapes every activity we undertake. The deepening crises of the American capitalist system and its reactionary interventions abroad do not imply any esoteric new "tactics" for building the party. They only reinforce the need to deepen our proletarian orientation and to take advantage of the new opportunities opening on all sides.

The perspective of increasing class struggle and class polarization indicates more than ever the need for a disciplined combat party of the working class.

The revolutionary party that seeks to lead the socialist revolution is a voluntary organization. Without a common bond of mutual confidence, experience, and loyalty to the program and goals on which it is founded, it will never accomplish the immense tasks before it. Thus, for us the concept of loyalty to the party we are building, pride and confidence in our collective efforts—what Trotsky referred to as party patriotism—is simply the proletarian orientation and internationalist perspective applied to the construction of the revolutionary instrument necessary to realize our program.

The conditions for victory

The "Manifesto of the Fourth International on the Imperialist War and the Proletarian World Revolution," drafted by Trotsky in May 1940, outlines the following basic conditions for the victory of the proletarian revolution:

"(1) the bourgeois impasse and the resulting confusion of the ruling class; (2) the sharp dissatisfaction and the striving towards decisive changes in the ranks of the petty bourgeoisie, without whose support the big bourgeoisie cannot maintain itself; (3) the consciousness of the intolerable situation and readiness for revolutionary actions in the ranks of the proletariat; (4) a clear program and a firm leadership of the proletarian vanguard."

The manifesto points out that the main reason for the defeat of so many revolutions is that these four conditions rarely attain the necessary degree of maturity at one and the same time.

In the period now opening, we can clearly see the forces building on a world scale that will bring these conditions to maturity in the United States. But the central question, the one over which we will have a decisive say, is that of gathering together the forces that are committed to forging a revolutionary party in time.

Jack Barnes

The Radicalization of the American Working Class

This is the report on the resolution "Prospects for Socialism in America" to the plenum of the SWP National Committee on May 1, 1975, in New York City. The text includes the summary remarks following the discussion on the report and resolution.

If there is a central thesis in "Prospects for Socialism in America," it is the judgment by the Political Committee that we are entering a new stage of the radicalization. We are at the beginning of the radicalization of the American working class. A corner has been turned in the objective circumstances, and the door has been opened for a new step forward in class consciousness and in the transformation of the political consciousness of American labor.

In many ways we've been pointing to aspects of this process for some time. We have pointed out time and again that the earlier stages of the radicalization had an impact on the working class as a whole. Individual workers and groups of workers, far from being immune, were affected in the same way others were affected by the struggles, social protests, mobilizations, and changing attitudes of the earlier stages of the radicalization. This was certainly true from the late sixties on.

We added another point over a year ago. We noted the confirmation of our judgment that a whole spectrum of radical attitudes was being picked up by young workers especially. Among other things, our view was verified by the Yankelovich public opinion survey and similar studies. [See SWP *Party Builder* Vol. 8, No. 2 in 1974.] This was basically an extension of the first stages of the radicalization.

We think the depression of 1974-75, the one we are still in, caps a four-year period, a period beginning in August 1971 with the wage freeze, going through the brief speculative boom, the meat and oil shocks, the double-digit inflation, and culminating in the depression. Something new has happened that is more than just

82

a quantitative extension of the attitudes of the young radicals and young protesters penetrating the younger layers of the working class. The working class as a whole is being affected— and gradually beginning to think they are affected—as a class by the new economic situation. The depression and its attendant uncertainty affects every worker. Over and above the impact of the political protests and changing attitudes, the impact of the depression—the direct pressure on the workers as producers, as workers on the job, and as working class consumers—has begun to alter their consciousness.

We are not talking in this resolution about tempo, about how fast this development will take place. But we think the fact that it is occurring is unassailable. The evolution on a world scale of the economic, social, military, and political contradictions that led to this new stage of the radicalization is also the very thing that precludes the ruling class from charting a course that can fundamentally reverse it.

We don't predict in this resolution what the tempo will be, or what precise forms coming struggles will take. But we are convinced we will not see a definitive reversal of the development of the radicalization of the working class before a showdown battle. The period following the 1975 depression and "loss" of Vietnam is going to be quite a bit different from the period in this country following the 1948 recession and the "loss" of China. If this is true, it follows that not only new struggles, but new forms of struggle, not identical to those of the last decade, are on the agenda. There are new political opportunities for the American revolutionary party in the mass movement and in the organizations of American labor. There are new opportunities for the party, necessitating a *turn* in our attitudes, consciousness, priorities, and modes of functioning. If there is a turn in the objective circumstances it is not enough to note it; the turn has to be reflected in the organizational functioning and priorities of the party and the focus of its campaigns. That is what we will discuss under Barry Sheppard's report on the party's tasks [see "To the Working Class!" later in this volume].

Preparing for the convention

In evaluating the new situation at this plenum, we want to look ahead to the party convention in August. It is important for the National Committee to discuss this here, to see if we have agreement on our fundamental analysis. We must then take this discussion back to the party. Our number-one job in the next three months is discussing the new situation and the tasks that flow from it, so that the party members can think things through and prepare all the practical conclusions necessary to go forward from the convention, taking further advantage of the new opportunities.

In preparing for the convention we also think it important to read and study a number of things along with the draft of "Prospects for Socialism in America." Most important is the document "The World Political Situation and the Tasks of the Fourth International," the general line of which the party adopted at our December 1973 convention. [See *Dynamics of World Revolution Today* (New York: Pathfinder Press, 1974), pp. 111-88.]

We should review the political resolutions and reports adopted by our conventions in 1969 and 1971. [See *Towards an American Socialist Revolution* (Pathfinder, 1971), and *A Revolutionary Strategy for the 70s* (Pathfinder, 1972).] The acquisitions codified by those documents laid the basis for this current resolution. There is a continuity in our analysis from 1969 to 1975 that should be studied and discussed.

And, in addition, it will become clear to comrades in the branches, as it was to us as we worked on the draft, that a rereading of the Transitional Program, along with Trotsky's conversations with the American comrades about the program, takes on an added educational value in light of what we see unfolding.

Pathfinder Press just published a new edition of the Transitional Program which now includes all the discussions with Trotsky on the Transitional Program, both before and after the final draft was adopted. These discussions give significant attention to the program's application to the United States. [See *The Transitional Program for Socialist Revolution,* Second Edition, 1974.]

Finally, there are two other things which would be valuable in helping to understand and absorb the resolution. The Education Department plans to publish an educational bulletin entitled *The Revolutionary Perspective for the United States* by James P. Cannon. The bulletin will include the 1946 American Theses, the speech on it presented to the 1946 party convention, the speech on it given to the Political Committee beforehand, Jim's letters to the members of the National Committee in the fifties about it, and some of the sections from Trotsky's writings on the future

American revolution, its characteristics, tempo, and perspectives.

In addition I would suggest that a rereading of Farrell's Teamster books, with their case study of how a revolutionary union came into existence and what it did, will reveal several things missed the first time around. Comrades may have read the first two volumes on the Teamsters when they came out but a rereading will be valuable. One of the central themes we want to grapple with in our discussion is the comparison between the present and the last big radicalization of the working class during the 1930s, as well as the present and the 1940s, which saw the process of radicalization begin to be reversed and the initiation of the period of conservatism that lasted until the new radicalization. [See *Teamster Rebellion, Teamster Power,* and *Teamster Politics* by Farrell Dobbs.]

In this new resolution we have also tried to incorporate some of the fundamental programmatic alterations and clarifications that the party has adopted in the last decade.

We include in the resolution the perspective that we discussed when we changed our governmental slogan from "for a workers' and farmers' government" to "for a workers' government" in 1967.

Second, we include in the resolution the modification of our proletarian military policy as adopted at our 1969 convention. [See *Revolutionary Strategy in the Fight Against the Vietnam War* (New York: SWP National Education Department, *Education for Socialists* bulletin, 1975).]

Third, we include the perspectives on proletarianizing the party which were spelled out in the organizational resolution adopted at the 1965 convention, and which were further explained and developed in the talks on "The Structure and Organizational Principles of the Party" which Farrell gave in 1970. [See *The Structure and Organizational Principles of the Party* by Farrell Dobbs (New York: SWP National Education Department, *Education for Socialists* bulletin, June 1971).]

Structure of "Prospects for Socialism in America"

I want to outline the basic structure and some of the key ideas of the draft resolution.

The first two sections of the resolution root our conclusions in the objective situation on a world and national scale. We could call the first two sections together, "Our Perspectives for the

Radicalization of the Working Class Are Rooted in the Contradictions of World Capitalism."

There is one point on which I want to put special emphasis. What we face in the world capitalist economy is the exhaustion of the internal sources of the great boom after World War II. It's not simply a cyclical recession. It's not just the effects of a war adventure in Vietnam. It's not just the exhaustion of the effects of the massive reconstruction after the destruction of World War II. Rather, the basic internal sources of the long boom have themselves been exhausted, and new contradictions bode a long wave of stagnation of the world capitalist economic forces, as opposed to the expansion which we saw for a quarter century.

This puts every new dip, every new cyclical turn, every new financial crisis, in a new light. As the resolution states, the ups are going to be lower and shorter and the downs are going to be longer and deeper. And we are not the only ones who are beginning to sense this.

We list three real perspectives of the American ruling class, ones they cannot avoid in the coming period.

One is the continued tendency to become involved in military adventures. The ruling class cannot allow the process of world revolution to unfold without attempting to intervene to reverse it, with all that implies.

Second, they are compelled to try to lower the standard of living of the American workers. There is a decline in the relative productivity rates and relative rate of extraction of surplus value compared to their biggest competitors, especially Germany and Japan, and ultimately, growing long-term pressure on their rate of profits.

And finally, what this clearly implies over time is the attempt by the rulers to restrict the gains and rights—economic, human, and even democratic rights—of the American workers, with the heaviest blows aimed at the oppressed minorities and women. This is the necessary political counterpart of forced economic belt-tightening.

Changing attitudes among the American workers

Section three is in many ways the most important because it states the fundamental theme of the resolution: the changing consciousness of the American working class. Some of the bourgeois sociologists, at least the more perspicacious ones, have been trying to analyze the same things that we have.

Comrades remember the public opinion survey by Daniel Yankelovich which we discussed at our last plenum when we discussed the changing attitudes of the young workers. Well, he did another one about a year after that in which he tried to explain to the ruling class the dreadful thing he sees happening. (His conclusions are published in the Fall 1974 issue of *Dissent*.) For a decade in this country we saw what Yankelovich calls a growing crisis of *moral legitimacy*. More and more people, including more and more young workers, began doubting the legitimacy of the government from a moral point of view. It was not doing the just thing; it was not doing the fair thing; it was not doing the correct thing—to the Black people, to the people of Vietnam, or to others who were demanding their rights. It was a crisis of legitimacy, but a restricted one, of moral legitimacy.

But then Yankelovich says something new began happening after 1971. What is added is what he calls in his jargon a crisis of *functional legitimacy*. What functional legitimacy means in simple terms is that the system is no longer producing as it should. Even if you are not affected by the moral inadequacies of a system; when it can't produce and give you security, that is another blow to its legitimacy.

He points out that when people reach that conclusion, and hold it long enough, when it comes on top of a crisis of moral legitimacy, it can lead to an even bigger problem for the ruling class. People may decide that there is really a crisis of *institutional legitimacy,* that only the changing of the institutions of capitalism can solve the problem.

Fortune also ran a special issue last month [April 1975] entirely dedicated to "The American System." You would expect it to be a celebration of the bicentennial. But the titles of the articles don't seem to celebrate very much. They run like: "Reshaping the American Dream"; "Ever-increasing Affluence Is Less of a Sure Thing"; "Battered Pillars of the American System: Religion, Education, Science"; "Black America: Still Waiting for Full Membership"; "Color the New Generation Very Light Green"; "Putting the Cuffs on Capitalism"; "The Revolution of Rising Entitlements."

"The Revolution of Rising Entitlements," by Daniel Bell, is the most interesting. His thesis is quite simple: Over the past twenty years the American working class has come to believe that they are *entitled* to certain things that the working class did not look upon as rights before. This began without anyone knowing it. It began as things that used to be dreams became realities and then became necessities. We shouldn't forget that necessity is a historical concept. What was not considered a necessity by a working person in one epoch can become a necessity in another. But the promise of plenty, Bell says, has been transformed into a revolution of rising entitlements, of rising expectations. The period of long boom got this going, and it has been discounted forward. In other words, workers began expecting not only that they should have what they were getting, but they should continue to receive more at the same pace. In Bell's opinion, the hard truth and fundamental fact of American life is that this is no longer possible in the coming period.

This same issue of *Fortune* has drawings which depict *Fortune*'s version of working people. It runs across the bottom of five pages—just a mass of angry people carrying picket signs with demands. This is the nightmare of *Fortune,* all in living color: "Jobs for Navajos," "More Funds for Senior Citizens," "Preserve the Wilderness," "Free Colleges Are a Necessity," "Don't Cut Funds for Medical Research," "Save the Dunes," "We Need Decent Pensions," "Gay Pride," "Consumers Need Protection," "Tax the Polluters," "Equal Opportunity for Blacks," "Extend Unemployment Benefits," "We Demand Low-Income Housing," "New Yorkers Need Daycare Centers," "More Money for Mass Transit," "We Can Afford Better Schools," "No Time to Cut Food Stamps," "Chicanos Need Jobs," "Support Student Aid," "Equal Pay for Women," "Decent Housing Is a Right," and there are many more.

In other words, *Fortune* is saying: "Fellow rulers, we have a wicked contradiction." And they are right.

The expectations of the working class—what they believe to be their right to a decent living and a decent future for themselves and their families—are at their highest level in history. This coincides with a basic turn in the world and American economy. The depression of 1974-75 comes down on at least a quarter of a century of an upward curve of rising expectations.

We exclude the possibility of a new "New Deal" adequate to fundamentally satisfy these expectations of the working class and decisively reverse the process of radicalization. In our earlier discussions the Political Committee thought that it was important to make one point in this regard clear. We do not say that a "New Deal-type" Democratic administration is impossible. In fact, in my opinion that is the most likely next thing on the agenda. Something like a Kennedy administration appealing to the mass of the American people with promises for this or that reform is certainly possible. We do not preclude an administration, in any single upturn of the cycle, taking some of the fat, which the American ruling class still has, and trying to buy off, channel, diffuse sectors of the population they judge the most susceptible. But what we preclude is an extended period of reform that is *adequate* to meet the demands and *expectations* of the working people and reverse the process of drawing labor toward a radicalization that began in 1971.

This is fundamental. We see in the future a revolutionary perspective, not a perspective of massive reform.

American capitalism's "revolution"

Sections four and five are "The Changing Character and Composition of the Working Class," and "The Radicalization and Mobilization of the Allies of the Proletariat." American capital has been concentrated, centralized, expanded, and has brought entire new layers into the work force; industrialized whole sectors of agriculture; automated and computerized whole sections of industry; and transformed the character of industry, technology, and labor in the United States. In many ways American capital has been the "revolutionary" factor, not American labor, for a couple of decades. What we are trying to look at in these sections —in the structure of the American working class, its composition, the changing character and weight of the potential allies of the proletariat—is what this tremendous explosion of the American economy and the growth of monopolization of capital have wrought in the last thirty years.

The growth of a massive credit structure and of imperialist trusts were prominent features of the great boom. This process wrought a change from the 1930s and the 1940s. Section five looks like a repetition to some degree of section four. There is a repetition and it's intentional. To drive home the point we look first at Black Americans, Chicanos, women, youth, etc., as components of the American working class. We look at them as workers. And then, we re-look at them through different eyes, as social groupings—with their own independent needs and struggles and demands — who are potential allies of the working class.

These great economic, demographic, and social changes have altered the composition of the American working class, and we try to show what the effects on the union movement have been. This is a different working class, with different features and a different composition, than the class we have seen in previous radicalizations in the United States.

We try to cut through some of the myths and fakery of the bourgeois sociologists and the so-called economic statisticians who try to blur class differences. They say there are no more classes, just plain folks who are better-off or worse-off. Or they peddle the theory of the petty-bourgeoisification of the working class. We try to indicate that this is not true; that there has been a change in the structure of American industry, but there has not been a merger of classes. On the contrary, the distinction and difference between the working class in all its sectors and the owners of capital, large and small, is wider than it has ever been before.

The intentional confusion in the statistics is manifold. For example, government statistics count all service workers as "non-blue-collar workers"; anyone who works for the government is listed as a "non-blue-collar worker"; the wife of a steelworker who is a key-punch operator or checks out groceries is listed as a "white collar salaried employee," not part of the working class. All this fakery has covered up the realities. That is, far from the transformation of the workers into a new petty bourgeoisie, we have seen instead the proletarianization and alienation of new layers of the work force in the United States.

Some of the changes have been striking. Even after the Second World War began—as late as 1941—the majority of Blacks lived on the land. These kinds of facts give an indication of the scope of the change in the working class in the United States in a few decades.

American labor's historical allies

The second way we look at these same workers—in section five—is as the allies of the proletariat. Here the resolution does a number of things. We look at the army, at the student movement, and at the traditional allies of the proletariat on the land; and we take note of the changes they have undergone. We re-look at some of the important weighty allies, the Blacks, Chicanos, the women, and we examine their potential in the coming American revolution.

We also look at the middle class, and its shadings into the

working class. Here we try to do several things. We try to differentiate potential friend from potential foe in the middle class. We try to differentiate those we are not going to win over from those we are, from those we can and must win over to the struggle for a humane socialist society. We try to indicate who it is most likely we can win, who we can neutralize, and who will be our foes. We point to the differnce between a cop and a computer programmer. We try to indicate how the working class can present demands for sections of the middle class which meet their own self-interest, and which point to their role in the future workers' state. We try to counter some of the divisions that the ruling class tries to perpetrate and play on, claiming the poor farmer and the worker have divergent interests, that the public worker rides on the back of the industrial worker who pays crushing taxes, etc.

The second thing we look at is the question of the so-called middle-class character of the working class itself. Here we discuss a process which we think is of great historical importance to the American socialist movement. It can be called the de-petty-bourgeoisification of the American proletariat. Historically the American proletariat, until relatively recently, was a working class which came out of, was involved with, and sometimes went back to being farmers, independent artisans, and small owners.

The central allies of the early socialist movement were the farmers. A worker's uncle or aunt or nephew, brothers or sisters, were often on the land, or owned their own tools as artisans, or their own shop. A worker would often be the first of a family of a generation in industry, in a factory, in an office. It was a common idea to think about saving enough out of wages to someday go back to the farm or to buy a little shop or to buy enough tools to become self-employed, like you remember your father or uncle was. Of course, the less privileged had fewer dreams of this sort. But the tendency was to look in this direction for a way out. That ideology has been greatly weakened.

Compare how many of our parents' kin were on the land with how many there are in our own generation, and think about your younger nephews and nieces. Many of them have no relatives on the land. Many have no relatives who are small shopkeepers, small artisans, small farmers, nor do they talk about returning to the farm, etc., as a way to survive. That's not where they look; that's not their way out. That's not the *realistic* way out. From this point of view the American working class is less petty bourgeois than ever before. Even for many of the skilled mechanics facing the reality of the industrialization of their trade, the way out is not to become a small artisan; the way out must be elsewhere—*with* the working class, not out of it.

What this means is that one of the barriers to class consciousness—which was not simply the relatively high standard of living of the American working class or the chicken they had in the pot or the Ford they began driving, but the particular structure of the working class itself—has been eroded. The proletarianization of millions more who must organize as workers if they are to find a way forward—that is a fundamental change, a change that has accelerated tremendously since the Second World War.

This process must be differentiated from the so-called middle-class standard of living of the American working class. Petty-bourgeois ideology was an obstacle, an obstacle to class consciousness, an obstacle to the organization of the American working class. It was not an insuperable one; a large enough revolutionary leadership in the 1930s would have solved it quickly. But it was an obstacle. The "middle-class standard of living" of the working class is not the same obstacle; in fact, as it is attacked by the rulers, it will become a motivating factor in the American revolution. Standards of consumption that are decent and expectations that have risen are not obstacles to class consciousness. Rather they become goals to fight for as the crunch intensifies. This helps explain a fundamental theoretical point raised by many Marxists, especially from afar, including some of the masters, who realized that the standard of living of the American workers alone was not and could not be enough to explain the lags in and the character of class consciousness among the American workers.

The resolution makes another differentiation. We differentiate between the bureaucracy of the American labor movement—a petty-bourgeois social layer that will have to be defeated, divided, broken up—and what you might call the labor aristocracy, the better off, the more regularly employed and skilled layers of workers who face the same problems fundamentally (taking into account their relative privileges) as the rest of the working class: unemployment, inflation, speedup, decline of standard of living. Far from being identical to the labor bureaucracy, it is among these aristocratic layers that some great struggles will break out.

The myth of American democracy

The resolution contains a section called "The Real Course of American Bourgeois Democracy." An alternative title could be "Prepare for the Rules to Change." If what we say is true, we are heading into a period of increased class struggle. And like night follows day, increased class struggle is accompanied by increased class polarization. Just as there will be moves toward independent working class political action and class-struggle wings and currents will grow—fascist and rightist groups will also develop with *their* answers to the crisis of American capitalism. This is the logic of future developments.

When the ruling class talks about nationalizations and economic planning, such programs have a different logic from when fought for by workers struggling for more and more control over their work and lives. They have the logic of restrictions on union rights and on broader democratic rights. The rise of expectations or entitlements, whatever one wants to call it, if it cannot be adequately controlled with the carrot, will be met by the stick, by restrictions of democratic rights, by probings, and confrontations along these lines. Thus the American workers themselves will see the other face of capitalism, the one that was always clear to Native Americans, slaves, the Caribbeans, and semicolonial masses around the world, the one that has periodically been seen by the working class. The other face of the American ruling class offers something else than concessions, steady work, and steady, even if modest, increases of the standard of living.

One point was put in the resolution in light of the experience the comrades had in the past with fascist movements. This is the phrase, referring to the fascist threat, "whatever its American camouflage." That is important. Having gone through the Hague and McCarthy experiences we know that the American fascist movement, a serious one, will not conveniently identify itself. We should be knowledgeable about the camouflages used by American fascist movements in the past. We should also note one of the differences between Europe and America concerning this question, and that is the color question. Black Americans will be the fundamental target of American fascism.

One thing should be made very clear here. We are not talking about a conjunctural perspective, what is around the corner tomorrow. We don't see the rise of a fascist movement or a fascist threat on the immediate agenda. We are the last ones who want to talk in such a way as to be misinterpreted in this respect. But we state that the perspective is of deepening class struggle and that means that there will inevitably be class polarization along with it. By stating this clearly and openly we underscore the need for a revolutionary, centralized party, based on fundamental programmatic homogeneity and loyalty.

The program for socialist revolution

The programmatic section is entitled "Labor's Strategic Line of March." Here we try to deal with the two big questions that Trotsky kept hammering away at in his discussions with the American comrades around the Transitional Program. That is, as he said, the American workers must learn to think socially and act politically.

They must learn to think socially, to see more and more that the problems they face cannot be solved on an individual level but only on a social level. They must learn that the big questions which they may not think are "their" questions—the problems of oppressed nationalities, of women, etc.—*are* "their" questions and are intimately tied to the solution of the growing crisis they are facing.

Second, they must learn to act politically, to find a road to their own political instrument, a party of labor, an *independent* party of labor, based on the powerfully organized union movement, that can begin to operate in the arena where all questions will be settled, the political arena.

The resolution brings the role of the allies of the proletariat into this politicalization process, and relates it to the logic of a class-struggle left wing arising within the union movement and struggling to transform the union power that exists today into a revolutionary force fighting for all the oppressed.

We have a long-term perspective in this section also. The decisive thing for us is not whether American capitalism comes out of this current depression or when. The odds are of course overwhelming that it will come out of the depression, and the "when" will probably not be that far down the road. But any single business cycle, and single crisis is not decisive. What is decisive is the growing uncertainty, growing insecurity caused by the ups and downs, more and more out of control, and the unexpected and sudden crises and breakdowns. As the past period of relative stability and prosperity—in which you more or less knew where you were going, what you could have, what you could plan for yourself and your children—begins being ripped apart, the uncertainty of the cyclical ups and downs of the value of the currency, of the crises, begins to dominate. The class-collaborationist ideology and perspectives of the labor bureaucracy will emerge as more and more out of tune with—contradictory to—the living reality that millions and millions of workers face.

We tried to go through the key sections of the Transitional Program, putting our demands in language that makes sense given the American workers' experience and the current stage of the radicalization.

Down with the war-makers

The first of the three programmatic sections deals with the struggle against the imperialist war machine. Here we tried to incorporate the fundamental lessons of the Vietnam War period and the adjustment in the proletarian military policy that Farrell drafted and we adopted at our 1969 convention. We look at the utilization by the ruling class of xenophobia, patriotism, and chauvinism that accompanies each threat of war. We look at the central role of the youth and the role of the army in this period.

We try to focus on two things. One is the permanent threat of the nuclear destruction of humanity, and we incorporate the demand for unilateral disarmament into the revolutionary program. The second is the permanent war budget and its massive size, which not only threatens the life and limb of the worker used as cannon fodder, but more and more is seen as a vicious and unjustifiable drain on the resources and products of our labor in a period when our living standards are under attack.

In addition we look at one other small thing—what for lack of anything else I call the role of television. The American ruling class faces a difficulty in fighting a war and implementing an imperialist foreign policy right in front of the American working class. Today they must fight their wars on TV. They must fight their wars in the newspapers. They must fight their wars with whole layers of their intelligentsia divided and exposing their aims and methods. They can no longer restrict the brutal reality of war to the families of those who are killed and maimed. The families of everyone who may grow up to be killed or maimed also have war made more real for them. The pace of communications and the widespread understanding of at least major aspects of

the realities of imperialist war and foreign policy are something
new and something favorable for revolutionaries.

The starting point of workers' struggles

The second section of the programmatic part is entitled "In
Defense of the Working Class," and this we could have titled
"The Fight for Workers' Control." The central idea here is
that the starting point for all struggles is the fight to defend the
workers' right to employment and to maintain their standard of
living, against the bosses and their government. Fundamental
demands of the Transitional Program are incorporated here—a
sliding scale of both hours and wages and our other basic
demands.

We have incorporated economic rights which workers feel they
have—the right to know what's going on; the right to veto
decisions which affect their lives, limbs, and the health and
welfare of the community; the right to organize everywhere; the
right to have veto power on the job. We put forward demands that
encroach upon the rights and secrecy of the bosses and their
government, demands whose logic leads toward workers' control,
planning, expropriation, etc. This is very important. What we try
to do is put these latter demands in the framework of the class-
struggle road, not make them an abstract presentation of goals.
Planning, nationalization, and so-called job enrichment—all
these in and of themselves have no value whatsoever. The
question is "job enrichment," planning, nationalization—by
whom, for what purposes, controlled by whom, achieved along
what path of struggle? We always place the logical line of march
of labor toward control, toward planning, toward expropriation,
in the unfolding of the class struggle and the development of a
class-struggle wing in the mass organizations.

If you read the discussions between Trotsky and the Americans, Shachtman just couldn't seem to get the meaning of
workers' control in the Transitional Program. He kept saying
that it didn't make any sense to the American workers. This
workers' control will never make any sense to them. Other things
they'll get, but this workers' control is way ahead of its time. You
know, if we reread the discussions and rethink what has been
happening and how we utilize this concept, not necessarily as a
slogan but as a concept, we'll see that Trotsky was more right
than Shachtman about workers' control and the American
workers.

For the class-struggle unity of the oppressed and exploited

The third part of the programmatic section in "Labor's Strategic Line of March" is titled "Human Rights, Not Property Rights." Here we deal with a fundamental question, the question of the divisions in the working class that are imposed by capitalism. The revolutionary bridging of these divisions and the mobilization of the whole class is decisive to the success of any revolutionary thrust. We try to note the three most important divisions.

The most fundamental division of all is the division between the employed and the unemployed, those with a job and those without a job. In a deep enough depression over a long period of time the ruling class tries to use this division to turn millions and millions of workers into a demoralized pariah section of the class which is no longer looked upon by their co-workers as part of the working class.

The second great division is that fostered by the ruling class through the historic role of racism and racial discrimination.

And the third one is discrimination by sex, the attempt to keep women a reserve and highly flexible source of labor to be used when capitalism needs them and then driven out of the labor market when capitalism does not need them, and to have women viewed as different from male workers in this respect.

The key to our approach is the integrity and unity of the working class itself. Against individual solutions based on any sort of privilege, and for social solutions based on overcoming the divisions in the working class that we don't foster but that are fostered by the ruling class. These historical divisions exist; we must work to overcome them. This can be done only on the basis of class-struggle unity, by putting the human rights of the class as a whole and its oppressed sectors above the relative privileges, divisions, and hopes for individual solutions that the ruling class breeds. Maybe it's another way of saying, "Workers of the World, Unite!" Tariffs, "Buy American," deporting foreign-born workers, setting workers against the working farmers, blaming public workers for higher taxes, blaming Blacks, women, etc.—all these chauvinist and divisive views are put forward by the bosses and nurtured by their ideology. Without this ideology the ruling class can't rule; capitalism can't survive.

In this way we try to show how the battle for jobs, for a decent standard of living for all, goes hand in hand with the battle against discrimination and against beating back by even one inch the gains made by the doubly oppressed and exploited layers of the working class. We try to show how yesterday's dream has become today's necessity, and how the rights that Malcolm X so aptly called "human rights," that go beyond the grudgingly given civil rights, are put forward and fought for.

We try to show that the logic of these struggles is the thrust toward direct democracy. In the course of struggle, committees— factory committees, strike committees, neighborhood committees, mobilization committees, action coalitions, whatever they are— are thrown forward and become the decision-making bodies, if for the moment, of struggles. The rise of these committees must go hand in hand with drawing the most oppressed into struggle. These must become the arenas where more and more decision-making power is fought for and more and more decision-making power is taken—taking power away from the government to declare war or to decide on nuclear tests; taking power away from the bosses to pollute, to make decisions on the job. On an institutional plane the logic of this is the fight for direct democracy, for councils, for soviets; against subordination of struggles to parliamentary institutions, their commissions, their appointees. Of course, this is the logic of the struggle of the united front, the united-front tactic.

The CP program—by comparison

One thing we might do as we discuss the resolution in the preconvention period is compare it to the program of the Communist Party. The CP is going to adopt their program on June 29 in Chicago and will immediately publish it. We sent a copy of their draft to all the members of the National Committee and organizers. It is very revealing to go through the CP's program section by section, step by step, section of the working class by section of the working class, and see what the class-collaborationist program is, compared to the class-struggle program. Take the two programs side by side, the program of the Socialist Workers Party for the American revolution and the program of the American Communist Party, and compare them. There are some useful things to discover.

For instance, we find that they think the real problem is to remove the power of war-making from the hands of the executive branch and to place it in the hands of the Congress! We say put it in the hands of the people, let the people vote on war. You'll see that contrary to any illusions arising from Gus Hall's "lame duck" pamphlet, the road to independent working class political action by necessity goes through the Democratic Party. You'll discover that in fifteen pages of discussion of women and the rise of women's struggles and the importance of women in the American revolution, neither the Equal Rights Amendment nor abortion are ever mentioned. You'll discover many good statistics on the exploitation and double oppression of the oppressed nationalities, its historical roots, and then you will find that the answer to this does not include preferential hiring, upgrading, or quotas. You'll even discover a new slogan, called "equal upgrading."

You'll discover that détente can be won only if the ruling class is divided and the antimonopoly forces are won over. The struggle to win détente can institutionalize détente, and that would open the road to American socialism. I've never seen the peaceful coexistence road to socialism more clearly and disgustingly presented.

You'll find that nationalization is called for but under "democratic" control, not under workers' control. This nationalization will not be the culmination of the revolutionary struggle of the working class for more and more control over the American economy, that is, expropriation of the exploiters, but the result of demands on the "antimonopoly" sectors of the American ruling class who see the necessity for nationalization under "democratic" control.

The same day I read this CP program I read that the California Democratic Council came out for nationalization of the energy industry under the democratic control of a public energy-control board. I suspect a drafter of that resolution read the CP's resolution first.

Section for section, stage of the class struggle after stage of the class struggle, two views of the strategic line of march for the American working class can be counterposed, a Trotskyist view and a Stalinist view.

The revolutionary party

The final section of the resolution is on the revolutionary party. In the past few years we have often compared and contrasted the current radicalization with the previous radicalizations in the Debs period and the 1930s. There is another comparison that should be noted if we are correct in our analysis. In many ways we are reminded of the depth of the contradictions growing in the period before the Civil War, the second American revolution.

While we recognize that there can be big fluctuations in the tempo of the unfolding struggle, and sudden explosions, and while no peaceful transition to socialism is possible, there is also no hopeless situation for the ruling class. The outcome depends ultimately on the subjective factor, the degree of consciousness, homogeneity, combativity, experience, and class consciousness of the working class, and the existence of an adequate leadership—that is, a revolutionary mass party able to lead the workers to power.

Trotsky repeats over and over that it is this subjective factor that has been missing in so many otherwise promising situations. In *Europe and America* he discusses Europe in the 1920s and he points out: "What then has been lacking is the final subjective precondition, the awareness of the proletariat of Europe of its position in society, and its corresponding organization, its corresponding training by the party capable of leading it." That is what was lacking. What was the price the working class paid for this lag? The price was the first imperialist war. But on the other hand, the imperialist war played a gigantic role in impelling this consciousness forward.

And in many ways that is what happened in this country. The price the American workers paid because of the weakness of the subjective side, the lack of a sizable enough revolutionary party to lead them to power, was the second imperialist slaughter and the subsequent period of quiescence, conservatism, and the great expansion of American capital in the last thirty years. But this had another side to it. It bred a new working class and imposed a new series of problems and contradictions that have begun opening doors for the resolution of the problem of the subjective factor.

Where are we in the process of building the party? We have to be clear on this, so that we don't try to jump ahead of ourselves.

We can say that there are three basic stages in the development of a revolutionary party. One is a propaganda nucleus. Second is a cadre group capable of initiating propaganda actions. And third is a party of mass action. In the first two stages a group is able to change the relationship of forces within the vanguard of the working class and its allies where relatively small forces are involved if they react in a timely way with the correct line to new developments, new protests, new crises; with the right kind of initiatives, the right kind of action campaigns, explanations;

with fusions, regroupments, and consolidation of cadres. Such initiatives help the party grow, develop its cadres, gain relative to its opponents. But such groups are not yet able to change the relationship of class forces.

We can say we are crossing the bridge from the first to the second stage, to a cadre nucleus capable of initiating propaganda actions. In a period of radicalization a group's ability to function realistically and correctly can prove in practice, on a limited scale, that it is the most capable of the competing organizations on the left. This is what we did in the antiwar movement, and in other movements. This helped in the accumulation of cadres and in changing the relationship of forces on the left.

The third stage cannot come until the radicalization of the working class is deepened to the point, and the revolutionary party is developed to the point, where we have displaced the domination of opponents in the mass movements to the degree that we can lead mass struggles that in and of themselves begin affecting the class relationship of forces. To recognize this and be clear about it is not to belittle our accomplishments to date, but to see clearly where we are, what we can do, and not do, in moving ahead toward the next stage.

There is always a little danger when we present a program or resolution that looks further ahead than the conjuncture. Comrades want to take the objective possibilities that the resolution shows are unfolding and act as if we were a much bigger party. This we cannot do. But if we act realistically, we will become a larger party much faster. Concerning this point it is worth rereading and studying the fifth section of the international resolution "World Political Situation and the Tasks of the Fourth International," the section called "The Maturing of the Subjective Conditions for Revolution." All of our experience on this question over the past decades is drawn together here.

The proletarianization of the Socialist Workers Party

Another thing the resolution takes up is the importance of the proletarianization of the party. It's important to recall something that I think got passed over a little bit. Comrades will remember that when we adopted the organizational resolution in 1965, the party's attention focused on drawing the organizational lessons of the Workers League and Spartacist splits. But the comrades on the committee who drafted it—Jim Cannon, Farrell Dobbs, and George Novack, who were assigned by the National Committee to draft it—included a section about proletarianizing the party. The new codification of our organizational principles called for us to look forward to penetrating all sectors of the mass movement. Paraphrasing the lectures on the organizational character of the party given by Farrell in 1970, this includes labor organizations within industry; the unemployed; the movements of the oppressed nationalities, the Blacks, the Chicanos, the Puerto Ricans, and others that were becoming radicalized and in which workers, by the way, predominate; the college campuses and high schools; and new movements, especially the women's liberation movement which was just beginning to develop. The opportunities and rewards of implementing this perspective are greater than they were five or ten years ago.

The continuity of American Trotskyism

One final thing, under this section on the revolutionary party, is worth discussing, and that is the character of the American Trotskyist movement. It is important for the younger comrades to absorb a little bit of history about what kind of party they are inheriting.

What kind of party is it that for almost five decades, including long stretches of reaction, imperialist wars, prosperity, and isolation has been able to maintain and develop the revolutionary program and the nucleus of the revolutionary cadres of the American revolutionary party? It is useful to look at a few of the factors that made this possible.

First, the original cadres of American Trotskyism came out of the leadership of the American Communist Party, which in its time had regrouped the best of the revolutionary and internationalist-minded cadres of the early American socialist and syndicalist movement.

Second, these founding cadres as a team had exceptional leadership abilities—that's clear from history—as politicians, theoreticians, organizers, and as mass leaders. They had the additional advantage, a unique historical advantage, of working with and learning directly from the central cadres of the Russian revolution, both in their participation in the leadership of the Comintern and later in a long period of close and direct collaboration with Trotsky.

The cadres of the party were never decimated by war, victorious fascism, or Stalinist assassination, as so many of the nuclei of the International Left Opposition and the Fourth International were. This has meant continuity of cadres, an overlapping and collaboration of generations, and a balanced preservation and transmission of the principle lessons, organizational experiences, and class-struggle experiences of decades of revolutionary struggle.

The SWP throughout its history has been largely proletarian in composition and leadership, as well as in orientation. And one of the advantages accruing from the advanced character of American capitalism has been, and will be even more, the yield of a relatively high percentage of revolutionary organizers, politicians, and intellectuals of proletarian origin.

Because of its internationalist origins and inspiration, the party was from its very inception conscious of its responsibility as a key component in the leadership of the Fourth International. In its first formative decade the Trotskyist movement was solidly grounded in class-struggle principles and when the formation of the party came in 1938 and the split with Shachtman and the war came in 1940, the basic cadres and the basic traditions of the party had been formed.

Following Trotsky's death, the party showed a capacity to react to new developments that made a new theoretical challenge. The overturns in Eastern Europe, China, Yugoslavia, and Cuba; the rise of Black nationalism, of the women's liberation movement, of the youth movement; the new problems of strategy and analysis posed by the development of American capitalism—each of these theoretical challenges has been met.

And we have been able to show over decades a Leninist understanding of political and organizational practice commensurate with the tasks before the party of the American revolution. It is a fortuitous but historic circumstance that such a nucleus of the revolutionary party exists in the decisive country for the world revolution.

Sometimes newer comrades take all this completely for granted, as if it is just in the course of things that when you become radical that is the kind of party, cadre, and tradition you join up with. But maybe as we consider this resolution and perspective it outlines it would by good to note the unique historic opportunity represented by the existence of the SWP.

So our job here is to discuss the draft as thoroughly as we can, and prepare a better draft to present to the party for discussion between now and the convention, to prepare what will be an important convention in the history of our party.

I also think that if we do a quality job on this resolution there will be interest in it around the world, among comrades trying to come to grips with and discuss out the place of the United States in the perspectives for world revolution.

Summary

The discussion has been a step forward both in unifying our thinking on the draft resolution and in gathering the suggested changes that will improve the resolution so that it can do the job we want it to do in advancing discussion in the party.

It's worth going back over some of the key themes of the resolution. These are richer after the discussion.

The turn

The first question is what is new, what is the turn we are talking about? Lynn [Henderson] addressed himself to this and so did Art [Sharon].

We begin with the objective fact that a fundamental turn has now definitely occurred in both the world and American capitalist economy, and as a result we see the beginning of a turn in the consciousness of the American working class. We do not simply mean an additional quantitative penetration into the working class of the attitudes engendered in the first stages of the radicalization which we have discussed before.

The qualitative turning point of this combined process is the 1974-75 American depression, which is part of the first world capitalist recession since 1937-38. We could not have made the same judgment at our last plenum, a year ago. It is not only the stagnation and lowering of real wages; it's more than that. 1971-75 was a period in which a process occurred, but it was the depression that culminated the process.

Starting roughly in 1965—as Art mentioned—there was a decade-long stagnation of the real income of the American working class.

With the turn in capitalist policy signaled by Nixon's wage-freeze, trade-war, devaluation speech in August 1971, something new occurs. On top of stagnation comes the lowering of real wages, and then the first of the big shocks and crises that the workers are completely unprepared for, and which send tremors through their consciousness.

For instance, all of a sudden there is a shortage of meat, in the

United States. I can remember when I was a kid back in the forties, we still only had meat several times a week, but after the mid-fifties it was there—almost like the water or the air. For young workers, a shortage of meat, soaring prices for meat—by god, take away meat!—it's something abnormal.

The whole country runs on oil and suddenly there's a giant oil crisis. You have to line up to get your tank partly filled!

We're used to relatively stable prices, but inflation, which began with the Vietnam War, all of a sudden begins soaring. And this is one of the most debilitating things that can happen to a worker. What will the dollar be worth tomorrow? What can I buy? How far ahead can I plan? Can we do the things we planned on doing? *Tremendous new uncertainty.* We were used to a little creeping inflation, a little bit in the fifties and early sixties, but not like this.

We faced the warped speculative boom in 1971-72 as we came out of the wage freeze. But it was an odd boom even when it was happening. It was a boom that was accompanied by accelerated inflation that soon reached double-digit proportions. There was great unevenness in the boom; the increase in employment didn't come close to keeping up with the money increase in Gross National Product. The boom seemed to consist of a tremendous export of wheat, the first fruits of the successful Nixon-Connally international offensive; and then the crash. The payoff for the big inflationary boom was the crash. And the crash marks a new stage.

The depression brings—not just to the youngest, not just to the most oppressed—but to the *working class as a whole*—the uncertainty about whether or not you'll have a job. Whether or not you can work and make a living. That's the greatest pressure of all on our class, which even if skilled and white, has only its labor power to sell.

It is this combination of things culminating in the depression that marks the turning of a corner on a world scale and in this country, as Lynn discussed. It has begun affecting the working class in a new way. The April 26 march on Washington for jobs, the smaller-scale protests that preceeded it, are reflections of this. Workers as workers, as unemployed and as unionists, marching on the question of jobs—that's new. And it was a popular march. It was a march that reflected the feelings of many people. I liked Frank Boehm's comments on this. It was a march that raised the idea that it would be a good thing for the public employees in

New York to repeat such a march where the Beame team hangs out. This new situation is the result of something in addition to the stagnation and then lowering of real wages. Today real wages, what you can really buy with your paycheck, are below what they were in late 1964. The government admits that; those are the facts, and any worker can tell you that.

But we could not yet have said that we were at the beginning stages of the radicalization of the working class at our last plenum, because it was not yet true. We were still at a stage—it turns out the end of a stage—in which we were anticipating this radicalization. Then we were looking at sectors and industries like construction and auto that began to crash first. We were looking at the attack on the workers' standard of living and their expectations and quality of life. We were looking for the blow from American capitalism that would generalize the turning point in the crisis of capitalism and do it in such way that the American workers would *know*.

And we got it with the depression. Now we can say a turn has occurred, and there is the beginning of its reflection in a new consciousness in the working class. About that there can be no ambiguity in the resolution.

Once we came to this conclusion, we found it useful to look at a few other things. What is this critter, the American working class?

So we go back and look at what capitalism has wrought in the last thirty years, and we see quite an animal. In numbers and size, in racial and sex composition, in age, in combativity, in attitudes and expectations, we see a whole series of changes from a previous period. And we look also at the powerful allies of the working class, to make our analysis and projections precise. What are the forces that are going to be the powerhouses of the coming battles, as we enter a period in which we can anticipate new class struggles and new class consciousness? We tried to answer that question, and that's why we looked at the structure of the working class and why we looked at the powerful allies.

In this resolution we look at these questions from a new vantage point. Many things in this resolution have been said in this or that place before, in the *Militant* or in previous resolutions, but not from the point of view of beginning with the changing character and structure of the American working class and the radicalization and mobilization of labor's allies. That's looking at this process from the point of view of charting a strategy of *labor to power*. That's the vantage point from which we look at the allies of the working class in this resolution. We'll look at the most important ally of the working class differently in the next report on the agenda. There we'll look at Afro-Americans as an independent component of the American revolution. But in the political resolution we intentionally have a different viewpoint.

Let me take the time to read two paragraphs of the summary of the report by Trotsky to the Third Congress of the Comintern that I referred to briefly in my report.

"The question, which is raised by many comrades abstractly, of just what will lead to revolution: impoverishment or prosperity, is completely false when so formulated. I have already tried to prove this in my report. One Spanish comrade told me in a private conversation that in his country it was precisely the prosperity which came to Spanish industry through the war that produced a revolutionary movement on a large scale, whereas previously stagnation had prevailed. Here we have an example that is not Russian but Spanish—an example from the other side of Europe. Comrades! Neither impoverishment nor prosperity as such can lead to revolution. But the alteration of prosperity and impoverishment, the crises, the uncertainty, the absence of stability—these are the motor factors of revolution.

"Why has the labor bureaucracy become so conservative? In most cases it consists of weak creatures who live on a moderate scale, whose existence is nowise marked by luxury; but they have grown accustomed to stable living conditions. They have no fear of unemployment so long as they can keep themselves within the framework of the normal party and trade union life. This tranquil mode of existence has also exerted its influence upon the psychology of a broad layer of workers who are better off. But today this blessed state, this stability of living conditions, has receded into the past; in place of artificial prosperity has come impoverishment. Prices are steeply rising, wages keep changing in or out of consonance with currency fluctuations. Currency leaps, prices leap, wages leap and then come the ups and downs of feverish fictitious conjunctures and profound crises. This lack of stability, the uncertainty of what tomorrow will bring in the personal life of every worker, is the most revolutionary factor of the epoch in which we live." [*The First Five Years of the Communist International* (New York: Monad Press, 1972), vol. 2, pp. 233-34.]

That comes close to being a description of the period which we have entered.

It's worth repeating what several comrades said. For the overwhelming majority of the members and leaders of this party, our entire political lives have been in another period, a period different from the one we are now entering. So I'm not worried about throwing the party off the tracks by calling this a turn. We're a homogeneous party, a party with a competent cadre. I'm most concerned about making the turn in everyone's consciousness, and on a nationwide scale, to prepare ourselves on all planes for the new situation. That's the first job.

Think socially and act politically

An important theme in the resolution is taken from Trotsky's discussions with the American comrades, in which he says several times, "The American workers must learn to think socially and act politically. There will be no revolution, there will be no revolutionary upsurge without those two factors." At least three times he makes that point in the discussion.

Act politically. What is involved here is quite simply the fact that labor's first giant step did not move onto the political plane. The organization of another million, two, or three million workers is not decisive, not in relation to the necessary next giant step forward for labor. What is decisive now is the political organization of the working class. A tool must be found, and there is only one—an independent political party—to take the struggles that lie ahead beyond the trade union plane and generalize them on the political level.

In the report I discussed the *Fortune* article by Daniel Bell about "The Revolution of Rising Entitlements." He raises another problem that the ruling class is trying to grapple with. More and more these expectations are formulated in demands aimed at the government. More and more working people are beginning to feel that only on the governmental level can these pressing problems of life be solved. The next step for the workers is to generalize and organize their struggle on this level, the political level. That means a labor party, not another employers' party like the Democrats or Republicans.

It's not a question of promissory notes. We don't guarantee that the labor party stage won't essentially be bypassed by a tremendous revolutionary upheaval and the rapid growth of the revolutionary party. If that is in the cards, so be it, that's great. But we start with the historic problem, and with the size of the SWP. There is massive power in the union movement. Frank Lovell described that organized power. There is massive power there, but it is blocked, at best, or tied to the employers' parties on the political level. It must move onto the political level. We don't propose a reformist or centrist program for this labor party. The program we propose for this labor party is in section 7 of our resolution; that's our program for a party of labor based on the unions. But the working class must take this step of organizing itself politically. And the most likely variant on how this step will first be taken is the organization of a labor party based on the unions. And it must be fought for. Without this fight the development of the class struggle toward posing the question of what class will rule will not have passed to the essential level of politics.

Think socially. Cease thinking that there are individual solutions. Cease thinking that there are solutions to your major problems on a plant level. Cease thinking there are solutions for you if you are relatively privileged, while many others are being driven down. Cease thinking the problems and solutions are solely national as opposed to international ones. Learn to think socially. Learn that the struggles of the oppressed outside your union, outside your plant, outside your neighborhood, outside your class, even, are *your* struggles and not only because they are right and just; but because without the forces of these layers joining with you, this horrendous capitalist society cannot and will not be changed.

The struggles of the Blacks, the Chicanos, the Puerto Ricans, the women will teach the labor movement to think socially. Everyone is going to be fighting for jobs. Maybe more Blacks and more women will be fighting for work, but job struggles are going to be broad struggles cutting across race and sex lines in American labor, as crises hit deeply. And a white male worker is going to find himself in the same boat with Blacks, women, and others once it hits him. Especially if he has been living high off the hog (relative to his own previous standards), and his family's expectations are high on the hog, it's going to hit even harder in some ways.

But on this question of learning to think socially the women and oppressed nationalities will take the lead, because by definition their struggles raise broader social questions. This is one of the things Nat [Weinstein] was pointing to when he stressed the historic tasks of the proletarian revolution, and how they can't be bypassed or postponed to the Greek Kalends; you can't cheat on them. Because what may look like historical tasks become the tasks for the moment, as a social crisis deepens on its way to a revolutionary situation. Not for moral reasons, but because of the need to mobilize enough clout to take power away from the capitalists. Labor can't cheat on this; because only if the oppressed nationalities, the women, these sectors of the working class, these allies, are mobilized in a gigantic struggle will the forces that can settle things in this country come forward. It's another way of saying that there is no way around principled politics.

Our refusal to subordinate the struggles of the most oppressed sections of the working class—whether they are fighting as superexploited workers or as an oppressed nationality or sex—is not some moral, utopian thing to make it look like we are a good party for all the oppressed. It is the realistic road, the class-struggle road, the *only* road to the mobilization of the forces that can transfer power from the capitalists to the workers.

What we are talking about here is not the same thing as the program a workers' state will carry out in the process of the construction of socialism. When we talk to women, to Blacks, to young people, to people who are worried about the ecology, to gay people, to all people whatever their attitude or situation in life, that find this society unbearable, we tell them that only a socialist society, a society that gets rid of classes, and the necessity for racial and sexual discrimination, can solve these problems. But the *essential first step* to reach that society is to fight together to establish a workers' government, a dictatorship of the proletariat—the most democratic government in history—to abolish the tyrannic dictatorship of capital. We need a new class in power to sweep the old crud aside, to begin the humane reconstruction of society. Unless the working class can be united around this perspective it will not be able to become a social and political fighting force. And without this perspective as part of its program, there are great limits to how far a class-struggle left wing in the unions can go.

In this sense the combined character of the American revolution refers to the struggle for power, not simply to the tasks of the revolution itself.

Against racist and sexist job discrimination

Now, if organizations like CLUW can't get straight on the question of discrimination in layoffs, they can't get anything straight and they don't deserve to exist. There's a reason we support a Coalition of Labor Union Women. We're not for dual unionism. We support CLUW because labor union women face some additional concrete historical forms of oppression, exploitation, discrimination, that labor union men don't. Right? We don't propose a coalition of labor union men. Some may—Shanker, Meany—but not us. It is the Coalition of Labor Union Women. And the one thing about which there can be no ambiguity is that it fights for labor union women, to eradicate and overcome the centuries of discrimination and special oppression of women. That's why it exists.

This has been very thoroughly discussed yesterday and today and I'm glad we're in solid agreement on this. This party is opposed to the bosses or capitalist government using layoffs to chop back any of the gains Blacks or women have made. Can you imagine what kind of party we would be if we didn't have this position? Here's a party that is for affirmative action, preferential hiring and upgrading during the big economic upswing when jobs are plentiful. We say, yes we're for it, not because it's an isolated problem here, but because it is a historic problem of discriminatory education patterns, racial and sexual discrimination on the job, in hiring and upgrading, etc. We say the bosses foster this discrimination because more than anything else they need the working class divided in order to maintain their rule. We say the road to equality can only be the rectification of past discrimination, through preferential methods. Everything else is fake liberalism. That's what we say when times are good.

And then when times are bad, what if there were any ambiguity in the stance of the SWP? What if we should say, well, cool it now, Blacks and women, seniority comes first. That would be read as bowing to the grossest prejudices emanating from the privileges of white male job-trusts and the union bureaucracy. And if that position were maintained over time, it would be. It would be.

The key thing is to turn this on the bosses and the employers. What we say is the *boss* cannot use his temporary monopoly over the means of production—which the workers who produce everything are going to take away from him someday but haven't yet, unfortunately—to reverse gains made by women and the oppressed nationalities. I think the formula we use in the resolution is not one percentage point less. Don't lower by a single percentage point the proportion of Black or women workers through discriminatory layoffs.

Within this framework we can educate and take on whatever confusion we have to take on in the ranks of labor. If in some places seniority is used by the bosses to cover discriminatory layoffs, well, we say, this is a higher principle than seniority and we figure a way to present our position. But we are always concrete. As Jean [Tussey] correctly said, what we don't do, is we don't get the two things mixed up. You don't go to a group of unorganized workers and say, brothers and sisters, one of the reasons to join the union is you won't have seniority.

Our opposition to *discrimination* in layoffs is completely different from our demand for jobs for all, for a sliding scale of hours, which is our platform for fighting against the massive layoffs of capitalist depressions. But until we can win jobs for all, there not only will be layoffs, but millions of discriminatory ones, and we are opposed to the bosses using them to reverse by one iota job gains made by the oppressed. On this we totally differentiate ourselves from the sectarian workerists and the straddling Stalinists.

The state of the unions

Do young workers look to their unions for solutions to their problems? Fred [Halstead] made the point that most do not today. But we should note the unevenness in relation to this, in the different industries, in different parts of the country. It's not true that miners who have problems don't look to their union. Obviously many of them do. It's not true that layers of workers in several unions, different industries, different parts of the country don't look to their unions. They do.

More important is that they must. Because there is an awesome question before the American workers, which they aren't aware of yet. In the epoch we're in and the period we're entering, the unions will be transformed into revolutionary instruments of class struggle that can lead social and political fights forward, or they will simply be turned into the police agencies for the bosses and their government.

The alternative we have before us is the alternative that Trotsky posed most strongly in "Trade Unions in the Epoch of

Imperialist Decay." That is the alternative that American workers face on a broad scale. It's not an optional question. It's a life and death struggle of the American working class to take from the bureaucrats the power and organization of the labor movement. The unions are many things to many people; they have been many things in the past. The CIO was a great social movement in the beginning, not just a union movement as many younger comrades think of it. And it will be many different things in the future.

We make no promises on this either. Whole sections of the union structure will be knocked down and new formations will come up. Whole sections will not meet the test. The problems of privilege, the problems of class collaboration, the problems of racism and sexism that Harry [Ring] pointed to that run so deep, can destroy certain unions. We don't offer promissory notes on this. What we offer is a commitment and a program to struggle, to struggle to transform these unions which belong to the workers, not to these bureaucratic cretins on top of them. They belong to the workers, and their power belongs to the workers, and they have to move forward to use this power. The American ruling class has not taken the union movement head-on at this stage of the crisis. They still try to skirt around it, go after its weakest links, probe it. But this can change rapidly and these questions will be posed.

At this stage we can only propagandize around the points of our program for the unions. Comrades asked me, well, are you proposing organizing class-struggle left wings in the unions? Well, the answer is yes, in a certain sense. That is what we should be doing. Yes. What can we do to organize class-struggle left wings at this stage? Well, mostly propaganda. Mostly explain. But there are many workers ready to listen, more ready to listen today than yesterday. We explain clearly and we keep explaining. That's part of organizing. You don't have to wait. We can't hot-house it, but a class-struggle left wing won't come full-blown from the forehead of Zeus. It won't blossom without the participation of revolutionists.

The program for socialist revolution

Finally there is the programmatic section. There wasn't much discussion on this part because comrades are comfortable with it. But we should go over that section carefully during the preconvention discussion, because we say some things in there in new ways. It's an attempt to apply aspects of our transitional program in ways that make sense for the coming period, in ways that we have not presented before.

It's worth repeating that it will be valuable during the discussion to reread the discussions with the Old Man on the Transitional Program. Reread the world political resolution which we adopted in December 1973. And reread Farrell's books. These books are the story of a revolutionary union, its rise and fall, what it did and how it was different from other unions. It's worth looking at these books from that point of view. How do you approach the question of thinking socially and acting politically? How do you approach the question of the pariah sections, the unemployed and oppressed? How did [Minneapolis Truck Drivers Local] 544 see its mission? How did its leaders think? How were its ranks mobilized? How was it different from what you see in unions today? How might the story of this union look to some young workers as the coming period of radicalization deepens?

We have not been talking about the immediate tasks and perspectives of the party under this point. One of the immediate tasks and perspectives of the party is to absorb this resolution if we agree on it and to make a turn in our thinking, to begin to come to grips with the fact that we are entering a period different from that most of us have lived through. We'll have to act differently, think differently, move in a different way. We'll have to have a different atmosphere in the party. We'll have to recruit in a different way. We won't recruit only people who are already professional revolutionists out of the YSA. I don't mean to jump ahead to the tasks and perspectives report and discussion. But we cannot accept the fact of this turn, make the turn in our thinking, and not prepare for the other turns that logically follow.

Let me say something about the word "turn." There was a discussion in the Political Committee concerning the term "turn." Joe [Hansen] pointed out it could be misinterpreted to mean something like the "French turn" in 1936 when we followed the example of the French Trotskyists and had our whole membership suddenly join the Socialist Party because of an opportunity to reach people in that milieu. Or a comrade could get the wrong idea that the turn means colonization of a certain industry that we're going to throw people into, something like that. Joe pointed out that it's an accumulation of a quantitative process that's outlined in our world political resolution. We don't want to misinterpret the word "turn." In an uneven way the changing objective situation is already reflected in the work of most branches. We're not missing many opportunities.

But from a fundamental point of view it is a turn. When we've gone through a period very different from the one opening up it's always useful to think this way. And we need it. There's an unevenness in the party. We need to use the preconvention discussion and convention discussion and workshops to pull the whole party together.

We're not talking about a narrow "union orientation." We say we are at the beginning of the radicalization of the *working class;* we are talking about throwing forces into important openings— reacting as a campaign cadre party to struggles such as the antiracist struggle that unfolded in Boston. We're talking about the growing possibilities of penetrating the mass movement, of the mass movement changing in all its sectors, of applying the proletarian orientation of the party as spelled out in the 1965 organizational resolution and in Farrell's explanation of it at the Socialist Activists and Educational Conference in 1970. We're talking about working to make this party and its leadership more Black, more Chicano, more Puerto Rican, more female, as well as more working class in composition.

We are convinced we can recruit over the coming period more workers, more Black fighters, more Puerto Ricans, more Chicanos, more women, more young people. And we intend to do so, because we will be fighting in the struggles that will be occurring and maximizing the chances of doing so.

We should be cautious about the concessions that can be made by the ruling class. Layers of the working class can win concessions; there may be a series of concessions. I thought George Breitman added a point that was valuable. It wasn't simply or primarily the New Deal that blocked the development of the radicalization of the American working class in the thirties. More important, it was the war and the turn the ruling class was able to make in extended preparation for the war— suppressing democratic rights, whipping up patriotism, utilizing war production, etc., that blocked independent political action by the labor movement. But the working class still could have done the job with the right leadership.

Given the changed composition, character, structure of the present working class, this radicalization presents even a better opportunity than the 1930s.

We shouldn't underestimate what the party section of this

resolution says. This resolution would not mean a damn thing, we'd be talking through our hats if over the last period we had not developed a cadre party that can implement this resolution in the years ahead.

How rich the opportunities are compared to what we would face if we had only a handful of members, or if we had not been through the struggles of the past four decades, or if we had not begun a transition in leadership, or if we had not had any experience in any sectors of the mass movement, or if we had no broad continuity. We have a cadre armed like very few cadres in the world have ever been.

We're not going to leap over ourselves and transform ourselves into a mass party overnight. No. But we think every single member of this party is going to make this turn, and we are going to enjoy making it. What did we join the party for? It wasn't to join a circle of friends, although there are pretty good people here and they are more interesting than most. That's true even when things are slow; but that's not what we joined for. We joined to participate in the next steps we see coming in the class struggle, to be part of them and to be part of the leadership of the mass movements.

We can add the point Fred Halstead made on the quality of life capitalism offers. He said, what do the capitalists really have to offer? Even the reformers. The *best* thing they have to offer, even if things go well, is another twenty years like the last twenty years of "prosperity." Another twenty years like that and we'll hardly be able to live in this country! This is the strongest capitalist power on the face of the earth, with the highest level of capitalist development, and that was the best they could do. The very best. And more and more workers in this country will come to see that.

Mary-Alice Waters

Toward a Mass Socialist Movement

This report on the resolution "Prospects for Socialism in America" was given to the Twenty-seventh National Convention of the Socialist Workers Party held in Ohio in August 1975.

"Prospects for Socialism in America" opens by summarizing what's new about the situation in the United States today. It says, "The effects of the combined social and economic shocks of the last half-decade, coming on top of the changes in attitudes wrought by the movements of social protest and the radicalization of the 1960s and 1970s have brought us to the threshold of a new period in the transformation of the political consciousness of the American working class.

"A different stage in the process of radicalization is opening; new types of struggles are coming onto the agenda."

We are stressing something that we did not say prior to the current depression, and that we could not have said with certainty two years ago. Changing economic and social conditions on a world scale are beginning to generate a new stage in the development of the political consciousness of the American working class, and most acutely among the most oppressed and exploited members and allies of the class. This necessitates a corresponding turn in the consciousness, priorities, and functioning of the Socialist Workers Party so that we can prepare to meet these new political challenges and opportunities.

Our goal is to play a role in the coming mass struggles of American labor and the oppressed nationalities, women, and youth that will advance this process of politicalization to the maximum. This is the essence of the turn that is analyzed in the political resolution and in the reports adopted by the National Committee that we have been discussing throughout the party for the past three-and-a-half months. This turn is the axis of our deliberations at this convention. We are confident that the SWP will leave the convention with a better understanding of this turn, having considered its implications and been alerted to the challenges it presents.

This report will not attempt to analyze the economic and political conjuncture in the capitalist world. The turn we are talking about is not predicated on specific immediate economic fluctuations or political lineups. We are not proposing immediate sweeping alterations in our activities—such as when we threw all our forces into the antiwar movement a decade ago. Nor are we discussing the kind of shift that the party made in the mid-1930s when we entered the Socialist Party for a time. Betsey Stone, who will give the report on tasks, Malik Miah, who will give the youth report, and Tony Thomas, who will present the report on "The Fight for Black Liberation: The Current Stage and Its Tasks," will be discussing the main areas of our activity for the coming months and the adjustments in our tasks that flow from the current political opportunities. This report and discussion will have a broader historical perspective and take a longer range view of the realities confronting our class today.

Three elements, or crossing a bridge

What is this turn in the objective situation that we have been talking about? It's a combination, or better yet, it's the cumulative effect of three interwoven elements.

First, there has been the radicalization process of the last fifteen years, which we have discussed, and written about extensively [see *Towards an American Socialist Revolution* and *A Revolutionary Strategy for the 70s* (New York: Pathfinder Press)]. The Black struggle, the Cuban revolution, youth rebellion, anti-Vietnam War movement, the women's radicalization, Watergate, the changing values of broad layers of the American population, the growing rejection by millions of the idea that the American government is *their* government ruling in *their* interest.

But there's more to the matter than a linear extension of this radicalization process or the continued penetration of these oppositional ideas into the working class. That second element is the change in the world economic situation. We are now seeing the end of the biggest and most extended boom in the history of modern capitalism. This postwar boom peaked in the 1968-71 period, ending what had been an unprecedented ten-year expansion without a downturn in the United States economy.

As the motor forces of the postwar boom increasingly exhausted themselves, we saw a deepening and exacerbation of all the contradictions inherent in the capitalist anarchy of production imprisoned within its outmoded framework of private property and national boundaries. Interimperialist conflict and competition has increased for the no-longer-rapidly-expanding world markets. The scramble to ensure sources of raw materials has intensified. European and Japanese capitalism's increasing productivity, narrowing the previous U.S. labor productivity advantage, brought mounting pressure on the U.S. capitalist economy, which could no longer pay for Vietnam, social and economic reforms, and maintain a competitive superiority on the world market.

The mortgage-credit explosion and war spending of the 1950s and 1960s helped to create the mountain of what Marx called fictitious capital, as inflation began tearing into the dollar. Further inflationary pressures, generated by the cost of Vietnam, undermined the privileged role of the dollar as world currency, and threatened the collapse of the world monetary system.

The rising combativity of European workers showed that it would not be easy to make them pay to maintain the profits and the competitive position of the capitalists of France, Britain, or Italy.

Then came the oil shock of 1973-74. Double-digit inflation, the most debilitating disease of modern capitalism, accelerated even faster in the first generalized international depression to hit all the major capitalist countries since 1937-38.

This second element, the downturn in the capitalist economy on an international scale, had engendered the third new factor in the objective situation: The American workers' consciousness of themselves as a class has begun to change. The end of the postwar boom did not have an immediate impact on that class consciousness, because the repercussions were not immediately felt by the average American worker. Between 1965 and 1970, money wages were rising, and inflation was running only 4-6 percent a year, so that real income remained steady, or fell only slightly. The gap between Black and white incomes even narrowed a little. There were some gains in social services.

The first big jolt came in August 1971 when the Nixon-Connally international economic offensive was launched, the wage freeze imposed, and the dollar devalued. This was followed by the Nixon administration's 1972-73 "rollback" of the gains in social services, especially those that had been made in the 1960s. The ruling class's policy, administered by Nixon, was to cut social welfare, to cut child care, to end the poverty programs, to reduce aid to education, aid to the cities, transportation and health appropriations. Inflation took its toll on the standard of living of the veterans, those who depend on Social Security, and the working class in general.

Then came the 1973-74 oil crisis and the 1974-75 depression, with double-digit inflation, with even official unemployment figures standing at more than 9 percent, with a sharp decline in real wages, with a widening of the Black-white gap, with the offensive against all the gains that had been won by Blacks and women through affirmative action suits and preferential hiring programs.

During this period, between the August 1971 wage freeze and the 1975 depression, a bridge was crossed in the state of consciousness and expectations of the American working class. On the 1971 side of the bridge, the working class was still relatively optimistic, with relative long-term security and confidence, even if there were growing doubts and questions. On the 1975 side of that bridge stands a working class with a growing sense of insecurity, with a fear of what the future will bring, and with the feeling that it will very likely be worse than what has been. Jobs are no longer plentiful, and even when you find work, inflation will erode your standard of living.

At the 1975 end of that bridge stands a working class that is beginning to sense that they face more than a temporary dip in an upward curve; they suspect that the future holds an enduring social crisis, an economic curve that is heading downward. Many will look back on this period as the beginning of hard times, not just a short bad spell in a period of increasing prosperity.

For the foreseeable future even the most optimistic bourgeois economists are predicting official unemployment rates of 6 to 8 percent. For many Black youths that means no hope whatsoever of ever finding a job. For many women that means being pushed out of the labor market.

Even the slightest upturn reraises the specter of runaway inflation.

The cities continue to rot, the social services deteriorate, and almost any day we can be faced with another sudden breakdown or shortage—oil, meat, water, bread, who knows what will be next? When we speak about a pronounced shift in the basic objective framework in which we function, we refer to the opening of this new period resulting from the impact of these three interrelated elements—the radicalization, the end of the boom, and the resultant changing consciousness of the American working class.

Our generation's "1930s"

The continuing instability and growing uncertainty that marks this new period is compelling workers to raise new questions, to be open to new answers, and to consider new perspectives. It will impel them into struggles that lead in a revolutionary direction.

We are not making predictions on the tempo of this process. We are not saying there won't be upturns in the economic cycle. We are not saying that revolutionary struggles are guaranteed around the corner. We are saying: Not only is the long postwar boom over but we have entered upon a new historical experience that is going to be for our generation the equivalent of the great social crisis of the 1930s.

The forms of the convulsions are not going to duplicate those of the Great Depression. But the duration and the scope of the coming social crisis and the revolutionary perspectives inherent in them are going to be comparable. With this basic framework in mind let us take a look at the state of the American working class, as it is confronted by and as it confronts this new situation.

Leon Trotsky, in discussion with SWP leaders in 1938 around the drafting of the program of the Fourth International, talked about the political backwardness of the American working class, what he called its petty-bourgeois mentality, its lack of class consciousness and class solidarity, its search for individual solutions to social problems [see *The Transitional Program for Socialist Revolution* by Leon Trotsky (New York: Pathfinder Press, 1974)]. His observations were accurate.

This political backwardness stems from the entire history of American society and its working population. Up to the very eve of the twentieth century the class conflicts that dominated American politics were not between wage-labor and capital, but between the slavocracy and expanding industrial capital, and between industrial capital and petty commodity producers.

In American working-class history we don't have the equivalents of the British Chartist movement, of the French and German revolutions of 1848, of the Paris Commune, of Russia's

1905. There was not even any large-scale unionization of American workers until we were one-third of the way through the twentieth century—and this unionization was not accompanied by the organization of a mass political party of the working class.

Trotsky insisted, of course, that this political backwardness was not an insuperable obstacle, an everlasting condition. It could be overcome—and rapidly—under the proper circumstances. The American working class learned a tremendous amount in a few years in the 1930s. But the progress of its political consciousness continued to be blocked by the betrayals of the AFL-CIO leaders, the Communist Party, and Social Democracy. Trotsky stresses over and over that before they would be able to play their historical role, the American workers had to learn to "think socially and to act politically."

That generalization is a good starting point for examining the changes that have come about in the character and composition of the American class structure since the 1930s. From that vantage point one thing becomes quite clear: these changes are serving to strengthen the working class in this country, numerically, socially, politically, and helping to lay the basis for overcoming the most serious weaknesses in the social and political consciousness of our class. These changes have affected the consciousness of the working class, and they have affected the forms of the class struggle in the United States, that is, the channels through which the working class tries to solve the problems imposed on it by capitalism's crisis.

Three major changes should be emphasized: (1) the scope of proletarianization in American society; (2) the forging of the American imperialist state as a modern prisonhouse of nations; and (3) the vastly increased role of the government in every aspect of economic and social life.

Decline of the "frontier mentality"

"Prospects for Socialism in America" emphasizes the extent to which industrialization, mechanization, automation, monopolization in every sector of economic activity have led to a massive increase in the size of the American working class, both absolutely and relative to other classes.

Two results of this process should be noted. First, the increased weight of the working class makes it easier for it to establish itself as the dominant class economically and politically and carry through the socialist transformation of society. Second, this process reflects the continued de-petty-bourgeoisification of the class structure of American society. This has led to a reduction of illusions that the solutions to one's problems lie in a personal escape—as a small farmer, artisan, or small businessman—rather than in collective struggle on one level or another. This is a crucially important aspect of the transformation of the social and class consciousness of the American workers. The changes that have taken place along this line have helped to alter the petty-bourgeois or individualist or frontier mentality that dominated American life so long and impeded the growth of proletarian class consciousness.

One of the most striking consequences is the relatively small role slated for the land question in the coming American socialist revolution. In the last decades monopoly capital has gone far toward reorganizing American agriculture on an industrial basis. The astronomical increases of its productivity have turned the plains and irrigated valleys of North America into the granary of the world.

The precipitous decline of the family farm as a weighty feature of American society has removed a whole avenue of retreat and refuge in distress for the individual worker in this country. It reinforces consciousness that the only road that is open leads to collective organization and struggle as part of the working class—not back to the old homestead on the family farm.

The second striking aspect of this process of proletarianization has been the incorporation of women into the labor force in proportions qualitatively higher than before the Second World War. This change has facilitated the new rise of the feminist movement we are aware of. And it is already becoming a major problem for the ruling class in a period of deepening economic and social crisis. Women who believe they have a right to a job, and many of whom believe they have a right to preferential treatment in order to overcome the centuries of discrimination, do not simply accept being pushed out of the job market when the crunch comes.

Compare what is happening today with the 1930s. In the short period between the crash at the end of 1929 and the 1930 census the proportion of the work force composed of women dropped by more than 10 percent. Thus working women bore a vastly disproportionate share of the unemployment following the crash of 1929. And it took fifteen years to recoup this lost ground.

The readiness of women today to fight to keep their jobs, the refusal to accept as normal their being cast out of the work force, their resistance to being relegated back into the home, is one of the most important changes in the character of the working class.

This factor has already begun to play a central part in altering the class consciousness of workers. It induces the working class toward thinking in broader social terms about the problems they face and begin to act collectively as a class force to politically resolve these larger social problems.

The centrality of the national question

Interrelated with proletarianization has been a second major change in the structure of American society in the past quarter century. That is the forging of imperialist America into a new and modern "prisonhouse of nations."

The weight of the national question as a component part of the American revolution has qualitatively increased since the 1930s. This is a result of the much greater size and political impact of the oppressed national minorities. Millions of Puerto Rican and Mexican immigrants have been proletarianized and incorporated into the labor market under conditions of superexploitation. The Black population has been transformed as a class force in less than thirty years. Even at the end of World War II the majority of the Black population was still a landless peasantry—share-croppers, to use American terminology. Today they are more urban and proletarian than the white sector.

When Trotsky talked about Black workers as the vanguard of the class, who were going to proceed to the American socialist revolution in giant strides, ahead of the white workers, he was talking about a vanguard of tens of thousands or at most hundreds of thousands. Nowadays we are talking about millions of Black workers in this category. The importance of this change for American politics as a whole—and our own perspectives in particular—should not be underestimated.

The radicalization, the independent mobilizations of the oppressed nationalities, their struggles for their democratic rights over the last twenty years are integral aspects of the striving of the American working class to resolve the problems that are imposed on it by American capitalism. These independent struggles flow from the alteration in the forms of the class struggle that stem from the changes in the character and composition of the American working class.

The importance of democratic struggles against oppression and discrimination make the nationalities question one of the driving forces of the coming American revolution. This is at the heart of our concept of the combined character of the third American revolution. Without an understanding of the dialectical interconnection between the class and the national struggle, without comprehending that the oppressed nationalities and national minorities are at the same time parts of the working class and allies of the working class, there can be no realistic and comprehensive revolutionary program and strategy for the United States.

The number-one problem of revolutionary strategy in the United States is overcoming the divisions among the American workers that are created, fostered, and maintained by the ruling class in order to weaken, disorient, divide, demoralize, and defeat the workers' collective efforts. These are the divisions between employed and unemployed, organized and unorganized, legals and "illegals," Black and white, male and female, skilled and unskilled, young and old, hourly wage workers and salaried personnel.

In recent years the independent mass mobilizations of the Black population have produced a significant alteration in the consciousness, not only of Black Americans, but of many more white Americans than realized. The racism and prejedice of white Americans remains colossal. Yet the changes that have been brought about by the independent battles of Blacks in the last decade makes the ruling class's use of racism to divide the American working people less effective today than ever before in our history.

Some of the contributions to the preconvention discussion on this question were very educational—for instance, Tom Kerry's recollections about conditions in the National Maritime Union after the war. We should stop and think for a moment about the meaning of the changes that have taken place over the fight for affirmative action, preferential hiring, and against discriminatory layoffs. The labor movement today is far advanced over the conditions that existed during the rise of the CIO. Frank Lovell pointed out in one of his contributions that when the CIO came along it was considered extremely radical that Blacks were accepted as members of the CIO unions alongside whites and that the principle of equal protection on the job was established. That was a landmark of progress. Up to that time Black workers were barred from most of the trade unions and craft structures of the AFL.

Today the battle is not over that settled question, nor over a liberal concept of equality which simply perpetuates inequality, but over the very revolutionary concept of the right to preferential treatment to overcome the centuries of discrimination. That battle is being fought out in principle and in everyday activity, not just in narrow left circles but in the mass organizations of the working class, in the unions, in the Black organizations, in the courts, on TV, in the newspapers.

For us there is something else involved in the nationwide debate over affirmative action and discriminatory layoffs. In this country a revolutionary party that lowers its banner one fraction of an inch in adaptation to the privileges of the American labor aristocracy that are being paid for by the slaves of American imperialism at home and abroad, that party will cease to be a genuine revolutionary party. We should stop and consider the lesson Marx and Engels taught revolutionists a hundred years ago, emphasizing the degree to which the English labor aristocracy was an obstacle to the development of revolutionary consciousness in Britain. That aristocracy was but a pale prototype of the labor aristocracy in this country which fattens on the crumbs from the table of American imperialism.

Our defense of preferential treatment and opposition to discriminatory layoffs is part of a policy designed to overcome the biggest obstacle on the road to the American revolution, the racial and sex divisions in the ranks of the working class. They cannot be overcome by pandering to or reinforcing the privileges of the relatively better off layers of the working class. Revolutionary unity can be forged only by combining the fight for broad social and economic goals of the class as a whole with an unconditional fight for the immediate needs of the most oppressed and exploited layers.

This is not a secondary, peripheral, or tactical question. It lies at the very heart of our revolutionary strategy. It implements our political line of how to break down the divisions within the working class. As Linda Jenness, Frank Lovell, and Baxter Smith pointed out in their contribution to the discussion bulletin, white male workers must be taught by experience that any attempt to maintain their relative privileges—and it's pretty damned relative in this economy—at the expense of their fellow workers is to side with the capitalist class and the bosses against their own interests as workers, and against their whole class. Understanding this truth is the beginning of class consciousness.

Our starting point is not concern for the attitudes of the relatively privileged workers. We know that the initial reaction of many of them will be to try to find some individual way to keep their small privileges at the expense of others. Our starting point is the material interests and needs of our class as a whole. We must base our party on those who understand this and those who will fight for this. We turn to the most oppressed, the most exploited, and we fight alongside them to educate and win the majority of our class, because it is only their struggle that can advance the education of the working class as a whole. We anticipate that just as the Black struggle has altered consciousness in recent years, so the struggle by the most oppressed and exploited layers of the working class is going to show the way toward a self-acting, self-conscious class force that is aware of its historical responsibilities and is striving to solve its class problems in the only way possible—along the road of revolutionary unity in struggle.

Increased role of government intervention

The third major change noted by "Prospects for Socialism in America" is the vastly increased role of the government in every aspect of economic and social life. We ordinarily think of this phenomenon in terms of the government as employer. We have often called attention to the tremendous growth of jobs in the public sector followed by the growth of public employee unionism. But this rapid rise in the size of the government payroll is one feature of something more extensive—that is the vast expansion of state intervention in every aspect of the society and economy.

The post-World War II generation is rarely conscious of this. For us it has always been there. But this is a very big change from the 1930s. When the crash came in 1929, there was no Social Security, no unemployment insurance, no wage boards, no phony price regulations. There was no payroll tax on the average worker's income, no massive military spending, no CIA, no poverty programs, etc., etc., etc.

Today the role of the government on every level as employer, contractor, regulator, arbitrator, controller, administrator of social and economic welface, world cop permanently armed to the teeth, is beginning to come forward in the general consciousness of the American working class. This is attended by the general attitude that the governement is responsible, both for the mess that has been created, whether it is inflation, gas shortages, unemployment, discrimination, or whatever, and also for the solutions to these problems. There is a feeling that only the government is powerful enough to resolve such colossal problems—and moreover it is obligated to do so.

In a recent public opinion survey on the American family, Daniel Yankelovich reports that one half the population believes that the government has the responsibility to see that everyone has a good standard of living. And he goes on to comment that what was once held to be the responsibility of the individual or family unit is now believed by one out of two people to be a right, just like unemployment insurance and Social Security. This he worriedly comments "does not make it easy to adapt to the realities of the present, and the evidence suggests that many American families are psychologically unprepared for a period of scarcity."

Of course what the ruling class refers to as a lack of "psychological" preparation is what we see as a step forward in political consciousness.

Two sides of this increased role of state intervention and the tendency to look to the government for solutions should be noted.

One, it reflects widespread illusions among the American people that the government is their government, that it represents some supraclass regulator that can be pressured into reconciling conflicting demands and interests on an equitable basis. In this sense it reflects the relative social peace of recent years and the fact that there was enough fat in this rich country for the ruling class to give some concessions under pressure.

But there is the other side to the tendency to look to the government for solutions. Such popular demands help to generate a greater degree of consciousness of the need to act politically because no individual boss, no individual industry, no individual family alone can solve the problems pressing upon them.

We shouldn't exaggerate this nascent trend. There is still an attitude among many that if you are unemployed, there is something wrong with *you* as a person, not with society. But that attitude is less prevalent than ever before.

The idea of political action continues to be pushed to the fore, the idea of directing political demands to the government as a whole, and searching for political solutions that take care of the needs of our class and its allies. It will help make our program of labor independence, of a need for a break with the political parties of the bosses, a more realistic and understandable prespective to the masses of the American workers.

Lessons of the New York crisis

This brings us to the question of the leadership of the American working class today and the state of the organized labor movement. We are forced to conclude, the union movement is in sorry shape. Despite their great potential strength, many unions today are being stalemated, driven back, or, as in the case of New York to date, routed without a fight.

The organized working class is now incomparably stronger than it was in 1929 when industrial unionism was barely on the horizon. But the *leadership* changes that have taken place in the union movement since the 1930s have not increased labor's fighting capacities. This leadership is a bigger obstacle today than then because of its size, its material stakes, and its greater degree of direct and indirect integration in the state apparatus. Trotsky outlined the basic elements of this picture thirty-five years ago when he drew up his notes on "Trade Unions in the Epoch of Imperialist Decay." And as Farrell Dobbs says in the introduction to the book where this article is reprinted, "There is more food for thought (and action) in this short unfinished piece than will be found in any book by anyone else on the union question" [*Leon Trotsky on the Trade Unions* (New York: Pathfinder Press, 1975), p. 44].

Trotsky pointed out that under monopoly capitalism, which does not rest on free competition and private initiative but on centralized command, there is a direct interconnection and collaboration at every step between the commanding heights of state power and the ruling capitalist families, the superrich, who dominate the trusts, the syndicates, and the banking consortiums. And the trade unions, deprived of the possibility of profiting from competition between various capitalist enterprises, "have to confront a centralized capitalist adversary intimately bound up with state power" (p. 69). Under these conditions, there is a tendency for the trade unions to more and more adapt to the capitalist state, to become integrated into it as an agency of capitalist rule. "The labor bureaucrats," Trotsky said, "do their level best in words and deeds to demonstrate to the 'democratic' state how reliable and indispensable they are" (ibid.).

Those words were written in 1940, but they sound as though they could have been penned last week, after witnessing the spectacle of New York's labor leaders grovelling at the feet of New York Mayor Abe Beame and Governor Hugh Carey. Bound hand and foot to the parties and policies of American imperialism, the Victor Gotbaums and Albert Shankers rush to praise the political leadership of their Democratic Party friends and to thank the banks for sharing their burdens with the workers.

What has happened in New York in recent months bears a closer look, because it is a dress rehearsal for the shape of things to come. All the elements reflecting the current relationship of forces, and the perspectives and solutions offered by the employers and by the labor bureaucracy, are present in the New York picture.

First, there is the broad social and economic framework, stemming from the world capitalist slump. The fiscal crisis it imposed on the cities and the effects of the depression were used month after month in a propaganda campaign to con the workers in New York into believing they were going to have to accept something bad in order to avoid something worse.

The scope of the social services in New York—welfare, medical care, city universities, and so forth—while deteriorated and inadequate, are still greater than exist in many other American cities. New York was one of the places where public employee unions won sizable wage increases in the 1960s. This made pacesetting New York a test case, a prime target of the ruling-class offensive on a national scale. The banks decided to test their strength against the public employee unions, against the Black and Puerto Rican communities, against the student movement. And they were determined to succeed in New York in order to set a pattern for the entire country.

The second element in New York was the division and disarray in the working class and its allies. The inability of the leaders of the unions, or the community organizations, to respond in a united way demonstrated the degree to which they fell easy prey to the ruling class's conscious strategy of divide and rule. This well-orchestrated campaign set taxpayers against the supposedly well-paid city workers, set one city service against another over which one was going to be rated "essential" and which one would have to be phased out. They counterposed the wages and working conditions of the teachers to the demands for better schools and better services. They set the teachers against the parents. They set one union against another as they argued among themselves about which ones were going to lose the most members and who was going to be fired first.

For good measure they threw the issue of the cops into the middle of the mess, with a racist campaign about how the muggers and rapists were going to take over the city if cops were fired. That ploy was designed to destroy any feelings of solidarity between the Black or Puerto Rican communities and the victims of the city payroll cut. It set the regular city workers against those who benefited from the special hiring program for Black, Puerto Rican, and women workers. Round one, in the divide and rule offensive, went to the bosses.

The third aspect in the New York events is what might be called the Gotbaum-Shanker show. On the one hand stands Shanker, a prize specimen of the cold-war, racist, Meany wing of the labor bureaucracy. And on the other, Gotbaum, who belongs to the liberal, "progressive," wing of the labor bureaucracy. Both vied with each other to try to prove their worth as "responsible civic leaders," helping the city out in a time of trouble.

And as the comitragedy unfolded, it became clearer and clearer just how crucial collaboration from the union leadership was to the bankers' plans. Without that, they could not have succeeded in averting a head-on confrontation with the working class in New York, could not have succeeded in their game of divide and rule. A solid united front against layoffs and cutbacks would have been a different ball game.

Gotbaum and Shanker, however, came through for them very well, campaigning for equality of sacrifice on the part of all, workers and Rockefellers alike. For instance, Rockefeller and I equally shell out the fifty cents for a subway ride.

The fourth element in the New York picture was the sanitation workers' wildcat strike. Though this was sold down the river in a matter of days, it evidenced the anger among broad layers of city workers and gave an indication of some of the militancy that exists.

Fifth, parallel to the Gotbaum-Shanker show, we were treated to the absolutely astounding performance of Big Mac—as the ruling class has fondly dubbed the Municipal Assistance Corporation, the "impartial" agency set up to beat down the living standards of the New York workers. Here the bankers came out from behind the scenes, and said, OK, we are going to run the city in the open. They moved representatives of finance capital right into the mayor's office and started putting out press releases and handing out their daily orders.

This is a dangerous game. When the commanders come out from behind their lieutenants such as Beame and Carey, this exposure helps educate the American working class on who really runs the city and the country, free, democratic elections notwithstanding. But the financiers decided that this risk was a lesser evil than to have the wrath of the workers of New York turned solely against the Democratic Party. They wanted Beame to look credible so he could say to the workers: "What can I do? We're all in the same boat. I have to take my orders too." They calculated that such a strategy would lessen the danger of a political break from the two-party system by any sector of the labor movement.

Just how well this shell-game was played by the labor bureaucrats was revealed by Albert Shanker in his United Federation of Teachers-sponsored column in the *New York Times*. After ten paragraphs of railing against the New York bankers who are sucking the city dry, what conclusions does Shanker reach? He says, "The crisis we face is not merely economic; it is political." So far, so good. Then he goes on, "It is a question whether, in this bicentennial year [that's when you know something crude is coming], democracy shall be ended in New York City; whether the decisions will be made by elected officials in accordance with the wishes and needs of the people—or by the banks" (*New York Times* advertisement, August 3, 1975).

They've always been made in accordance with the wishes of the people up to now, you see. Then he says, "The banks . . . have won the first round." But how did they do it? How were they able to put this over on the people of New York?

They succeeded, Shanker argues, "only by discrediting the Mayor and our other elected officials. We are now witnessing the beginning of a massive, finely orchestrated campaign to convince us that Mayor Beame is incompetent, paralyzed in the face of the city's problems, etc."

That won't do. "In the weeks and months to come," says Shanker, "we will need Mayor Beame more and more. . . . Only he, as our elected chief executive [these are his words], can mobilize the people to fight against the monied interests for the preservation of elected government. . . . Mr. Mayor. . . . We need you—and you need us."

There is *one* thing that Shanker is correct about, and that is that the Big Mac operation has only begun to hurt. New Yorkers are only beginning to feel the blows of what is coming. And the bankers simply cannot believe everything they have gotten away with. It is beyond their fondest dreams.

They have already axed almost 15,000 workers from the payroll. They have cut millions from desperately needed social services. They even made the sanitation workers' union put up a bond to pay their own salaries. They have announced the closing of half-a-dozen hospitals. They have almost doubled the transit fare. They slashed the school budget. They have even forced the city workers to invest their pension funds in the bonds that are being put up, in order to blackmail them against making future pay demands.

And what about the resistance? There have been a few small demonstrations, the biggest one about 20,000. There was a wildcat strike of the sanitation workers for a few days. And what answer does the labor bureaucracy give to workers who want to stand and fight back before they are cut to ribbons and don't have the strength to fight? Their position was adequately summed up by Lillian Roberts, one of the leaders of District Council 37 of the American Federation of State, County, and Municipal Employees (AFSCME). When challenged by some of the workers in the District Council about why the unions weren't fighting back, she answered: "We are fighting back, we are loaning the city money so people can work. That's unionism."

Indeed, that *is* unionism to the Gotbaum-Shanker school, and that is precisely where things must be changed. The Gotbaums and the Shankers are not going to change. They are going to have to be pushed aside in the process. They are preparing further losses and setbacks right now.

But the working class, starting with the Black workers, the Puerto Rican workers, and women workers, and the young workers, will have to bring their own methods of struggle onto the scene. They want to fight to win, not lose. They are going to be looking for a program of struggle that corresponds to their interests, and they are going to be looking for a leadership that can offer them a class-struggle alternative, as our small forces sought to do.

In "Trade Unions in the Epoch of Imperialist Decay," Trotsky notes that there are only two alternative functions for unions today. "The trade unions of our time can either serve as secondary instruments of imperialist capitalism for the subordination and disciplining of workers and for obstructing the revolution, or, on the contrary, the trade unions can become the instruments of the revolutionary movement of the proletariat" [*Leon Trotsky on the Trade Unions*, p. 71].

Those are the two fundamental options; there are no others. And we are fighting to assure that they will take the latter road. Along that road we can look forward to building a class-struggle wing of millions of workers who are striving for the complete independence of the unions from the capitalist state and its political parties. Such an organized force in the union movement can provide leadership for the class on all social issues. It can struggle to turn the unions into popular organizations of the broad exploited masses, not organizations dominated by the labor aristocracy.

The challenge before us

What does this period we are entering upon mean for the future of the Socialist Workers Party? If the perspective ahead is one of broad social crisis several things logically follow.

One, the scope and character of the coming struggles are going to be broader, deeper, sharper than anything we have seen for a number of decades. The struggles occurring this month over desegregation in Boston, cutbacks and layoffs in New York, the farm workers in the Rio Grande valley, are small glimpses of what's on the agenda.

Two, the interest in our ideas, in our program of struggle, will be greater. It is going to become increasingly clear to more and more workers that something has to change. And our ideas, our perspectives are going to get a better hearing—in the unions, in the plants, among the oppressed nationalities, and all the victims of capitalism's degradations. Working people are going to be looking for clear, definite answers to the big questions, and they will be more receptive to joining an organization fighting for that kind of program. Our kind of program will make more sense to them. They will be more easily persuaded to add their strength to ours, to see how powerless we are as individuals but how strong we can be as an organized political force.

The one thing we can be the most confident of is the power of our program. The basic program outlined in "Prospects for Socialism in America" is not new. We have tried to formulate its points in a language and framework that is understandable to the American workers today, as they face the last quarter of the twentieth century. We have adapted its approach to the peculiar historical, class, and national features of American society, shaped by the international role of American imperialism.

But basically, the program contains nothing new. It has a continuity that goes all the way back to the beginning of Marxism. It is linked most immediately with the SWP political resolutions of recent years, our analysis of the radicalization. But it is also a continuation of the party's central resolutions since its formation. It conforms to the Transitional Program that was adopted at the founding of the Fourth International in 1938; as well as to Trotsky's criticisms of Stalin's draft program for the Sixth Congress of the Communist International in 1928, which was the founding document of the International Left Opposition; with the first four congresses of the Comintern; with the 1917 program of the Bolsheviks; with the revolutionary traditions of the Second International; with the *Communist Manifesto* of 1847. In the 128 years since then, we can say that this program has been tested time and again, not in every conceivable way, because every new development in the class struggle poses new tests and poses them in new ways, but through the experiences of victories and defeats for the world working class, that program has been confirmed and reconfirmed many times over.

The challenge before us is to prove ourselves capable of understanding that program fully and applying it. What really counts in the mass movement is what we do and how well we do it. We are going to have many opportunities to apply our program, as the broad outlines of the transitional program become increasingly applicable to mass struggle.

The turn that we are talking about is not a narrow, exclusively trade union turn, even though we are all excited about the increasing possibilities for political work in the unions, and rightly so. This is the first occasion in thirty years that there have been significant openings for revolutionists in the union movement. But that is just part of the picture. This is not a "turn to the working class" in the abstract. There are tens of millions of workers in this country, and only a few thousands of us. We must have a clear idea of whom we are addressing ourselves to in the main.

Tom Leonard made a good point in his statement that a turn to the workers in no way means turning away from the priorities we place on the struggles of Chicanos, Blacks, youth, women, defense of civil liberties, and so forth. Just the opposite.

Trotsky outlined what we have in view in the Transitional Program, where he said that our perspective is to open the road to the Black worker, to the woman worker, to the young worker, to the most oppressed and exploited, and all potentially combative layers. They are the forces of the future. They are not going to be found only in the unions or the plants. We are going to find some of those young and combative working women and men in the NAACP, in the National Student Coalition Against Racism, in the Nation of Islam, in the streets of Boston, in Chicano organizations, in the community control struggles, in the women's liberation movement, in defense committees, on the campuses, in the prisons, on the unemployed lines, as well as in the factories and the union halls.

There are openings for us in all the sectors of the mass movement, and our job is to get out there and find them. We can't create them out of thin air—or hot air. But neither do we sit and wait until they come knocking at our headquarters door.

Our job is to be prepared to recognize the changes that are taking place, to make rapid and sensitive readjustments, to be able to take advantage of every opening that comes along. Sometimes the initiatives we take won't make too much difference in the total picture. At other times, they can play a crucial role, as the evolution of the struggles in Boston over the last year have made abundantly plain.

Nor do we need to huddle together in bigger and bigger party units. Our direction is outward into the mass movement, for more members, for growing numbers of branches, and for smaller branches to carry out this orientation. The expansion plans we have been discussing for Newark, Baltimore, New Orleans, San Antonio, San Jose, New York's Lower East Side, the Chicago South Side and West Side are outgrowths of the turn we are making to augment the prospects for growth in the coming period.

We know we are stronger vis-à-vis our main competitors on the left in the working class movement than at the beginning of the 1930s—stronger vis-à-vis the Stalinists and the Social Democracy than we were then. But we also know the gains we have made have not definitively settled anything. The tasks before us remain essentially the same as in the 1930s. That is to provide the program and perspective to help our class move faster and further on the road to the socialist revolution, and, for that, to construct a mass revolutionary party that is capable of leading the way to victory.

Jack Barnes

The Economic Squeeze and the Workers' Response

This is the main political report to the SWP National Committee plenum, January 2, 1976, in Milwaukee, Wisconsin. The text includes the summary remarks after the discussion.

Our point of departure and our framework are the two resolutions adopted at the SWP convention last August— "Prospects for Socialism in America" and "The Fight for Black Liberation: The Current Stage and Its Tasks." We do not need to recapitulate those documents. Instead we can take a look at the objective developments in several of the key areas treated in the political resolution so as to further our discussion of the strategic line of march of American labor, of the burning need for American workers to think socially and act politically. What has transpired in the four months since our August 1975 convention?

Angola: a new imperialist adventure

Our political resolution placed special emphasis on the fact that "the threat of military adventures, and along with them the possibility of nuclear annihilation, will continue. Rivalries among the imperialist powers will sharpen as they compete for markets and raw materials. There will be increased efforts to impose American imperialist needs and perspectives on the masses of the colonial and semicolonial world with the inevitable resistance this will generate."

We did not know at the time we wrote the resolution that the next adventure was already being prepared—in Angola. The immediate reaction in the country was: "Not another Vietnam!" A public debate began at once. This time not five years or so after we had been dragged into a war, but at a very early stage. This debate is, of course, distorted because the loudest voices are presenting the ideas and perspectives of the ruling class. It is fed by information "leaked" out because of the tactical divisions among the powers that be. But the debate is qualitatively different from the one in the early stages of the Vietnam War.

In this case, at the very beginning of a new imperialist venture—even before advisers are sent—there is widespread public knowledge and awareness of, debate over, and opposition to a "new Vietnam," outcries against a new foreign military involvement.

"Leaks" began gushing from ruling circles themselves. Fear of the growth of a new antiwar movement and fear of an explosive reaction by Black Americans to any direct military involvement in southern Africa weighed heavily on Washington. Differences in the State Department were exacerbated as each side rushed to expose the other's lies. For example, they had the debate over the dollar value of covert "aid" being sent. It was revealed that machine guns were being marked down to 50 cents and bazookas to $1.29, or something similar. And then the factions started arguing about *when* the covert "aid" began. Soon after the leaks began, Walter Cronkite's CBS news announced a week of special presentations on Angola and the danger of another Vietnam.

This course of events confirms three conclusions we had reached at the convention and what their lessons were for the American working class and its allies:

1. More adventures are inevitably going to occur. They are part and parcel of the decline of imperialism and they go along with and are not contradicted by détente.

2. Mass public reaction is going to be at a qualitatively different level than at the beginning of previous adventures initiated by American imperialism after World War II. The last fifteen years have seen a signal change in mass consciousness in this country. This has deepened the tactical differences over foreign policy within the ruling class itself, a factor that accelerates and legitimizes dissension and leaks. The officials in charge are pulled into the debate right from the beginning.

3. The third conclusion is the most important. Working people can't count on Congress or either of its two parties to prevent new military adventures from happening again or to solve the contradictions that generate them. On the contrary, these flow fundamentally from the decline of American imperialism, not the particular qualities or "program" of the capitalist politician occupying the White House at the time.

The real face of the American rulers

The second area in which important developments have occurred is what we have called "the crisis of perspective" of the American ruling class, which is bound up with the continuing exposure of the real face of declining bourgeois democracy. What used to be called the credibility gap and later "Watergate" continues to develop apace. For the time being, the ruling class cannot stop wave after wave of exposés of the undemocratic and illegal methods, or elements of these methods, practiced by the American rulers. Such scandals have become an everyday feature of American life.

Just in the four months since the convention, there have been damaging new exposés concerning the CIA's use of American missionaries and journalists, CIA funding of foreign political parties, and the international assassination plots against Castro, Lumumba, and others. Today a great percentage of the Black population and a growing number of whites firmly believe that Martin Luther King—let alone militants like Fred Hampton—was assassinated by agents originally hired and trained by the Federal Bureau of Investigation.

As this process of exposure unfolds it has repercussions that are unwanted by any sector of the ruling class. One result is a spreading comprehension that assassinations and similar activities are not just exceptional international policies used only in Chile or the Congo. These same policies are utilized in one form or another at home. They assassinate Lumumba, they assassinate King.

Another idea gains credence: the notion that maybe these policies are not of recent origin, unfortunate excesses of the "turbulent" Vietnam years and the "terrible" Nixon years. Growing numbers become convinced that it may go back farther—to the Johnson years, the Kennedy years. More Americans are discovering that Camelot was really a bunch of mobsters in tuxedos, deciding our fate. If you read Farrell Dobbs's books on the Teamsters carefully, you will see that the trail goes back to the Roosevelt years. In fact, that's where its present form originated.

A further idea that gains currency is the realization that these policies are not simply aberrations. They are not the individual acts of a J. Edgar Hoover, a Colby, a Nixon—someone you can fire, or impeach; the acts of an officeholder who flipped out. On the contrary, they are the necessary policies of the American ruling class today. These are the policies of the most liberal and respected (i.e., those not caught red-handed) of the leaders of the capitalist elite. The tendency toward spying, provocation, assassination, the use of police-state methods—this is not the work of a few demented individuals. It is the direction of a declining, thus objectively demented, class.

The policies are not just decided by a few heinous Republicans. They are carried out by the whole two-party lot, as they have been for a long time. *They* are the terrorists, *they* are the assassins, *they* are the advocates and practitioners of minority violence. *They* are the ones who organize conspiracies of a small minority to impose their ends on the great majority of the American people.

The rulers can't openly defend and justify these methods. The great majority, who benefit less and less from this system and who reject these methods, would not accept it. Yet there is no way the rulers can completely hide what they are doing behind the scenes. As on the war question—like Angola—the tactical divisions in the ruling class, stemming from all the pressures they are subjected to, lead to exposures, "leaks," debates, new divisions, and mutual distrust. This is the source of much raw material for us and for other sections of the working class movement and its allies to put to use for educating the American people to the truth of capitalist society today.

I was struck by some of the coverage given the assassination of the CIA station chief in Athens, Greece, recently. Several days ago on CBS TV morning news they showed the body being brought back and the burial with full-scale military honors at Arlington. Then they interviewed a spokesman for the Retired Intelligence Officers Association. The retired spook pointed to what he considered a "new problem." The danger, he said, doesn't come from the intelligence apparatus of the "other side." In fact, the rival services now are forced to collaborate more and more. The danger, he explained, comes from "people at home who don't understand our mission."

Immediately following this, another person was interviewed by Daniel Schorr. Cameras wouldn't show his face, but Schorr identified him as a former high-ranking CIA agent who had resigned a year and a half ago. Far from drawing the conclusion from the death of the Greek station chief that further exposés should be hushed up, he announced that he was publishing in the next months a list of 750 names of various chiefs, secondary officers, and affiliated CIA figures around the world.

These three incidents were presented all within five or six minutes on a television news show watched by millions of Americans.

Rights and rising expectations

What about the state of democracy, democratic rights, and rising expectations? The party's political resolution, "Prospects for Socialism in America," examines the way in which the defense of traditional political liberties can today be extended to include social and economic rights for working people, rights that the bosses and their governments had previously looked on as their sole prerogative to give or take away. The most important of these have been listed in the "Bill of Rights for Working People" issued by Peter Camejo and Willie Mae Reid, the party's 1976 presidential and vice-presidential candidates. Our resolution examines the expectations of the masses that encroach on private property and the relations of production of capitalism itself.

From an opposite point of view, the ruling class shares our assessment of the situation. But where we are optimistic, they despair. *Business Week* recently published an end-of-the-year series of commentaries on the growth of "egalitarian" sentiments among American workers (December 1, 8, and 15, 1975). The theme was their deep concern that the demand for economic rights is the latest threat to a free market. The series begins by quoting Voltaire, who said, "Equality is at once the most natural and most chimerical thing in the world: natural when it is limited to rights, unnatural when it attempts to level goods and powers." That is the text for their sermon.

They point out that more and more rights are being demanded by the people, and the character of these rights tends to "override the classic principle that what a man consumes must be determined by what he produces or what he owns." In fact, they emphasize, "the American economy, based on private property, uses the market to determine rewards and allocate resources. Differences in pay and profit are essential to it." At some point, they conclude, a move toward equality requires a shift from capitalism to socialism.

Business Week notes that "the most obvious examples of

egalitarian actions today are busing to integrate school districts and affirmative action programs designed to force employers to hire more women and more members of minorities." These affirmative action programs create all kinds of new problems that weren't foreseen ten years ago. The very fact that the United States has made a start toward equality has created a demand for faster progress, for more equality and added rights.

Then they draw the horrible, pessimistic conclusion: "Since the Middle Ages, the general will—or at least, the will of the majority—has been asserting itself against the rights of property." They pose this dilemma: A choice must be made between the rights of property and the unlimited extension of democracy. *Business Week* takes a firm and open stand: for the rights of property. And on that note they wish us all a Merry Christmas and a Happy New Year.

Business Week's observations reflect not only capitalism's crisis and the resulting radicalization we have analyzed, but the growing polarization in this society. There is no contradiction in all these things happening at once. With various ups and downs and shifts in form, the crisis of the system will deepen. The radicalization will also evolve, change its forms, and deepen. And simultaneously a class polarization will take place.

The question will be more and more clearly posed: are rights, even the traditional bourgeois constitutional ones, let alone those that are anticipated, compatible with the needs of the capitalist economic system? A growing number in the ruling class will draw the same conclusion we do. The answer is no. But the ruling class will have a different solution than ours. They will come down on the side of the rights of property; we will be on the side of extending democracy and equality into the social and economic spheres through the struggle for workers' power and socialism.

Economic prospects

But shouldn't all these problems be growing less acute for the powers that be? After all, the economy, by all their accounts, is well into a recovery from the depression of 1974-75. In this light it's worth taking a glance at the recovery and its character to date.

The value of the dollar has gone up. The balance of trade has improved significantly. The stock market looks as if it will soon be several hundred points above its low. The estimate for profits, especially in 1976 and 1977, has gone way up. Industrial production has risen in the last few months. All these indices look like standard signs of recovery, similar to all the recessions we've lived through since the end of World War II.

But another side of this development is more important, though it is not peculiar to this recovery either. That is the extent of unemployment. Official unemployment figures vary between 8 and 11 percent, depending on whether Gerald Ford or Hubert Humphrey is doing the measuring. And no bourgeois source estimates that it will go below 7 percent! A number of experts now predict that 1976-77 auto production will top the 1973 record—yet all agree it will be accomplished with fewer auto workers. Inflation remains in the 7 to 8 percent range, well ahead of most of labor's wage increases. And the threat of another dose of double-digit inflation, more shortages, and breakdowns continues to hang over our heads.

The government statisticians tell us that real spendable earnings finally rose by 0.2 percent in December, so we can all feel richer. But then they forget to tell us that beginning January 1 we are scheduled to pay more in Social Security taxes and for every single social service. This means that our real income—let alone the quality of living conditions—has continued to slide. For the working class this kind of "recovery" is going to be hard to recover from.

This has been acutely exemplified by the crisis in New York City where 37,000 workers were "recovered" right out of the economy in 1975. Union contracts have been torn up, simply ripped apart. Social services that have been fought for over decades and decades have been dumped. And the budget chops have been regressive. The increase in taxes, in subway fares, slashes in child care, school budgets, hospitals, etc., are the kind of chops that hurt working people the most. The modest affirmative action gains of the last few years by Blacks, by Puerto Ricans, by women, have been brutally shoved back—with the blessing of the New York courts in the name of opposing "reverse discrimination."

This is an omen of what the rulers plan, not only in other cities, but in the basic industries. Not only the weak unions, but the strongest industrial unions will eventually become the targets.

Recoveries in a period of accelerated expansion were one thing, even though the "American century" didn't live up to expectations. The standard of living for many, many workers rose. But spasmodic recoveries in a long period of stagnation, in a period of a growing social tension such as we have now entered, are something different. We are now getting a picture of the best that can be expected.

Socialism is not creeping in under the auspices of monopoly capitalism. But there has been a big increase in the socialization of the accumulation of capital. The capitalist state has stepped in with workers' taxes to bail out bankrupt railroads and airplane trusts. Chrysler in Britain was bailed out to the tune of $300 million. The big New York financial families and banks have been bailed out. But this is "socialism" for the superrich. Every time one of these government bailouts takes place, it does so at the cost of jobs, wages, social gains, living and working conditions. They are put over in a way that exacerbates to the utmost the divisions within the working class.

The total absence of any leadership capacity among the officials of the New York unions—where the workers were ready to resist and looked to their unions for some answer as the crisis deepened—was a gift the rulers had hardly dared anticipate. There is no question that a whole section of the ruling class has the taste of blood. They are going to probe further.

Their offensive will take diverse forms. They will probe other cities like New York. They will try to bust relatively weak unions or those in an exposed position, as they are trying to do to the pressmen at the *Washington Post*. They will try to see how much of labor's gains the Democratic "friends of labor" can take back, as they did in San Francisco when they backed the antilabor referenda in the last elections. They will try to curb the teachers, whose unprecedented wave of strikes is not a "good lesson" any way the boss class figures it. They will try to convince a growing number of crafts to take "voluntary" wage cuts. Two weeks ago the bricklayers in New York agreed to take a 25 percent wage cut and a 40 percent cut in fringe benefits. The purpose, they were told, was to spread out the work. But, of course, that won't be the result.

The doubly and triply oppressed

This has happened during only the first half-year of the "recovery"! From the point of view of the ruling class, the slashes of the last several years have resulted in great strides toward something that Marx explained to the workers a long time ago. Whenever there has been a long period of high employment the ruling class must reconstitute an industrial reserve army. It is an absolute necessity if the capitalist system is to survive and thrive, i.e., to continue to produce profits for those who own the means of production. The ruling class must create a pariah section of the working class, a special pool, accepted as such by the relatively more privileged sections of the wage workers, which can be pushed in and out of the labor market and used to exert downward pressure on the wages and working conditions of the working class as a whole.

These are the doubly oppressed sections of the working class: the Blacks, the Chicanos, the Puerto Ricans, the women, the youngest, the least trained workers. Like other workers, they feel the effects of the bosses' blows—on the job, in education, in real wages, in social services. But for them the blows almost always have a double whammy. They always end up more, not less, segregated than before. Not only are there fewer teachers, but a smaller percentage of Black teachers, Puerto Rican teachers, Chicano teachers. Not only are real wages in general being cut, but the unprivileged have less chance at equal pay. Discriminatory layoffs increase. Social gains that made it possible to become a full-fledged part of the work force, such as child care or bilingual education, are special targets. Discriminatory layoffs, and anything like them, always give the employing class a bonus. Not only do they chop the labor force down, but they divide it a little bit more, and thus place the industrial reserve army in a still worse position.

What have the oppressed nationalities and women seen as this process accelerates? They have seen the liberal vote catchers retreat—on busing, on the Equal Rights Amendment, on the extension of services such as child care. They have seen, not less but more racist practices, more segregation, more sex discrimination. They have seen the misleaders of labor turn their backs on them.

The ruling class needs this industrial reserve army. It is a fundamental precondition for the success of its offensive against the wages, working conditions, and social welfare of the working class as a whole. But the ruling class's strategy can work only if this reserve army section of the working class is seen to one degree or another by the rest of the working class, by the labor movement, as "the others," as pariahs, as the "outsiders" whose fate is not as important as what happens to "us." They must be the at-home version of the "foreigners" or the "illegals." At the same time this ruling-class operation is a delicate one, which has to be carefully handled because it can be self-defeating if it spurs the doubly and triply oppressed to further struggles.

Class polarization

As the social crisis remains unresolved and this offensive of the rulers continues, a growing class polarization occurs. The rulers try to do everything they can to camouflage this reality and portray it as a race war, or a battle of the sexes, or the righteous anger of the honest taxpayers. ROAR, anti-ERA groups, the antiabortion cabal, the reactionary posses in California against the farm workers, are presented as people who simply oppose busing, or who have their own views on the rights of women, or different opinions on the character of Mexicans. To be sure, they do have their own reactionary opinions on all these things. But they represent something more. They are the advance guard of the antilabor forces in this country who have their own definitive labor-hating opinions on the rights, future, and character of the working class.

This kind of polarization, fanned by the ruling class offensive against labor and its allies that comes on top of the social and economic crises and radicalization of the last decade, throws all sorts of organizations into a crisis of perspectives. Organizations like the Nation of Islam, the NAACP, NOW, who want to represent or are based on some sizable sections of the oppressed, more and more fall into a crisis of perspective, a crisis of strategy, a crisis over what to do. Problems of policy and direction come up for review and discussion within their leaderships and memberships.

The degree to which this is a class offensive, camouflaged and reinforced by racist and sexist attitudes, is shown even by the reflexes of a George Meany. His statements in favor of busing and the ERA are very much out of character for the AFL-CIO head. But even to some of those like Meany, the organized oppositions that defeated the ERA in New Jersey and New York, and are trying to drive back busing to desegregate the schools, smelled too much like the most vicious, reactionary, potentially union-busting forces in American society.

It would be useful to take a look at four developments in the

American labor movement that reflect the specific characteristics of this social crisis, the radicalization, and the coming polarization. We picked out for special examination the Farm Workers, the Coalition of Labor Union Women, Ed Sadlowski's campaign, called Steelworkers Fight Back, and the union response to the New York crisis. In the labor movement too, as among the Black, Chicano, and women's organizations, there is a crisis of strategy, of orientation. Do the old methods work? What is the correct road to take? What is a winning strategy? A certain number of workers are beginning to see that the very existence of the labor movement is and will be threatened by the bosses' offensive and that no section of the labor movement is safe if that goes far enough. Transforming the labor movement to think socially and act politically has become a life-and-death matter for the American working class.

The United Farm Workers

The strength of the Farm Workers' struggle comes from something radically different from the methods and strategies of the current misleaders of American labor. The very deep nationalist appeal, an appeal to the farm workers as *la raza*, as a doubly oppressed people, has been its central feature from the beginning. It is *la causa*. At every critical turning point this has been a key element in orienting or reorienting the farm workers' struggle. The actions that paved the way for steps forward have been those that went beyond the forces of the farm workers themselves, toward whatever help was available from the labor movement and its supporters.

Take the grape boycott. It was a broad, popular action that depended for its success on becoming a significant social protest movement. Its weaknesses aside, this was the only way that contingents from outside could be brought to bear and help improve the poor relationship of forces vis-à-vis the growers. The AFL-CIO leadership basically ignored the farm workers' struggle from the beginning; their methods, exemplified by the business unionism of the Teamster bureaucracy, could only lead to its total defeat. The Farm Workers have always sought to think socially, in their own terms. This helped them recover from the low point in 1973. It reoriented them and helped them correct a disastrously wrong policy in refusing to defend the so-called illegal workers. It led them to reconsider their inclination to give up on the boycott.

And it has brought them to where they are today.

Besides the special difficulties entailed in organizing the farm industry, the Farm Workers have complicated matters by their politics, the correlative side of thinking socially. They remain tied to the Democratic Party both in their leadership and their political thinking. They have no perspective of independent labor politics. That weakness stands as a big obstacle to further progress and is a continual danger to the gains and growth of the last couple of years.

Coalition of Labor Union Women

CLUW offers striking proof of the character of the radicalization, as well as the nature of the social crisis, and its effect on the labor movement. None of our various sectarian opponents understand this and all drew basically similar conclusions from last month's CLUW convention. *Workers Power,* organ of the International Socialists, was the clearest wrong expression. They announced (1) the convention exhausted both its delegates and any remaining hopes for an effective organization; (2) the new CLUW constitution rules out any activity by any members of CLUW to fight for working women's rights; and (3) CLUW is now totally useless as a potential organization for working women. One, Two, Three—out! That was their analysis of CLUW at the end of the convention.

In none of the articles by the sectarians is there the foggiest notion of the real origins and character of CLUW, or what strategic course to chart to realize its potential. CLUW is rooted in two interrelated phenomena: first, the changes brought about by American capital in the post-World War II years that drew millions of women into wage-labor, and second, the rise of the women's movement. Thus the origins of CLUW are not to be found within the labor movement or the policies of its misleaders but rather in the changing consciousness and role of women in the work force and the resurgence of the nationwide struggle for women's rights.

CLUW would have been inconceivable even ten years ago. It is based on something very new and real—a revolt against their permanent second-class status by 35 million women in American society. The main goal of CLUW must be very simple. This goal is to change the American labor movement by mobilizing its power to help fight for the needs and demands of women.

CLUW's objective is to use union power to fight for women's rights, on the job, in the union, and in society. This implies changing the labor movement as a whole, and in the process changing the consciousness and conduct of men in the labor movement to see the correctness and necessity of this fight.

In this sense, CLUW has a crucial role to play in the broad fight that must be carried on to transform the unions into a powerful leading component of a popular social movement. The union movement will have to begin showing women in practice that it champions women's struggles, understands and fights for their needs. This is indispensable, not only to put the labor movement on the road to becoming a popular social movement, but to enable the unions to organize the unorganized women, a task the current labor leadership cannot and will not undertake in any qualitatively new way.

The logic of this course, if carried out, is to establish CLUW as the leading organization of women in this country, an organization that would attract millions. That does not mean there would then be no need for other organizations of women, or that other organizations of women would disappear. On the contrary. But a fighting union women's organization, forcing labor to use its power to fight for women, could take the lead in the struggle for women's rights in this country. It would be in the vanguard of the working class.

Whether this goal can be achieved is another question. But that is our strategic aim. That's what we fight for.

There are many obstacles in the way. CLUW, as it is now constituted, is still in its infancy. And it has demonstrated some major defaults in its obligation to fight unconditionally for the rights of women. For instance, CLUW has refused to campaign unsparingly against discriminatory layoffs. This must be overcome. There are hesitations about turning to the ranks, the only place where a mass CLUW can be built, around an action program to meet women's needs and demands. Of course, a major obstacle involves the question of political action. Like the Farm Workers, the ties to the Democratic Party exert a constant enfeebling pressure.

Only by overcoming these obstacles can CLUW move toward playing its potentially historic role. By going to the ranks, fighting unconditionally for the needs of women on the job, in the union, in society, CLUW can begin to realize that potential.

Our opponents are unable to grasp what CLUW is *not*. CLUW

is not an organization that can solve the problems of labor in general. It cannot solve the problem of jobs. It cannot solve the problem of inflation. It cannot solve the problem of organizing the unorganized. In fact, to the degree that these are put forward as the central tasks of CLUW, they become fake. They become a cover for not orienting CLUW toward fighting in the unions to support action campaigns for women. They become empty platitudes that poorly disguise a reluctance to fight to make CLUW what it can be: an organization whose goal is to transform the union movement into a powerful social force that fights for women. The big pitch of the Stalinists and to some degree the *Guardian* on the CLUW convention reflected this error. The great betrayal of the CLUW convention, they said, was the failure to recognize that the fight for jobs is the number one job of this several-thousand-strong women's organization.

The second mistake to avoid is declaring something to be dead when it is not yet born and standing on its own feet. To declare CLUW dead is simply to be unwilling to struggle to give it life. This winged judgment was the sectarians' big contribution to an analysis of the CLUW convention.

Whether CLUW can grow, whether it can put forward a class-struggle leadership, whether it can organize into its ranks the tens or hundreds of thousands of union women needed to accomplish CLUW's task, of course, remains to be seen. But CLUW is not dead; it has yet to be really born.

The third mistake to avoid is the idea that CLUW will be built right now around some sort of power caucus to replace its incumbent officers. That's another item all our sectarian opponents had at the top of their worry list at the constitutional convention of CLUW. They weren't thinking about implementing CLUW's constitution and statement of purpose by organizing action campaigns around the ERA, affirmative action, abortion, etc., which is the only road to building CLUW and attracting women to it. No, they were worrying about who is going to replace Olga Madar, who is going to replace Addie Wyatt, etc., etc., ad exhaustum. Along that road they would only capture themselves. The idea of taking the statement of purpose of the constitution, drawing women into struggles for CLUW's stated goals, finding action programs to do this through committees in every union in the country, and thus driving forward to build CLUW—that simple idea seems beyond them.

This is 1976, not 1950. We speak for the ranks of laboring

women. Those ranks are growing and they will change still more under the blows of this unfolding social crisis. And we are confident that the program that speaks for them and charts a path in their interests can succeed. We are convinced that social struggles will continue to have a deep effect on all sections of the working people, including the union movement. These social struggles, the struggles of the doubly oppressed, both within and without the labor movement, will be decisive forces in initiating the required changes in the labor movement and preparing it to meet the more direct frontal assault that is coming.

The refusal of women to accept second-class status in society and in the work force is here to stay. That social consciousness can only improve. More women will come forward to fight. And the ruling class attempts to reconstitute this section, the female section, of the industrial reserve army will backfire on them in a most unanticipated way. That perspective guides our course of action.

Steelworkers Fight Back

Ed Sadlowski's campaign for president of the Steelworkers goes under the name Steelworkers Fight Back. It is an important phenomenon.

As with CLUW, we make no promises about the results of the Sadlowski campaign or how big a role it can play in beginning to alter the United Steelworkers of America. That remains to be seen. But the Sadlowski drive is qualitatively different from Abel's fight to replace McDonald in 1965. We supported Abel against McDonald, though we recognized that Abel was not interested in much more than getting enough of the USW staff behind him to oust McDonald.

The Sadlowski campaign is often compared to the Miller insurgency in the Mineworkers. The Miners for Democracy took on the bureaucracy and won, even though they had to rely on federal government intervention to get the challenge off the ground. This is a legitimate comparison.

But we think the differences between Miners for Democracy and Steelworkers Fight Back are as important as the similarities. These times are different from the period that led up to the revolt in the Mineworkers. This is a different generation. Sadlowski belongs and appeals to a different generation from that of Miller; he reflects the new layers that came into the plants in the 1960s.

Steelworkers Fight Back is more typical of what is coming in a regenerated union movement.

If he is going to win, Sadlowski must take the fight for democracy in the Steelworkers back where he himself came from. His campaign has to go to the rank-and-file steelworkers. That's the only chance to beat Abel's stand-in. The age clause in the constitution precludes Abel from running, but we can be sure that the bureaucracy will find a worthy replacement.

The most important thing about the Sadlowski campaign is not what happens in the USW itself, important as that is. This can be the beginning of a reform movement to democratize the American labor movement. That is the way it is posed by Sadlowski in much that he writes and much that is written about him. In the letters Sadlowski sent out asking for funds, in the article he wrote for the *Nation,* in interviews he gave to Studs Terkel, to the *Rolling Stone,* to Sidney Lens, he hammers away on the theme that his efforts are the beginning of a movement to democratize the American trade unions. And that's how those who support him seem to view his campaign.

And that's the framework we also should take as a starter—a movement fighting to take control of the labor movement out of the hands of those who don't work—maybe have never worked—and get it into the hands of those who do labor and are facing the bosses' offensive. We support any step in this direction. For this reason we side with Sadlowski's fight to throw Abel out on the way to democratize the Steelworkers.

We don't consider Steelworkers Fight Back an embryonic left-wing caucus at this stage. Nor is it some special kind of organization like the Coalition of Labor Union Women, or Coalition of Black Trade Unionists, whose job is to press for the special needs, demands, and rights of women and of Blacks.

We say we too want a democratic labor movement. On that issue we're with you. Yes, we want a tough labor movement. On that issue we're with you too. We want to use labor's power. But democratization for what purpose? Use labor's power to what end? Those are questions the *Militant* wants to talk to workers about. That's what *we* want to address ourselves to. That's what everyone who supports Sadlowski is obliged to discuss. We fight for democratization in order to transform the unions into revolutionary organizations of class struggle. It is part of the struggle to transform labor into a movement that will think and act socially, that will champion the oppressed and draw them to it. It is part of the struggle to transform labor into a movement that will act politically, independent of the employers and their political parties, and combat the crisis of their system.

In Sadlowski's articles and interviews he points out that the most fundamental rights of labor—the right to bargain, to strike, to some elementary job security—are being threatened. No section of the labor movement can escape the threat. And if these rights are not effectively defended, a stupendous defeat will be recorded in this country.

The second important thing to note about Sadlowski's interviews is what he says about Black workers, the Black movement. He states unambiguously that racism and unionism are incompatible. You can't be a union fighter and be a racist of any kind. He points out that the entire history of this country from the time of slavery to today has been marked by the bosses' successful attempts to divide and conquer. That's how they have always won. And that's how they can continue to win. He points out the racist bias, as well as the class bias, in cutbacks, in the abuse of seniority. He talks about things like the murder of the Black Panther leader Fred Hampton and draws some of the correct conclusions. In one place he indicates the importance of women's struggles, although on this he says much less than on racist oppression.

Third, Sadlowski accurately describes what the unions have become, what the leadership of the unions has become. Here we have a big contribution to make and we should begin writing about this. What policies have led the unions to their current state? When and how did this develop? Only if workers know how their unions became so conservatized and bureaucratized can they figure out a strategy to change the labor movement.

Sadlowski doesn't say much about the decline of the CIO. He describes early heroic struggles, and then he jumps to the problems facing workers today caught in the vise of "tuxedo unionism." There is quite a gap there. And that gap in labor history has to be discussed by steelworkers, by all workers. It covers the rise of Roosevelt's War Deal and the support from most of the labor movement to the bosses' war. The inescapable result was a decline of union democracy, the bureaucratization, and integration of the unions into the state machinery during World War II. The ties to the Democratic Party were consolidated and every thrust toward a labor party, toward independent labor political action, was killed. As it was misled down this path, the

CIO moved away from being a social movement, a popular movement, a movement that draws the oppressed of society into struggle, fights alongside them, champions the struggles of all of capitalism's victims, and solicits their aid in labor's struggles. The social-patriotic capitulation of the Socialist Party, Communist Party, and labor leaderships to the imperialists in World War II made the second capitulation in the cold war that much easier.

The percentage of the working class in the organized labor movement declined and the CIO leadership itself turned into a conservative element in the labor aristocracy. The new leaders relied less and less on the class struggles of labor; they protected fewer and fewer jobs, and excluded more and more oppressed workers. If the deterioration of the American labor movement has been due to these wretched policies, the new rise of labor as a fighting social and political movement of class struggle will be based on the reversal of these policies.

Sadlowski has little to say whenever he gets to politics. He makes comments like "I have no isms." When asked what he thinks about the Democrats and Republicans, he replies, "They're all pricks." What should we do about them? "I don't have any strategy." What is your answer? One word: "Organize." When people are hungry you feed them. When people don't have any democracy you fight for their rights. As a sympathetic reporter might say, he is still thinking out the key questions. And so will many who support him.

The fight to democratize the Steelworkers union, to throw Abel and his ilk out, to mobilize everyone who wants this, to proclaim this as a struggle for the entire working class that deserves everyone's support—that is our approach. For union democracy; for control by the members of their unions. And along the way more and more workers will begin to read, think about, and discuss these broader questions posed by the fight to democratize the labor movement.

New York crisis

New York has become the code word in the ruling class for every single city and every single public workers' union. It is also part of a broader ruling class offensive—things like the bosses' drive at the *Washington Post,* against the New York bricklayers, give us a glimpse of what's planned for the rest of American labor.

In the four months since we last discussed what is happening in New York, the head-on attack has accelerated. The Democratic administration admits it has eliminated 35,000 jobs. Shanker claims they plan to get rid of another 55,000 in the next two-and-a-half years. Ninety thousand working people in one city! That is what is happening. It's not just that wages have been frozen and every collective bargaining session is conducted under heavy pressure. Contracts have simply been torn up. Working conditions have deteriorated. Social services have deteriorated. And every single squeeze hits the working class where it hurts, starting with the Black, Puerto Rican, and women workers, whose hard fought gains of recent years are being wiped out. This highlights the dead-end of the strategy based on the assumption of permanent prosperity and clubhouse politics with the Democratic Party in a period of expansion.

It is important to remember the origins of many New York employees unions. They did not arise out of great organizing campaigns in a period of working class radicalization. They grew under cover of a special relationship with the Democratic Party. The municipal work force swelled tremendously in the postwar period. The unions and their members were key supporters, doorbell ringers, and campaign subsidizers for the big-city Democratic politicians. In return (given what they assumed to be an ever-growing GNP, ever-ascending tax revenues), at one minute to midnight on the last day of contract negotiations, the Democratic city administration could always make concessions. In return, the union leaders would promise favors at the polls. In return for which more unionization was agreed to. Etc.

This mutual backscratching reached the point that the teachers in New York, the largest union local in the country, gave tacit support to the union-busting Taylor Law, which also contained provisions for dues checkoff and recognition—which was all Shanker wanted. And, as the Teachers union was consolidated, Shanker pandered to the most reactionary stance against the oppressed.

The leaders of the municipal workers' unions thrived on this special relationship with the Democratic Party and clubhouse politics.

There is a set of clippings from the *New York Times* that reads like a novel, especially if you think about what has happened to teachers over the last six months in New York. In the spring of 1973 (May 19, 1973, to be exact), the *New York Times* ran an article under the headline, "Two Labor Groups Endorse Beame's Nomination." One was the Central Labor Council. The other was the United Federation of Teachers. This was the first time the UFT ever endorsed a candidate in a New York City election. Who did they endorse? Abe Beame.

Why did the UFT take such a step? According to Albert Shanker, "Our endorsement of Abe Beame reflects teachers' growing political awareness." He praised Beame as "a progressive and enlightened public official," able "to get people working together," to improve wages and working conditions in New York City schools. Shanker also attacked Beame's opponents for having "closely allied themselves with the forces of community control." So reads the first clipping.

The second clipping is a year or so later, September 19, 1974. The headline reads, "Teachers Groups Increase Election Campaign Outlay." The article simply details the millions that Shanker and his allies were pouring into the coffers of the capitalist politicians like Beame.

The third clipping is about the same time, September 16, 1974. It has the headline: "Teachers Union Supporting Carey." The article explains how the "surprising" decision was reached. No one expected the teachers' state convention to endorse a candidate for governor of New York, but, as Shanker said, discussion began "spontaneously." It lasted all of ninety minutes and ended in a *unanimous vote!* He said that was hard to explain. "It was a real ground swell, a tremendous feeling of excitement." This ninety-minute ground swell was built on Carey's "labor record in Congress and his excellent program from the educational point of view."

Then another article appeared: "Teachers Union Violates U.S. Code on Political Aid" (September 19, 1974). Shanker had gotten so carried away with the political "friends of labor" like Carey that the Teachers union poured more money into their coffers than the law allowed. In 1973-74, Beame and Carey. That was the prelude to 1975. And all this was organized against "the forces of community control." That's another code word, enunciated in the same manner that George Wallace says "federal guidelines."

On December 21, Shanker published a Christmas message to the workers of New York: "There is some hope. Help may come in time. Maybe the economy will turn around. . . . Or perhaps the federal government will relieve states and cities of the burdensome costs of welfare and medical care. We can also hope that tax reform will bring increased revenues. . ." (*New York Times*). But meanwhile we must simply hang on. "We must develop a 'wartime' frame of mind. We must be willing to sacrifice, to stick it out until the 'lights go on again.' That will not be easy. . . . Like wartime, this is a time for everyone to pitch in, to help bring the city through its darkest period."

Shanker goes on to plead with the ruling class. After all, labor is sacrificing, so it is wrong for the New York City Board of Education and the Board of Higher Education to take advantage of the situation, "to make war on their employees—to break their contracts." But all is not lost. "The courts are bound to rule that a contract is a contract and must be upheld." In the meantime, "everyone has been pitching in. Everyone has been working beyond what is legally required. That is the way it must be and should be, in a period like this."

That is the sum total of the labor bureaucracy's strategy! Theirs is not a policy for today's reality, for growing social and economic crisis. Even on the crudest level, their policies have become a reactionary utopia. Capitalism can no longer make available the resources for the clubhouse politicians to pay off the union leaders that "go along." That's over and done with. The relative gains won through that policy were possible only in a different period. Neither the hopes that some new prosperity will come along, nor the hope for an electoral victory of a powerful and benevolent "friend of labor," can improve the desperate situation labor faces. The ruling class can no longer extend the kinds of concessions it did before.

For public employees, every problem immediately manifests itself as a political problem. They have no single boss. They are not in a single industry. They deal directly with the city, the county, the state, or the federal government. And instead of helping them, the friends of labor they elected turn on them. Not because they were the "wrong" bourgeois politicians to support but because Mayor Beame and Governor Carey must enforce the antilabor policy the ruling class finds necessary. The public employee unions must become political animals, but independent of the employers' parties.

The results are felt not only in New York but far beyond. We must emphasize that New York is a trial run for other cities. It is a trial run against the weak components of the labor movement. The plutocrats and their agents are probing, pushing, testing. And every single union in this country is the eventual target.

The axes of our work

In the report later by Doug Jenness we will discuss our political campaigns and organizational tasks. But certain broad axes to our work flow from the analysis we have given.

1. *No more Vietnams.* On Angola, our obligation is to demand that the imperialists get out, stay out, and keep their hands off southern Africa. No more Vietnams! That is a popular slogan in this country. Use that monstrous hundred-billion-dollar war budget for social needs. Those bombs and planes, spies and assassins, are of no use to any working person anywhere in the world.

2. *The right to know.* We must take advantage of the continuing exposés of the real face of the declining bourgeois democracy in this country. The scandals that continue to rock every capitalist institution from the CIA to industry to every two-bit politician. Our central demand is: Open the books! The American people have the right to know what is being done in government, in industry, in finance. We must aid those who are striving to expose any hidden cranny of capitalist rule. We are for publishing every government file that can be obtained, every secret corporation ledger that can be pried open. The right to know is connected to the class polarization that is coming in this country. Working people have to find out everything about the real character of the Legions of Justice, the reactionary lynch mobs that roam Boston's streets, the Ku Kluxers. What are their real connections? Who is really behind them? What are their goals?

3. *Capitalism's responsibility.* We have to keep pointing to the real architects of these obscene policies. They are the leaders of the two parties of American capitalism who are charged with the political administration of a more and more irrational and antihuman social system.

A campaign party

We must use the national strength and mobility of the party, in cooperation with the YSA, to throw ourselves into key struggles that can pave the way for educating the consciousness of American labor and changing the class relationship of forces. We participate in struggles that develop around busing, bilingual education, government cutbacks, the ERA, the farm workers, affirmative action, defense cases. One of our greatest assets is to be mobile enough and cohesive enough to act with maximum force.

We should take the issues raised by these struggles to the labor movement, to the entire working class. The AFT must reverse its policies, must support busing. The fight for the ERA should be supported not only in words but in deeds by the labor movement. Affirmative action and adjustments in the seniority system to prevent discriminatory layoffs should be pushed forward. Opposition to the bosses' campaign against so-called illegals should be mounted. The struggles against discrimination led by the NAACP and other such groups should be supported. That is part and parcel of the effort to think socially and act politically.

For independent working class political action

We should take a step forward in our propaganda and education, through our press and our election campaigns, on the need for a labor party and a Black party. We are convinced that there can be no class-struggle left wing of the American labor movement that doesn't inscribe on its banner the need for independent political action. No popular social movement will grow, let alone become a revolutionary instrument of class struggle, without taking this step. Learning to think socially and act politically are intimately intertwined.

None of the major problems that the crisis of capitalism poses before the American workers can be solved simply at the trade union level. The most that can be accomplished is a few more temporary gains for a smaller and smaller percentage of the work force. The labor movement as it exists today cannot organize the unorganized or reorganize itself on an industrial basis. It finds it increasingly difficult even to bargain for the members it has, let alone the ones it is losing, or the millions of unorganized.

The ruling class strategy is a step-by-step "zap labor" campaign. They eventually aim to co-opt the union bureaucracy more and more and break the strength of the remaining bastions of the industrial unions. We do not foresee another division within the labor bureaucracy of the kind that spurred the rise of the CIO and industrial unionism—and held the working class within those limits. The challenge today is much greater. The transformation of the labor movement must be social and political from the beginning. And the big social struggles outside the unions are very important to this process.

It is worthwhile to observe the alternatives the ruling class is debating. These are illustrated by Ford's veto of Labor Secretary Dunlop's picketing bill. There you saw two intertwined perspectives of the ruling class to deal with labor resistance in a period of employer offensive. Dunlop's bill, of course, was designed to further integrate the construction trades into the state, to further centralize and regularize the government's relations with the skilled trades bureaucracy.

Ford's veto of the bill reflected, even if unconsciously, a further perspective: that of hammering and smashing the unions. Frank Lovell emphasized in our Political Committee discussion that there are a lot of bosses in this country who never reconciled themselves to the rise of the CIO. They do not consider industrial unionism to be a historically necessary development that they are obliged to accept and live with forever.

These two alternative perspectives of the boss class are interrelated and combined: the attempt to integrate the unions, through their misleadership, into the state apparatus, and concurrently the desire of growing numbers of the ruling class to probe, to move toward the ultimate fascist-like solution. That is to break the unions altogether and prevent them from being organizations that fight for the economic needs of the workers they serve.

We want to enhance our propaganda for independent political action in a way that avoids some errors. We don't want to present the idea in a maximalist way. We don't go around saying, "to build socialism we need a labor party," or "the labor party is the crowning demand of the transitional program," or anything like that. This doesn't mean the time for a labor party is far off in the future. The time for a labor party is now.

Look at the facts of this American capitalist society as we have just outlined them, the facts that dictated the party's turn. It is unassailable that the time for independent political action is now. There is no discernible motion in that direction; we don't pretend that there is. But objectively that is what is needed, and this way forward can be made clear to growing numbers of people.

The demand for a labor party is not a tactic. This is not something we demand along with a whole series of other items. Independent labor political action represents a fundamental strategic break from being tied politically to the needs of the employers. This break must be made not only to move ahead but even to save the gains we have won.

We do not see propaganda for a labor party as a substitute for participating in progressive actions. That would be the most sectarian and abstentionist mistake imaginable. A campaign for a labor party can never be a substitute for throwing yourself into the major social struggles that erupt. In fact no other course gets across the idea of the kind of independent political action we are talking about.

This is not an agitational campaign. We are not forming, or announcing the intention to form, labor party clubs. We are not trying to beat out the various sectarian grouplets in calling a labor party conference.

We do not want to go about this in a routinist manner. The objective is not to end each article in the press with a paragraph that says: "We need a labor party. We need to break with the Democrats to move forward."

We think we can avoid such errors and at the same time step up this campaign. Willie Mae Reid's speech in New York that the *Militant* printed last week was a good example of the way we can integrate this question into our educational campaign.

We should look at every major struggle or capitalist breakdown as an opportunity to present the need for a labor party: the New York crisis, the campaign against so-called illegal aliens, busing, the battle for the ERA. We should say what a labor government in New York would do when the bankers claim there is no money. Point after point after point, our propaganda and our action lend themselves to saying that the oppressed and exploited need to break from the twin parties of oppression and exploitation. We will do this primarily through the *Militant* and our candidates across the country.

Simultaneously we must educate on the need for a Black party and for a Chicano party. We cannot dissolve the need for independent Black political action into a nonexistent labor party or into our propaganda for one. Here there is an even greater growing objective need. Every liberal politician has been in open or disguised retreat on the busing question, desegregation, bilingual education, affirmative action, cutbacks. The election of thousands of Black Democratic and Republican politicians has raised more problems than solutions. What Baxter Smith in the *Militant* calls the BEOs, the Black elected officials, have produced nothing for their constituents. And they *can* produce nothing in a declining social order so long as they are handcuffed to the parties and class of that decaying order.

The problems that the Black population as a whole, as well as the Chicano population, face can't be solved on the job or on the union level alone. They are *doubly* political, in that racism and discrimination are clear political questions. What we are calling for is not a Black Democratic Party but a *new* kind of party, a party that lives up to the principle of not subordinating the struggles and needs of the Black population to anything or anyone. Like the labor party, we are not presenting this with any maximalist, routinist, or agitational excesses. Nor are we operating under any illusions. It is not our assessment that there is tangible motion toward an independent Black party, any more than there is any real motion toward a labor party at present. But that doesn't change the objective need for such political action. We must explain this or we can't give honest answers to any of the crises capitalism engenders. We would find ourselves saying what Ed Sadlowski says—"Organize!"—and no more.

But we are revolutionary socialists, not merely radical trade unionists. This report has concentrated on the labor movement for the reasons outlined at the beginning. But we should end by emphasizing that for us the key is not what is happening in the unions per se right now. The key is the social crisis as a whole and the struggles it engenders, which will have a growing reflection inside the unions. These, combined with what workers face on the job, are essential for the transformation of the unions. And the struggles outside the labor movement will not go away as the radicalization deepens and as the labor movement changes. They will deepen. Only the coming struggles will determine which unions will be integrated and housebroken and what section of the labor movement will be won to a perspective of using its power as an instrument of revolutionary social change.

Summary

Several speakers emphasized in the discussion that we can't give the answers to the concrete effects of the ruling-class offensive without raising the labor party perspective, the Black and Chicano independent party perspective, and their interconnection. I think this is correct. We're not talking about a future need or some far distant stage. Without explaining the labor party question we cannot even answer how we, the American working people, got into the bind we are in today and why it s getting worse.

Jeff Mackler discussed the AFT-NEA merger question. Let us think back to the 1955 merger of the AFL and the CIO. What happened after that merger, when almost all of organized labor came together under a single roof? Were the goals the leaders loudly proclaimed met? What were the goals? One, organize the South. Two, reverse the trend toward a decreasing percentage of American labor being unionized. Three, repeal the Taft Hartley antistrike law. And four, change the political and social climate in this country so that the union movement could be strengthened and working people could get a greater share of the wealth they produce.

Those were the goals presented at the time of merger, which took place at the midpoint of almost a quarter century of relative prosperity. What were the results under the AFL-CIO leadership? None of these goals were reached. In fact, the reverse occurred. The large-scale organization of the South never got off the ground. Today a smaller percentage of the work force is in the organized labor movement than at the time of the AFL-CIO merger. There are more and stronger antiunion laws on the books now than in 1955. And certainly, if the last year is any example, the situation that working people face when they try to defend their most minimal gains, try to prevent slashes in their standard of living, let alone achieve advances, is the worst since the Great Depression.

Union mergers, increases in the potential organizational power of the movement, can accomplish nothing substantial without a fundamental change in policy. The potential power of the unions has not declined. Labor's potential social and political power remains immense. But the current policy of the bureaucracy simply wastes, cripples, and (to the degree that it uses it) abuses this power.

Union militants can't win an argument with Shanker supporters by simply discussing whether Shanker was right or wrong when he opposed last fall's New York teachers' strike. If the Shanker framework is accepted, Shanker was dead right. The strike was bound to be a loser. And, to top it off, the contract was torn up a few months later by Big Mac. The correct course cannot be explained by someone who accepts Shanker's framework of (1) ride out the recession and wait for the return of prosperity; (2)

push "the community control people" into the other camp by opposing their just demands; and (3) count on your relationship with the Democratic Party to bring a few contract gains, as it has for the last decade or two. As long as teachers accept that framework, strikes are doomed and all the potential power of the labor movement is hamstrung. Only by concretely and emphatically rejecting all these premises can an alternative course be charted for the teachers from coast to coast.

The noose about their necks today consists of the very things that many organized teachers and public workers accepted for a quarter of a century as the road to gains—cling to the illusion of permanent prosperity, ignore the oppressed outside the union, keep lobbying within the two-party system. It was always a dead end but it's hard to convince people of that when the policy seems to be yielding results of some kind. But that is no longer the case. The economic and social necessities faced by the ruling class and its two parties preclude any other course at this time. That is why a different party is needed—a class party of a new type.

In the same issue of the *Nation* that printed the article by Sadlowski (September 6, 1975), there is an article on Meany by B. J. Widick. He quotes Meany's response to a question about the jobs march on Washington last April. Would the AFL-CIO try to organize the rank-and-file sentiment expressed by the massive turnout there?

Meany says, "No, the AFL-CIO is pretty conservative in certain ways. We believe in the American system. We believe in working within the American system. When we get laws passed over on Capitol Hill that we feel are detrimental to us, we just bat away and try to change them. We don't man the barricades, and we don't take to the streets. And we don't call general strikes, and we don't call political strikes."

That is an excellent description of Meany's policy. We cannot explain the predicament the labor movement is in and the reality of what lies ahead in places like New York unless we deal with these policies that have guided Meany and Shanker and placed the union movement in the straightjacket it wears today.

The social and political policies of the labor movement have crippled it. It is not only crippled in the fight for gains, it's hamstrung even when it comes to defending its existence. What's going on in the construction trades and at the *Washington Post* today are examples. Labor will not even be able to protect its own organizational existence without a reversal of these policies of retreat and defeat.

The labor party we advocate

The kind of program we advocate for a prospective labor party is our program. When we talk about a labor party, about a break by labor from its enemy, the bosses, who are organized in the two-party system in this country, we are always addressing ourselves to some concrete problem: the layoffs and cutbacks in New York, the situation that the steelworkers face, the attempt to break the pressmen's union at the *Washington Post*, the task of getting the support of the oppressed minorities for the teachers, and vice versa.

Whatever the specific problem, we explain the labor party perspective as part of our answer, part of our proposal on what is to be done, and in that way we present the labor party idea intermeshed with our action program drawn from our transitional program. We don't pose this step as a precondition for everything else. But the need for a new type of party is intertwined with the concrete demands we are fighting for.

The question was posed: Why is the demand for a labor party a transitional one? After all, there is no more visible motion toward a labor party than there is toward the SWP. The answer is simple. The SWP is small. The labor movement is very large. The union movement exists. It has organized almost a quarter of the work force of the most powerful capitalist country on earth. Much of it is organized on an industrial basis.

How much of this movement will be integrated into the capitalist state apparatus and destroyed, and how much of it will be transformed into a revolutionary instrument of struggle for the oppressed and exploited? This question will be answered in a fight with historic repercussions that will deeply affect the class relationship of forces in this country, and the odds of the success of the American socialist revolution. This is the point of departure for all of our thinking on the unions.

We present the labor party along the same line as we present the Black party. It is an instrument to fight for the objectives we are for, and for the goals we are after—to break from the employers, to fight for the workers and their allies, to get rid of the domination of capital. Our goal is to build a mass revolutionary workers' party that can lead the struggle for power.

We exist as a program and a cadre. But unions exist as mass class institutions. And these institutions don't belong to the bureaucrats who have usurped them, although they would like to claim possession. They belong to the workers, who must learn to use them politically or they will continue to be used against the interests of the workers.

There is a second transitional side to our proposal for a labor party. This is a transition in consciousness. We try to raise class consciousness. Union consciousness, which is strong in this country, is one elementary form of class consciousness. We try to advance political class consciousness, a higher stage. We explain: You can't do battle with the bosses and their agents, fight against cutbacks, layoffs, race and sex discrimination, rampant inflation, and at the same time be tied to the political instruments that carry out these policies.

In the Sadlowski articles and interviews he underlines that there are bosses and there are workers, and you can't fudge the line between the two. In other words, you can't cross class lines. He'll even take an Abel ahead of a steel boss. Abel's a bastard but he's our bastard.

But this elementary class consciousness has to be applied on the *political* level where class relationships are generalized and the capitalist regime is run. We don't counterpose the SWP to a labor party. We counterpose the powerlessness and helplessness of the labor movement in this country to the mighty force it can be if it becomes truly independent—a popular social movement of the oppressed and exploited. Our program includes not only goals and ends but also *how* to get there. A class struggle includes economic and social demands, but it culminates in an overall political perspective for our class.

It is a waste of time to speculate: Will there be a Black party first? Will there be a labor party first? Will a mass Chicano party precede both? Will a labor party get off the ground and will a big SWP then develop? How many of the unions will be transformed into revolutionary instruments of class struggle? How many will be busted up by the bosses and their state in this process? What different forms of popular organization will come forward and lead mass struggles? What will be the American form of soviets?

All these things will be decided in the course of struggle. The labor party may be bypassed in this country by the rapid growth of a revolutionary party. That remains a historical possibility. But the struggle for a labor party can't be bypassed because that's part of the process of building the revolutionary working class vanguard.

Does our ability to get a hearing for our explanation of the need for independent political organization vary from industry to industry and from city to city? In certain secondary ways, yes. But in the most fundamental sense, no. Right now in New York we can get a hearing from a whole layer of working people that is different from a year ago. Perhaps the crisis-ridden New York workers are more receptive than in some other city. But there are many signs coming from dissimilar sources—the Farm Workers, a basic industry like steel, the birth of a fighting coalition of labor union women, the shakeup of perspective in the Nation of Islam, and new stirrings in the NAACP. Hence we draw the conclusion that it's not going to vary fundamentally from city to city or from industry to industry.

Ironically it is in some of the most "aristocratic" sections of the labor movement, the craft unions, that the current crisis is most acute. The workers in these trades haven't even solved the question of industrial organization, let alone affirmative action and political organization. And now they will have to take on all these questions at the same time. In fact the former will be impossible without the latter.

We don't counterpose the labor party to class-struggle action. The labor party perspective is a necessary component of taking action in a new way, in a new situation. If we are to be successful we must link it to action.

When we talk about a labor party or a Black party it is too bad we have to use the word party, because, as Andrew Pulley said, no one has ever seen the kind of parties we are talking about. They haven't seen them because they have never existed in the experience of the American workers. We are talking about a party of a new type that leads struggles, fights on all levels, unconditionally, for the oppressed and the exploited.

There is a world of difference between us and the Benjamin Spocks and Eugene McCarthys who start from the premises and practices of what's gone wrong with the Democrats. We begin with the idea of what's right about using the power of the working people to realize their economic and social goals. To do this, you can't be chained to the two parties of the employers on the political level. That's what we are talking about. We are talking about political action to use the power of a class, even though it is manacled and misled today. We begin with the realities of the two major classes in American society, not the moral failings—although they are many—of the two capitalist parties.

The CIO was built in a period when the forces leading it were not linked to the Democratic Party in anything like the way they are today. Think of the great battles of 1934. They were led by three forces: the Stalinists in San Francisco, still in their Third Period ultraleftism, the Trotskyists in Minneapolis, and the Musteites in Toledo. None of these was linked to the Democratic Party, in their perspectives, in their politics, or in their methods of action. It took the preparation of the War Deal and the war to thoroughly integrate an entire layer of the labor bureaucracy, with the help of the Social Democracy and the Stalinists. Even so, it took the gutting of the labor movement by the witch-hunt and prosperity after World War II to stifle the last tendencies toward labor political action. These were still evident in the UAW in 1950.

Malik Miah's point on the Black party was important. There is an additional problem in presenting the perspective of the Black party compared to the labor party. When we talk about the Black party we are not talking about transforming potentially powerful existing institutions. There is no equivalent of unions in the Black or Chicano communities, no comparable organized power.

The problem with the Black elected officials is that they front for a party that's led by the capitalists and by people who have no interest in the struggles of Black people as an oppressed nationality or as workers. Some Black people draw the conclusion from the experience of the BEOs that there's no point in getting involved in politics at all. There's a progressive side to that, because the Black party we are talking about is a party with politics of a *new* type that fights for the needs of people 365 days a year. Not a political machine that comes around on election day to get into office.

The Black Richard Hatcher and Coleman Young and the white Abe Beame and Hugh Carey are interchangeable as long as they are tied to the perspectives of the Democratic Party and responsible for administering capitalism in its decline. The offensive against workers, Blacks, and women, in New York, Gary, or Detroit, can't be turned back through the liberal capitalist politics they practice.

The polls show that more young people are independents, not Republicans or Democrats, than at any time since polling began.

Many have the attitude, to hell with politics, it stinks. And they are right; capitalist politics stinks. We don't start with voting. We start with the ongoing struggles and how to carry them forward, breaking with your enemies and organizing the kind of instrument that can fight effectively and win. That's how we can explain the reasons for a Black party, a Raza Unida party, or any other kind of working class party independent of the ruling class.

The Fight for Black Liberation: The Current Stage and Its Tasks

This resolution was adopted by the Twenty-seventh National Convention of the Socialist Workers Party, held in Ohio in August 1975.

More than a hundred years after the Emancipation Proclamation and twenty years after the Supreme Court decision outlawing school segregation, we see that racism, discrimination, and de facto segregation still exclude Afro-Americans from equal political, social, and economic opportunities.

The gap between the income of Black and white families increased 5 percent between 1970 and 1975. Black unemployment has consistently been twice as high as white unemployment since the Korean War. Government statistics placed Black unemployment at the beginning of 1975 at 14.2 percent compared to an overall figure of 8.4 percent. Blacks who do get jobs tend to be segregated into the lowest paying positions with the worst working conditions and the least job security. Even those Blacks who have broken through the educational, job-training, and employment barriers to become skilled workers or technicians are usually paid at rates far below those of whites with the same qualifications.

The plight of Black youth is a notorious scandal. In 1973 the Department of Labor estimated that unemployment for Black teen-agers was 30 percent, about two-and-a-half times the rate for white teen-agers. In the wake of the 1974-75 depression the press today puts the figure at 60 percent or higher.

Schools in the Black communities are rundown, under-staffed, and under-funded; the further cuts in state and federal funds will make them worse. The high pushout rates and low reading scores register the effects of systematic discrimination in education. Inner-city boards of education direct school administrations toward using ghetto schools not as places of education, but as detention centers to keep Black youth off the streets. Blacks are shunted away from courses that lead toward college or better-paying salaried and industrial jobs.

These conditions breed the disillusionment and hopelessness that have driven tens of thousands of Black youth to drugs for escape.

Bank red-lining and landlord discrimination make it difficult to buy or rent decent housing. Most Blacks are crowded into segregated neighborhoods with inferior housing at exorbitant rates.

The police prey upon the Black communities. While protecting and profiting from rent-gouging landlords and organized crime, the cops harass, shake down, beat up, and murder Blacks. Special tactical squads, ostensibly established to cut down crime, are used to terrorize Blacks. At the same time, Blacks are more victimized by crime than whites.

Even the miserable conditions that Blacks are condemned to are precarious and grow worse with every economic downturn. Inflation is most disastrous for those frozen into the lowest paying jobs. Black workers are among the first hit by large-scale layoffs.

On top of this the ruling class is trying to divert attention from its responsibility for the growing social crisis of American capitalism by whipping up racist prejudices against all non-whites—Blacks, other oppressed minorities, and nonwhite foreign-born workers. This reinforces the present campaign to roll back concessions and rights won by Black people in their struggles during the 1960s.

The persistence of such pervasive discrimination in spite of the civil rights movement and ghetto revolts of the 1960s—the largest and most powerful movement of Blacks in the United States since Reconstruction—shows not only the deep roots of racial oppression but that it is constantly regenerated by the workings of capitalist exploitation.

Racism and capitalism

Racial oppression of Blacks has been a pillar of capitalist rule since the founding of the United States. Its historical roots are in the slave-labor system that was the basis for the Southern plantation economy until the Civil War. Anti-Black prejudice originated to justify the enslavement of Blacks. In the North racial discrimination and prejudices were reinforced by the existence of slavery in the South and by proslavery governments in Washington.

But racial oppression against Blacks did not disappear with the abolition of slavery. Instead it continued in new forms. After the Civil War and Reconstruction it was retained for use by the industrial capitalist class, forerunner of the present-day monopoly capitalists. In the South this took the form of the apartheid-like system of Jim Crow laws, imposed and maintained by a reign of terror. In the country as a whole it took the form of discrimination and de facto segregation in virtually every aspect of life. And although the Black upsurge of the 1960s smashed the legal Jim Crow system in the South, racial oppression continues to be a fundamental feature of American capitalism.

Racism has been retained because it economically benefits and politically strengthens the capitalist rulers. It is one of their essential weapons in dividing the working class.

Blacks, who in their overwhelming majority are workers, are part of capitalism's reserve force of unemployed. As the last hired and first fired they function as an auxiliary labor force from which workers can be drawn during periods of economic upswing and laid off in any recession or depression. At all times their lower wages help depress the wage levels of all workers.

The billions of dollars in additional profits the capitalists reap as a result of racial oppression is very substantial. In addition to weakening the labor movement and helping to depress wage levels, racial discrimination means that Blacks receive a much smaller proportion of the national income than whites.

In 1971, for example, Black income was $46 billion. This was 6.6 percent of the total income for the country. However, Black people were 11.3 percent of the total population. If Black people had received 11.3 percent of the total income—their proportionate share—then their income for 1971 would have been an additional $32.6 billion. These billions go into the coffers of the ruling rich.

Billions are also made by charging Blacks higher rents for rotten housing. Billions more are diverted to other uses by the rulers by not providing decent schools, child-care centers, transportation, recreational facilities, and other social services for Black people.

The capitalists try to make white workers believe that their relatively better conditions compared to Blacks can be maintained by keeping Blacks down rather than by fighting the domination of the capitalists. To the extent they hold this attitude, white workers are led to view the unions as white job-trusts, which undercuts the development of class consciousness, solidarity, and the advancement of all workers.

The results can be seen in the racist attitudes of top trade union bureaucrats. Leaders of the construction unions, for example, strongly oppose admitting Blacks into the skilled building trades. Albert Shanker, president of the American Federation of Teachers, one of the most notorious white job-trusters, has won a national reputation as an opponent of preferential hiring of Blacks and other oppressed minorities, and of the struggles of oppressed minorities for improving or controlling their schools.

These reactionary policies have weakened trade unions by depriving them of the support they could receive from Blacks and other minorities.

By injecting racist prejudices into the white working class in order to create suspicions, hatred, and conflicts, the ruling class divides and weakens the working class as a whole and reinforces reaction. They brand an entire section of the working class as pariahs and try to get relatively better-off workers to view this layer as "them" rather than "us."

By undermining class solidarity the capitalists get racist-minded whites to tolerate high unemployment, rundown housing, and bad schools in the Black community as a product of Black "inferiority."

This helps convince white workers to accept the large-scale Black poverty and unemployment that would otherwise seem shocking to them, given the wealth of American society. This is especially true during a depression or recession when the conditions of Blacks relative to whites are worsened.

The national oppression of Black people also reinforces the political rule of the capitalist class by strengthening reactionary political ideas.

Racism has proved a useful ideological prop for justifying U.S. imperialist oppression of nonwhite peoples in Africa, Asia, Latin America, and the Caribbean. The fact that the Japanese are a people of color was used by the American rulers to win acceptance for dropping atomic bombs on Hiroshima and Nagasaki. Likewise, racism was utilized to make the savage atrocities committed against the Korean and then the Vietnamese people appear less heinous to the American people.

Whites who believe that their school, housing, and job problems can be solved by keeping Blacks out, are echoing the rulers' concept that the only way change can take place is within the guidelines dictated by the capitalist regime. This runs contrary to the truth that these problems can be solved only by struggling against the capitalist class, not against Blacks.

The ruling class tries to convince white workers that they have a *racial* interest as whites opposed to Blacks, rather than a *class* interest as workers opposed to the capitalists.

Racist codewords such as "law and order" and "crime in the streets" have been used to justify strengthening police forces and restricting civil liberties. In this way racism is used to whip up support for increasing political repression and eroding the democratic rights of all workers.

Racial discrimination provides a social basis for extralegal violence against Blacks and others fighting against capitalist oppression. This can be seen in the racist mobs mobilized in Boston against busing. Violence of this type has also encouraged smaller right-wing groups such as the Ku Klux Klan and the Nazis to more aggressively distribute their hate-mongering literature and launch terrorist attacks against Blacks and their supporters. The same reactionaries who are behind the antibusing campaign can be found organizing to defeat the ERA, outlaw abortion rights, and smash the unions.

Capitalist politicians—liberal and conservative—bear a large share of the responsibility for these attacks, both for retreating on the question of school desegregation and for refusing to arrest and convict the racist terrorists. This shows that their real interests are not in helping Blacks achieve equality and that Blacks cannot rely on the capitalist politicians to realize their goals.

During periods of extreme political and economic crisis, when capitalist political rule is threatened, capitalism is forced to rely on extralegal violence to roll back and crush the working class movement. In Germany, Italy, Spain, and other countries it utilized mass fascist movements to terrorize and smash the unions and working class parties, demoralize the working class, and end all political rights including those of oppressed nationalities.

As the class struggle sharpens in this country and the ruling class feels more threatened by a radicalized working class, it will increasingly encourage fascist demagogues and preachers of race hatred. They will attempt to make Blacks the scapegoats for capitalism's ills and take advantage of every source of friction to inflame white prejudices and incite whites against Blacks. Racism is a spawning ground for, and will be an integral part of, fascist ideology and fascist movements.

If the working class is not united against capitalist attacks, it will be crushed. Unity can be achieved only by winning the workers' movement to a policy of complete and unconditional support for the struggle of Afro-Americans.

The privileged position of whites relative to Blacks has made the question of how working class unity will be attained more difficult. The possibility of overcoming this difficulty is easier to grasp if it is recognized that this society is not only divided along national lines—between oppressed nationalities and the white majority—but is objectively even more deeply divided along class lines, between the capitalist class and the workers. In fact, the key function of racist oppression is to divide and weaken the working masses and bolster the system of class exploitation.

Thus white and Black workers have a very significant thing in common—an enemy that economically and politically dominates them and benefits from their divisions. Many white workers will only recognize this common problem when they learn by bitter experience that racial divisions result in defeats for them.

Unity will not be achieved by Blacks subordinating their struggle for equality to the present racist setup, but by white workers supporting Black rights. This process will be advanced by the Black struggle itself as it mobilizes for its own democratic demands and for economic and social demands which answer the needs of all working people. A strong, independent Black movement with its own organizations and caucuses will increase the prospects of winning respect and support from white workers.

Combined character of the American revolution

Centuries of oppression have welded Black people into a distinct nationality with an identity that differentiates them both from other oppressed nationalities in this country and from white Americans. Consciousness of their national identity has deepened with the urbanization and proletarianization of Black people in this century.

The Black struggle has a dual character, flowing from the class and national aspects of Black oppression. On the one hand, Blacks are fighting against the oppression they face as a people, as a nationality. On the other, they are fighting against their exploitation as workers. These two aspects of their struggle are deeply intertwined. The oppression that Blacks face as a people is conditioned by their largely proletarian status, and the exploitation of Blacks as workers becomes superexploitation as a result of the racial discrimination they face as Blacks.

The Black struggle has been a permanent component at the center of political life in America. Despite ups and downs, setbacks and diversions, the general tendency has been toward greater Black self-confidence in asserting demands. Every wave of Black militancy in the twentieth century has led the most militant fighters, like Malcolm X, to develop anticapitalist convictions as they saw America's capitalist rulers in their dual role as both class and national enemies of Black people.

The spread of Black nationalism over the past thirty years and the growing radicalization of Afro-Americans has confirmed Trotsky's prediction that Blacks "are convoked by the historic development to become a vanguard of the working class." The Black struggle has surged ahead during the past decades while the labor movement was conservatized and remained relatively quiescent.

Blacks are playing a leading role in the political radicalization of the working class. Their importance is indicated by the strategic place of Blacks in the work force—their concentration in basic industry and in urban employment, as well as their growing numbers in the major industrial centers of the country. The nationalist self-identity and self-reliance of Blacks will not diminish in importance as organized labor regains its militant character. As labor begins to move, Black people will become even more outspoken and militant in their demands for human rights. The power of an insurgent labor movement will inspire Blacks with greater confidence to push ahead. This in turn will add weight to those forces in the unions seeking to commit their organizations to the fight for the social and political interests of all the victims of capitalist society.

The heightened political consciousness and independent struggle of the Black movement will make it a powerful force *alongside of* as well as *inside of* the labor movement in the fight against capitalism.

The coming American revolution has the job of winning equality and freedom from racial oppression for Blacks and other oppressed nationalities along with the liberation of the working class from capitalist exploitation. In theory these two tasks should have been solved hundreds of years apart in two different historical epochs. No one could expect the capitalist overlords to give up their wealth and power and create an egalitarian, classless society. That could only be the job of the working class, which has no stake in private ownership of industry, and which could only reorganize society on the basis of common ownership of social wealth by the whole working population. But the American revolution two hundred years ago did promise "liberty and equality for all."

The capitalist revolutions against feudalism, while defending private ownership of the means of production, at least promised that everyone would be equal before the law, that there would be no special persecution of groups in society because of their racial or national origin. It is because bourgeois democracy defaulted on this promise and institutionalized racism as a tool of its minority rule that the job of stamping out racial and national oppression today can only be accomplished by the united struggle of the oppressed minorities and the working class through the overthrow of capitalism and the creation of a socialist society. That is why the American socialist revolution will have a "combined character"—it will combine the fight for socialism with the fight to complete the unfinished and betrayed tasks of the bourgeois-democratic revolution of 1776 and of the Civil War.

Neither the first nor second American revolution resulted in full equality for Black people. Although the Civil War abolished chattel slavery, the Reconstruction period that followed did not bring the radical land reform or any other basic economic and social transformation that could lift the mass of Afro-Americans out of the lowest depths of poverty and oppression. The bourgeois reaction in the late 1870s snatched political liberties won during the post-Civil War period from Afro-Americans, relegalized racial oppression, and reduced Blacks to the condition of an intensely exploited pariah section of the toiling masses.

The equality that the capitalist class failed to extend at the height of its radicalism could certainly not be granted as it became a more and more hardened imperialist force. In fact, the rise of American imperialism at the end of the nineteenth century created a *new* need for racism to serve as justification for the superexploitation of, and brutal wars against, nonwhite peoples. It is not that American "democracy" has been agonizingly slow in fulfilling its promises. The capitalist rulers are moving in the opposite direction entirely and have no intention of abandoning racism as a central prop of their class power.

The democratic task of providing equality, left over from the past, has been handed down to the present generation for solution. This historic default of the bourgeoisie has to be corrected by the progressive anticapitalist forces of our time.

This conforms to Leon Trotsky's theory of the permanent revolution, which holds that whatever progressive tasks the bourgeois revolutions have been incapable of carrying through have to be made good by the working class.

The size, social weight, and nationalist consciousness of the Black population indicate that the coming American revolution, as part of carrying through the democratic task of equalizing opportunities in all aspects of social life, will also be a revolution for the self-determination of Black people; that is, Black people will have the right to decide for themselves what state form they need to guarantee their complete liberation from racial oppression. At this stage it is not clear what their decision will be—whether a federation of councils exercising community control of the Black community, a separate state, integration in a common state with whites, or some other solution. If it turns out that the legacy of racism and degree of oppression are so great that Blacks feel it is necessary to separate from this country and set up a separate Black state, it will not only be the obligation of the new workers' state to defend the right of Black people to do this, but to provide all the material assistance necessary.

The defeat of Jim Crow

The Jim Crow system of legally sanctioned segregation, enforced by extralegal terror, was created in the South as part of the defeat of Reconstruction. Its purpose was to provide cheap labor for the production of cotton and other agricultural crops formerly produced by slaves. The rights to vote, move, organize, speak, and assemble, won during Reconstruction, were taken away from Blacks. Every aspect of life was segregated by law. This entire social and juridical system was rigorously enforced by the police and courts and the extralegal terror of reactionary organizations like the Ku Klux Klan.

This system molded Southern Blacks into a distinct oppressed grouping defined by race with legal and social rights sharply circumscribed. Blacks were forced to work at very low wages, or, as in the case of many sharecroppers, for no wages at all.

This was different from the forms of national oppression and de facto segregation Black people faced in the North and now face in the South. Jim Crow aimed to exclude Southern rural Blacks from the free labor market in order to provide the type of cheap labor needed in Southern agriculture. De facto segregation, on the other hand, aims to keep Black people on or near the bottom of the free labor market. De facto segregation, which has existed in the North for years, has replaced legal segregation in the South. It is being consciously established in virtually every area of life by landlords, employers, school boards, city governments, and other ruling institutions.

While Jim Crow disenfranchised Southern Blacks, under today's de facto segregation the legal barriers to Blacks voting have been eliminated in the South. The ruling class attempts to politically subordinate Blacks in the South the same way they have been doing for years in the North, by deceiving them into voting for the capitalist politicians of the two-party system.

The economic structure on which Jim Crow was based began to break down after World War II with the stepped-up migration of Blacks to urban industrial centers and the big advances in the mechanization of Southern agriculture.

Despite these changes, the capitalists found it politically and economically useful to continue Jim Crow practices that reinforced racism in general and helped keep nonwhites in all parts of the country as special pariah sectors of the industrial reserve army.

The 1954 Supreme Court decision declaring school segregation illegal, for example, was not prompted by a desire to end segregation in education or anywhere else. This ruling was intended as a face-saving measure because of two problems facing the ruling class.

The first was the embarrassment Jim Crow created for the rulers in their foreign relations and diplomatic maneuvers, especially with the countries of Africa and Asia. The American imperialists needed to make it appear that they were doing something about this social blight which most of the world viewed with horror.

A second factor was the rise in struggles for Black rights that followed the migration of Blacks to the urban centers in the 1930s and 1940s. Black people had already forced the government to establish fair-employment laws in government jobs and to desegregate the armed forces by the time of the 1954 Supreme Court decision.

The central, although unintended, effect of this court decision was the encouragement it gave Blacks to launch a struggle that finally abolished the Jim Crow laws that legitimized segregation in the South. This struggle was inspired by the victories of independence movements in the colonial world.

The first of the major civil rights actions was the 1955 bus boycott by the Black community in Montgomery, Alabama. This set the pace for nearly ten years of demonstrations, marches, sit-ins, wade-ins, freedom rides, and other actions which involved masses of Blacks, students, and other supporters of equality.

Advances in agricultural technology and the large-scale migration of Blacks laid the basis for the elimination of Jim Crow on an economic level. However, it required the massive extraparliamentary actions of the Black liberation movement to carry through the job.

Eliminating Jim Crow did not end racial oppression of Southern Blacks. But it cut out the legal justification for racial discrimination, putting the law formally on the side of Blacks fighting segregation in whatever form it appears. It opened the door to a new and more favorable stage of the fight for social, economic, and political gains.

Just as Jim Crow strengthened racism all over the country, its defeat was a blow to racists everywhere and spurred actions in Black communities throughout the country.

The struggle for the abolition of Jim Crow accelerated the struggle against de facto segregation that had been established outside the South. This posed the need for major social and economic changes in this country in a way that the struggle against Jim Crow did not.

The inability of the moderate civil rights leaders such as Martin Luther King, Jr., to deal with these problems, and the limits of the civil rights victories in the mid-1960s, led to the spread of Black power consciousness. This development also went under the names of Black nationalism and Pan Africanism.

The aim of Black power advocates tended toward establishing Black control over the economic, educational, political, and cultural life of the Black community. This objective was concretized in the demand by masses of Afro-Americans for Black control over the Black community and the demand, by a smaller number, for a separate Black state. Black nationalism increased identification with the colonial and semicolonial countries, particularly in Africa. It also stimulated and increased interest in the socialist alternative to capitalism and imperialism.

There were major community struggles around the demand for Black control of Black schools, widespread student actions, the emergence of Black caucuses in the unions and the Democratic Party, Black GI organizations, prison revolts, and Black power and nationalist conferences that drew thousands of militants.

The most significant development of this period was the massive ghetto rebellions that took place in almost every major city between 1964 and 1968, culminating in outbreaks across the country after the assassination of Martin Luther King, Jr. These struggles displayed the massive anger that had developed in the Black community at the government's recalcitrance in meeting the demands of the civil rights movement and its total failure to offer improvements in the social and economic conditions of the urban ghettos.

This upsurge helped force the ruling class not only to end the Jim Crow system in the South, but also to grant other concessions. These moves were made easier for the ruling class because of the economic boom of the early and middle 1960s.

Some better-paying industrial and white collar jobs were opened up to Black people. A small layer of Blacks was given executive positions in the government and private industry. Most white collar jobs Blacks gained were in professions like teaching and social work. A much larger layer of Blacks is now employed in federal and municipal service jobs where they are concentrated in the lower-paying levels.

Larger numbers of Blacks are finishing high school and substantially more have been admitted to colleges and universities since the mid-1960s. While many of these changes reflected shifts in the composition and character of the work force, others were products of the struggle for civil rights and Black power.

Increased numbers of Black students made student actions a more important aspect of the Black struggle. In the late 1960s, Black students were able to win Black studies departments on many campuses, along with increased admission of Black students.

As a result of these changes and of the final stages of the migration of Blacks out of the rural South, there was a slight narrowing in the income differential between Blacks and whites during the middle 1960s. However, even during that period of economic improvement the masses of Black people remained on the bottom of the economic ladder.

The power of the civil rights movement, the mass ghetto explosions, and the Black power struggles won respect for Blacks from many whites and helped break down racist prejudices. The civil rights movement, for example, was the spark for the student movement in the early 1960s. It helped prepare a new generation to morally reject U.S. aggression abroad and the oppression and alienation bred by American capitalism at home.

The battles of the 1950s and 1960s significantly raised the political consciousness, self-identity, and confidence of Black people. The struggle against Jim Crow, one of the forms of national oppression Black people have faced, passed over into a recognition of and struggle against other forms of national oppression. This in turn produced greater nationalist conscious- ness throughout the Black community and greater recognition of the fact that racism is an intrinsic part of the American system, not an aberration.

The net result of the victories and the new consciousness created by the civil rights movement and the Black power struggles was to substantially alter political life in the United States, and to improve the relationship of forces for Blacks and all oppressed and exploited nationalities, social groups, and classes.

Ruling class shift

At the height of the Black struggles of the mid-1960s, particularly after the ghetto rebellions, the ruling class recog- nized that it had to change its strategy in regard to the Black community. This shift included granting the concessions that have already been enumerated. Taking advantage of the deficiencies in the leadership of the Black liberation movement at that time, the rulers' new strategy combined both cooptation and repression. Its aim was to break apart the militant civil rights and Black power movements and channel them into the Democratic Party and government apparatuses.

To maximize the power of the Black liberation struggle after the civil rights victories, the movement required a leadership willing to mobilize the masses of Afro-Americans around the problems facing them in their schools, communities, and work places. It needed a leadership willing to take the Black movement forward toward political independence from the Democrats and Republicans through the formation of a mass Black political party.

The Socialist Workers Party has mapped out this type of program for the Black struggle. Its key elements are contained in the *Transitional Program for Black Liberation,* adopted by the 1969 SWP convention. [See *Black Liberation and Socialism,* edited by Tony Thomas (New York: Pathfinder Press, 1974).] Despite the exemplary role of the SWP in the struggles of the 1960s and despite the SWP's development of a program that could advance the Black movement, the Black revolutionary socialist cadres were too few to make up for the leadership deficiencies the Black struggle faced in the mid-1960s and early 1970s.

Most civil rights and Black power activists believed that the problems of the Black community could be solved through the capitalist system and the Democratic Party. This trend stood in the way of the development of the Black liberation movement, because many tended to subordinate mass action to the goal of pressuring the Democrats. This view was shared by those who followed Martin Luther King, Jr., as well as by many nationalists such as the leaders of the Congress of Racial Equality.

More revolutionary minded militants were not able to develop an effective program to continue the mass struggles that led to the civil rights and Black power victories. Groups like the Student Non-Violent Coordinating Committee (SNCC) and the Black Panther Party developed ultraleft strategies based on their misconception that the revolutionary movements of Africa, Asia, and Latin America could serve as models applicable to the realities of American capitalism.

This crisis of leadership was aggravated by the fact that demands for community control and the abolition of de facto segregation required more far-reaching social and economic changes than did the struggle against Jim Crow. Today's tasks require a deeper understanding of the relationship between racism and American capitalism, as well as the mobilization of more powerful social forces than were required for the destruction of the Jim Crow practices which were no longer essential to the capitalists when the civil rights movement appeared in the 1950s.

Poverty programs, Democrats, and repression

The ruling class counteroffensive against the Black liberation movement in the 1960s was centered around the poverty programs, opening up the Democratic Party to Blacks, and repression.

Lyndon Johnson's "War on Poverty" was primarily a way of putting thousands of local Black leaders and potential leaders on the government payroll where they could be pressured to moderate their demands and methods. Others were corrupted by "grants" from private corporate and church foundations.

While the poverty programs have been curtailed during the economic downturn, they still keep thousands of Black activists on government payrolls, drawing many of them deeper into the government apparatus and the Democratic Party.

Second, the ruling class opened up the doors of the Democratic Party to Blacks on an unprecedented scale. This was a way of channeling the desire for Black political power that came out of the civil rights and Black power struggles into the capitalist political machine. More than 3,500 Blacks now hold state and local elected office, and token numbers have been appointed to posts in the higher echelons of the party and the federal government.

Black mayors in several of the country's major cities symbolize the ruling class's strategy to shift the blame for the "urban crisis" from decaying capitalism to Black politicians. Their attitude is symbolized by telling Blacks, "O.K., let's see one of *your* people do better." What they don't add is, "in *our* capitalist two-party framework."

The increased number of Black Democratic politicians has reinforced the illusion that progress for Blacks can be achieved by supporting Democrats and has encouraged the policy of confining struggles to limits acceptable to the Democratic Party leadership.

Another obstacle in the way of developing a nationwide, struggle-oriented leadership has been the government's ferocious repression against Black leaders who threatened to take an independent course or projected the mobilization of the masses. This was particularly shown by their assassination of Malcolm X, the most promising Black revolutionary mass leader yet to appear.

The extent of this effort has been partially revealed with the release of documents from the FBI's Counterintelligence Program

(COINTELPRO). Repression against SNCC and the Panthers was facilitated by the adventurist errors and superrevolutionary rhetoric of these groups. Despite massive sympathy for these victims of government persecution, within the Black community and beyond, their ultraleft and sectarian attitudes increased the difficulties of organizing an adequate campaign of defense against government repression.

The difficulties in developing a leadership prepared to cope with the government offensive were reinforced by the conservatism and stagnation of the labor movement for the three decades following World War II. What this means can perhaps best be seen by imagining the impact an upsurge in the working class as a whole, with a powerful class-struggle left-wing development in the unions, would have on the Black movement.

An insurgent labor movement, fighting the same enemy Black people are fighting—the capitalist class and its two-party con game—would by its very power offer encouragement and inspiration. It would end the present skepticism as to whether the labor movement will ever radicalize, and would pose the perspective of a majority of the American people powerfully organized to fight against the evils of capitalist society.

As a minority of the population, Black people cannot topple capitalist rule and end racial oppression by themselves, even though they have shown that independent mobilization of their forces can have a powerful impact on American politics. The lack of a labor radicalization after the brief post-World War II strike wave contributed to the periodic frustration, cynicism, and hunts for shortcuts by many Black leaders.

The current stage

The combined impact of the poverty programs, the disruption tactics, and the cooptation of many Black leaders into Democratic Party politicking has been to bring to a halt the tide of mass action and victories that began with the 1955 Montgomery bus boycott.

This does not mean that nationalist and radical consciousness in the Black community has been set back. In fact it has broadened and deepened since the 1960s. What is lacking are the confidence and readiness to use mass action to move the struggle forward.

In the current economic crisis the state of disarray within the

Black movement makes it easier for the ruling class to launch new attacks aimed at taking away gains previously won by Black people, and making them bear a disproportionate share of the unemployment and social costs of the depression.

Among the sharpest attacks today are those in response to attempts to desegregate schools by busing Black children to predominantly white schools. The antibusing forces were given a big boost by the Supreme Court decision in 1974 outlawing the use of busing between some city and suburban school districts. This ruling is an important step toward trying to reverse the 1954 decision declaring that separate schools for Blacks and whites are inherently unequal.

The goal of busing is to break down the inequality in education that prepares Blacks for inferior jobs. It asserts the democratic right of Black people to have access to equal educational facilities denied them by racial discrimination in housing and gerrymandered school districts.

A ten-year effort has been organized by Boston's school board and city government to prevent school desegregation. This effort has served as a model for racist and reactionary forces throughout the country determined to hold back access by Blacks to decent education, housing and jobs. This racist offensive has made Boston the hottest battleground in the struggle for equality in education. Lynch-minded racist mobs are demonstrating the boldness of the antibusing forces.

The racist forces, who sense that nationally the present leadership of the Black struggle is politically weak and atomized, are probing to test how far they can go. If the racists are successful in preventing school desegregation in Boston and other cities where busing plans are being implemented or planned, it will be a severe blow to the Black struggle. Not only would it set back the fight for equal education, but it would demoralize and discourage those fighting for equality in housing and jobs, rights for women, bilingual education programs, democratization of the labor movement, and all others fighting for progressive social change. At the same time it would give the racists more confidence to push ahead.

The Boston reactionaries have received the support of top leaders of the Democratic and Republican parties, including President Ford who "sympathizes" with their opposition to busing. Antibusing legislation supported by racist groups has been sponsored by congressional leaders from both the Republican and Democratic parties. This reactionary offensive in Boston is not simply a local aberration, but part of a national campaign acquiesced in by some of the top leaders of American capitalism.

In the atmosphere created by the ruling class's drive against Black gains, there has been a revival of theories of Black inferiority, ranging from those of the Ku Klux Klan to more "scientific" myths such as those being peddled by William Shockley and others. Shockley has lectured on his racist theories at colleges and universities across the country. Even Klan and fascist spokespersons are finding more openness among "anti-busing militants" to their views.

If the civil rights movement and the Black power struggles demonstrated the enormous capacities of the Black struggle even without an adequate leadership, the past ten years of ruling class co-optation, repression and attacks have shown the limitations of the existing leaderships and the need to construct another one.

Present trends and organizations

The more direct-action-oriented organizations such as the Southern Christian Leadership Conference (SCLC), the Congress of Racial Equality, and SNCC, which were prominent in the civil rights movement of the 1960s, have disappeared, split, or significantly lost ground. Other groups, such as the Black Panther Party, that grew out of the Black power phase have suffered a similar fate. Black student organizations that were once centers for Black nationalist activity have been transformed in many cases from political organizations into purely social and cultural groups.

However, a number of important organizations and trends remain that are a reflection both of the weakness of the Black struggle and of important new changes.

1. The National Black Political Conventions held in Gary, Indiana, in 1972, and Little Rock, Arkansas, in 1974, rallied thousands of Black activists from all over the country. These gatherings confirmed the growing political awareness of Blacks and demonstrated the potential that exists for establishing a powerful national voice for Blacks. Unfortunately, the results were meager. The leadership of these conventions oriented the participants toward getting more Black Democrats elected rather than initiating political action and struggles independent of the capitalist political parties. The National Black Agenda, a

program of specific demands adopted at the Gary convention, was never utilized as a call to action by the National Black Assembly, the organization created by the convention.

2. Another attempt to establish a national voice was the Congressional Black Caucus. Consisting of the elected Black representatives in Congress, this group of Black Democrats drew up a program and promised to launch a campaign to fight for the needs of Black people. But little came of it because the CBC's activities centered around personal advancement within the framework of the capitalist political parties. Thus it looked on mobilizing Black people as irrelevant or dangerous.

On a local scale many Black elected officials are looked to by Blacks for leadership. But the primary orientation of this entire layer of politicians is to convince Black people to rely on the Democratic and Republican two-party system to fight racism rather than on their own independent initiatives.

3. Since the murder of Martin Luther King, Jr., in 1968, the Southern Christian Leadership Conference has split and declined. The wing led by Ralph Abernathy no longer has the national standing that it did. The wing led by Jesse Jackson, which has become Operation PUSH, has initiated some direct actions including nationally coordinated rallies against unemployment. It is attempting to expand nationally from its Chicago base. But PUSH has a religious character and is heavily dominated by Jesse Jackson. It is deeply involved in Democratic Party politics and played a major role in the efforts to get a Black Democratic candidate nominated for mayor in Chicago's 1975 election.

4. An important organized component of the Black struggle is in the trade unions. Large numbers of Blacks are concentrated in the auto, steel, and other basic industries, in service industries, and among public workers. This is reflected in predominantly Black memberships in some unions, the emergence of Black caucuses, and in the election of an increasing number of Blacks to official positions in the trade unions on a local and a union-wide level.

The Coalition of Black Trade Unionists (CBTU) primarily represents Black trade union officials organized on a national level, although rank-and-file unionists can join. While it was created in order to give support to McGovern's 1972 campaign, the CBTU has supported actions against Black oppression including the December 14, 1974, demonstration against racism in Boston.

A number of Black women trade unionists have been active in the Coalition of Labor Union Women (CLUW). Six to eight hundred Blacks attended that organization's founding conference in 1974. CLUW, which includes both officials and rank-and-file members, has taken stands in favor of Black rights in a number of local areas.

5. There have also been some significant changes in the NAACP, the largest and oldest civil rights organization, and for a long time the dominant one. Many of its older leaders are cold-war liberals. However, in many chapters and among the national leadership, there is a new generation that became active during the radicalization of the 1960s.

During the rise of the civil rights and Black power movements, the size and relative influence of the NAACP declined. Its failure, with some exceptions, to go beyond court action, however important that is at certain points, and take the lead in building mass actions, meant that the NAACP was outflanked and bypassed by more militant organizations.

The NAACP, however, despite its decline and loss of prestige among militants, remains the largest national Black organization, and it has been thrust into current struggles. The work the NAACP has done in defending Black rights and gains in the courts makes it an important component of campaigns around issues like busing, housing, and jobs. The pressure of the racist offensive, and the difficulties of compelling the government to enforce the law against segregation, is in some instances stimulating younger leaders to initiate mass actions such as the May 17, 1975, demonstration of 15,000 in Boston for school desegregation, which was supported by the national NAACP. They have also taken positions in defense of the Black community against those held by many liberals, Social Democrats, and union officials. For example, the discriminatory layoffs of Blacks during the current depression have led the NAACP into basic conflict with the top AFL-CIO bureaucracy. The NAACP has opposed discriminatory layoffs while the bureaucracy has defended "strict seniority" used as a cover by the bosses to carry them out.

6. A wing of the Black nationalists, particularly those who identify with Pan Africanism, are turning to socialist ideas. Many take a favorable view of Maoism, mistakenly believing that it is genuine Marxism. Some belong to one or another of the many small Black Maoist groups; most don't belong to any organization.

The most prominent leader among this layer has been Amiri Baraka, who heads the Congress of African People. Baraka emerged as a spokesman of nationalist-minded students and youth in the late 1960s because he articulated what many felt about the dead-end ultraleftism of the Black Panther Party. His stature rose even higher as a result of his role in helping to elect Kenneth Gibson mayor of Newark in 1970.

He advocated forming an independent Black Party, but proposed that this be done by working in and through the Democratic Party and supporting certain Black Democrats. At the National Black Political Conventions in Gary and Little Rock he opposed the call for an independent Black party and oriented the participants toward supporting Democrats.

Once Mayor Gibson consolidated his power he didn't need Baraka and his organization any longer. He denied Baraka's supporters any positions of power within the Democratic administration and used the police to harass his organization. This experience, along with his turn to Maoism, culminated in Baraka's break with Gibson. During its period as a Maoist organization the Congress of African People has declined in influence.

7. The Nation of Islam, one of the oldest organizations identified with Black nationalism in this country, has experienced some important changes since the death of its long-time leader, Elijah Muhammad. These include ending the restriction of membership to Blacks only, steps in the direction of getting involved in struggles of the Black community (for example, Muhammad Ali's support for the Hurricane Carter defense case), a modification of the group's reactionary views on the status of women, and a greater openness to exchanging opinions with other groups, including socialists.

Previous to this, the Nation of Islam had abstained from struggles against Black oppression, counterposing to such actions their strategy of attempting to win liberation through self-help economic projects and total devotion to Islam. The Nation is also a rigidly hierarchical organization with a long-standing practice of avoiding conflicts with the capitalist ruling powers.

Since they are still in the process of evolving their new approach, it is impossible to say how far, or exactly in what direction, the changes in the Nation will go. Given their widespread influence, there is no question that any turn toward more direct involvement in political or social action will have an important impact on the Black community.

Counter the racist offensive

To overcome the problems imposed on the Black community, it is necessary to organize to counter the current racist offensive. The organizations and individuals willing to participate should be brought together to help reestablish lost confidence in mass action and united struggle, and to awaken the Black community, the labor movement, and their allies to the dangers presented by the racist assault.

In preparing such countermobilizations, Black people are defending rights supposedly granted by law, such as the right to desegregated education. They can build on the positive social and political consciousness that has been achieved by the Black movement in past decades. Initial protest actions calling attention to the need to defend such rights are a necessary first step toward preparing future advances.

To carry out this objective, united-action coalitions of various groups and individuals involved in struggle should be formed. Such coalitions can have the potential of expanding to a national level given that the problems Black people face are national in scope and require national action to deal with them.

Local struggles can win important gains, but they can be considerably strengthened by a powerfully organized national opposition to racism.

A good example of this relationship is the development of local coalitions that were part of the national campaign to build the May 17, 1975, Boston demonstration called by the NAACP. While the focus of these coalitions and the local chapters of the National Student Coalition Against Racism (NSCAR) was around the struggle in Boston, they linked that fight to others on a local scale, whether it was student cutback struggles in New England and New York, the community control fight in New York City's School District One, or busing struggles in Pasadena and other cities.

Through the organization of such united-front-type actions and action coalitions, the fragmentation of the Black movement can begin to be overcome, and a new leadership emerge. Blacks can be remobilized and not only beat back the racist offensive, but make further gains on various fronts of the struggle.

Three of the most important issues facing Afro-Americans are the racist offensive in the areas of jobs, education, and housing.

Jobs

The question of job discrimination and unemployment, an important problem for Blacks during periods of prosperity, has become an even more pressing problem as a result of the current economic depression.

Massive support from Blacks should be organized for actions called by the labor movement for more jobs, such as the April 26, 1975, demonstration in Washington. To combat unemployment of Blacks and other workers, an emergency public works program should be established to create millions of socially useful jobs. The workweek should be reduced with no reduction in pay, to spread the work. These demands relate to the need for the labor movement to refuse to allow the capitalists to shove the burden of the economic depression on workers' backs.

Special measures are also needed to protect Black workers against discriminatory employment policies, and Blacks must take the lead in fighting for them. In many industries Black workers face discriminatory layoffs. This occurs especially where Blacks are the most recently hired. In some cases the bosses have used such layoffs to nullify affirmative action programs won by Black workers. Some racist union bureaucrats have tried to use the seniority system as a justification for these moves.

Seniority was won in struggle by workers to protect them from the bosses' arbitrarily firing whomever they pleased, especially union militants. However, the seniority system should not be perverted to be used as a tool by the bosses or the bureaucrats to carry out racially or sexually discriminatory layoffs.

One demand that Blacks, progressive unionists, and the Socialist Workers Party raise in connection with this problem is that where layoffs take place, the same percentage of Blacks be retained after the layoffs as were working before. This demand should be linked closely with the fight for jobs for all.

Maintaining this position is important. The bosses are trying to use racism to divide the workers, to make them think that there is an individual solution to the economic crisis. The demand that the percentage of Black workers be maintained despite layoffs poses the need for the working class to refuse to be divided over this issue, as well as the need to convert the trade unions into a fighting social movement championing the rights of Blacks and other oppressed groups.

Any program to expand jobs must be linked with a program to abolish job discrimination and upgrade Black workers into higher-paying jobs. To equalize employment opportunities for Black workers, preferential hiring, promotions, and upgrading linked with a special program to train them for skilled and professional positions are needed.

Blacks have been fighting for elements of this demand in struggles around hiring quotas and affirmative action programs. While in some cases these actions have forced court rulings that grant some of these demands, existing programs are inadequate and largely unenforced. They are also being obliterated by the layoffs.

Preferential hiring and the demand to maintain existing percentages of Black employment are under stiff attack from the employers because they cut into the capitalists' prerogative of hiring and firing whom they please and their desire to keep a large majority of Blacks on the bottom.

Education

Another key area where a national effort is needed to strengthen local struggles is education. Education is closely linked to job opportunities, political and cultural outlook, and political control. Schools in the Black community give Black youth a poor education, assuring that they wind up in bad jobs, if they are able to find jobs at all.

Black people have been trying for decades to break out of the straitjacket of inferior segregated schools and to end racist practices in "desegregated" school systems.

The 1954 Supreme Court decision and the subsequent struggles and decisions to enforce them marked an important advance for the Black movement. While desegregation laws have been in effect since 1954, de facto segregation continues in the schools. Segregation is maintained through what are called "neighborhood" school systems. Housing segregation and gerrymandering of school district lines are used to maintain de facto school segregation.

Even where individual schools are formally desegregated, "tracking" and other divisions segregate Black education from white education to maintain white privilege.

To eliminate this inequality, Black people are demanding that their children be bused to better schools across neighborhood lines. In some cities support for these demands has won favorable court decisions and laws.

In Boston and other cities, busing is one of the focal points of the racist offensive against Black rights. The racists contend that busing is "forced" upon white children and violates their freedom. For years the same racists have used force to keep Blacks out of predominantly white schools and prevent them from moving into white neighborhoods.

The issue is not the use of "force" versus "freedom," but whether force is to be used in defense of Black rights, or whether it will continue to be used to keep Black people down, depriving their children of equal educational opportunities.

Where existing institutions and housing patterns are used to deprive Blacks of the right to the same educational facilities as whites or to go to school unmolested by racist threats, counter-force is necessary. This is why leaders of the desegregation fight in Boston have called for the use of all force necessary, including federal troops, to implement school desegregation.

The demand for federal troops in situations such as the Black community faces in Boston is a necessary and legitimate expression of the struggle for Black equality. It points up the government's obligation to enforce its own laws and protect the rights of Black people against racist mobs. The demand for troops helps to indict the racists as the intigators of violence, to expose the government for its failure to act, and to convince masses of people, Black and white, that forcible action must be taken to halt the vigilante terror—if not by the government, then by Blacks themselves.

The racist violence in Boston and other cities shows the need for Blacks to organize in their own defense. Self-defense is a traditional democratic right in this country. It has been increasingly accepted and used by Black communities under vigilante attack. Movement activists should begin the organization of demonstration marshals, bodyguards for threatened Black leaders, and defense guards at the first signs of racist terrorism. Experience has shown that self-defense actions are most effective when based on a large movement and integrated with a perspective of mass mobilizations.

The racists have chosen to make the issue of busing the battleground where they hope to administer a serious defeat to the Black movement. Their challenge cannot be evaded; to concede the point without a fight would only embolden the enemies of Black rights. This does not imply any lessening of the long-run importance of the efforts to win community control over ghetto schools. These two prongs of the fight for equal education should be seen as complementary and should not be counterposed, as some Black groups have tended to do.

Inferior education for Blacks is maintained in two ways: not only by denying maximum funds to schools in the Black community or preventing Black parents and students from making decisions that affect them, but also by refusing to allow Blacks to attend better-financed schools in segregated white neighborhoods. There will be no equality for Blacks in education until both evils are eliminated.

The common thread that unites the effort to desegregate predominantly white schools and the effort to wrest control of Black community schools away from their white, capitalist, absentee administrators is the right of the Black community to have the final say on how its children are educated and to be the final judge of whether the treatment its children receive is equal to that of others. These two sides of the fight can be further unified under the general demand for more state and federal funds to improve and expand schools in the Black community under Black community control.

Housing

Housing discrimination dictates the areas where Black people have to live. It establishes the so-called geographical justification for school segregation, and the geographical definition of the area subjected to specialized police terror, inferior social services, and other forms of oppression Blacks face. Segregation forces Blacks to pay inflated rents for inferior housing. It is one of the most blatant manifestations of how capitalist property rights are used to abuse Black people. Housing discrimination is perpetuated by racist terror and by openly discriminatory practices of landlords, real estate agents, bankers, and contractors.

Racist opposition to attempts by Blacks to move into predominantly white areas frequently erupts in savage attacks on Black homes.

The Black community needs equalized housing opportunities. It needs full enforcement of all laws banning housing segregation and their enactment where they don't yet exist. All apartments and homes on the market should be available for rental or purchase by Blacks on the same terms offered to whites. The federal government should launch a crash program to build low-cost housing for the Black community. City governments should be compelled to provide protection against racist attempts to force Blacks out of previously all-white neighborhoods, and Black organizations should organize effective self-defense of threatened tenants and home owners if no protection is guaranteed by the government. The labor movement has a fundamental responsibility to pitch in and help with such efforts.

Political independence

The increase in the number of Black elected officials is not only a result of the decision of the ruling class to attempt to co-opt the Black movement; it is also a political reflection of nationalist consciousness in the Black community. It indicates the strong desire of Blacks to be *represented* in the political arena. Blacks who previously voted for white candidates or did not vote at all now vote for Blacks hoping that Black officeholders will be more sensitive to the needs of Black people. They hope concessions can be wrested by these Black Democrats to bring some relief to the Black community. Many well-intentioned militants mistakenly see Black participation in the Democratic Party as a step toward eventual Black political independence.

These illusions have enhanced the equally false notion that Black people should refrain from engaging in direct action and taking militant stands because such tactics might offend or embarrass Democratic politicians.

Experience has shown that these policies have set back the prospects for Black liberation. When Afro-Americans with the reputation of being militant representatives of the Black community participate in the Democratic Party, they divert and hold back the progress of the movement. They miseducate Black people on the roots of their oppression and the solution to their problems.

Most important, they nurture the misconception that the problems of the Black community can be solved without a mass political confrontation with the upholders and servants of the capitalist system.

Black participation in the Democratic Party as a way to freedom is totally unrealistic because it advises Blacks to operate within an institution which is one of the main instruments perpetuating the oppression and exploitation of Black people. The financial power and behind-the-scenes intervention of the big corporations far outweigh any influence Blacks can exert in such an organization.

The proof of this is that along with the big increase in the number of Black elected officials in the late 1960s there was no accompanying increase in the concessions granted to the Black community. On the contrary, there has been a steady whittling away at the little that Black people had. And in exchange for these powerless figureheads who front for the white capitalist power structure, Blacks paid heavily by being diverted from strengthening their own independent organizations.

The road to Black self-determination and economic gains lies through organizing actions that mobilize the independent power of the Black community and other working people, not through reliance on the Democrats or Republicans, Black or white. Our party's educational campaign to explain the need to break the Democratic Party's hold on the Black community is a central part of our work.

Black Democratic Party supporters can be involved in action coalitions and organizations around specific issues in the interest of Black people. Such experiences will show that independent mass action and not Democratic Party politics is the way to get things done. Such coalitions and struggles can draw Democratic Party supporters into contact with Blacks who are more conscious of the need for political independence and thereby help convince them to break from the Democrats.

Only by combining mass action and independent Black electoral politics can the Black community be freed from the domination of leaders bound to the two-party system and the capitalists who control it.

To fight for their interests against the capitalist exploiters and their parties, Blacks, like other workers, need their own independent organizations. An advanced form of organization would be an independent Black party that could fight in the electoral arena as well as on all other fronts. Unlike the capitalist political parties, a Black party would not counterpose electoral activity to demonstrations, rallies, and pickets; it would use its electoral campaigns to reach broader forces, win them to its perspectives, and help advance the mobilization of the Black community.

Independent Black candidates who were elected could use their legislative or municipal offices to serve the interests of the struggle against oppression, instead of crippling and crushing it, as the capitalist politicians now do.

Given the overwhelmingly proletarian composition of the Black people, the formation of an independent Black party would be a working class break with capitalist politics. It would attract Black unionists and make an impact in the labor movement, giving a big impetus to the formation of a labor party based on the unions.

The formation of such a mass Black party seems very distant at this time because of the overall dominance of the Black Democrats. Several attempts during the 1960s to set up Black parties failed, as in the case of the Black Panther Party, Baraka's Committee for a Unified Newark, the Lowndes County (Alabama) Freedom Organization (LCFO), and the Michigan Freedom Now Party.

It is important to remember *why* they failed, because failure was not necessary and the errors made do not have to be repeated. The Panthers failed because of their ultraleft positions and activities, Baraka because of his illusions in the Black Democrats, the LCFO because of its illusions in the national Democratic Party, and the Michigan Freedom Now Party because of its lack of a long-term perspective for winning over the Black community.

More positive strides toward political independence will undoubtedly be the product of future actions by the Black community to defend itself from ruling class attacks. Mass actions and demonstrations will educate the Black community on the need for relying on its own political forces.

Blacks and labor

An important feature of the present situation is that while the deepening economic crisis leads to more ruling class attacks against Black rights and gains it also generates increased opposition by workers—both Black and white—in defense of their deteriorating living standards. Many key actions of Blacks are linked to the struggle of the working class as a whole, which gives greater impetus to both movements. And labor actions such as the AFL-CIO sponsored April 26, 1975, March for Jobs strengthen the forces that oppose racism.

This brings into relief the fact that the fight for Black

liberation is more closely intertwined with the fate of the labor movement than ever before. The number of Blacks in industry has grown considerably in the last thirty years as has Black union membership. Moreover, the greater numbers of Blacks in the working class and in major industrial cities means that the trade union movement is more and more forced to confront the questions posed by the Black movement both inside and outside the plants and offices.

Unfortunately a narrow-minded, conservative bureaucracy presides over the trade unions. Its outlook and policies are based on collaborating with the capitalist class rather than struggling against it. This includes its failure to organize any significant fight for jobs, wages, and working conditions. The prostration of the union officialdom is capped by its subordination to the two capitalist political parties.

The labor bureaucracy fundamentally refused to fight the discrimination against Blacks on and off the job. Union leaders from AFL-CIO President George Meany to American Federation of Teachers President Albert Shanker on down try to convince workers to oppose preferential hiring, community control, and other demands to achieve equality for Black people, echoing the capitalist lie that this threatens the living standards and security of American labor.

This stand is in marked contrast to the policies carried out by the CIO in the 1930s. Unlike the unions of today, the CIO was a rank-and-file organization basing itself on the mass action of the workers. It was a social movement as well as a trade union movement. A large number of its members and some leaders aspired to working class political independence through the formation of a labor party, but the class-collaborationist policies of the Stalinists and Social Democrats prevented labor from taking this important step.

Even though there were fewer Blacks in industry as a whole at that time, CIO unions, especially in the auto and steel industries, opposed discrimination against Blacks and fought for Black rights both on and off the job. Previous racist policies of the unions had led to defeats for organizing drives in the steel, meatpacking, and other industries. Many CIO militants learned the lesson that the only way to unite Black and white workers, which was the only way to win against the bosses, was to support Black rights.

During World War II, and the postwar economic boom and

McCarthyite witch-hunt, the trade union bureaucrats, with the aid of the Communist and Socialist parties, consolidated their grip on the unions and reversed the more radical policies of the CIO unions and abridged their democracy.

Efforts toward political action were diverted into subservience to the Democratic Party. The attempt of the union movement to speak out as a working class voice on social and political questions was replaced by a narrow trade union outlook. At best the union officials trailed behind the Democratic Party liberals as they became more and more integrated into government boards and other state institutions. Part of this shift was the virtual disappearance of union action in defense of Black rights.

To defend the interests of Blacks and other workers against ruling class political and economic attacks, the trade union movement must be transformed into the type of radical social movement that the CIO at its best was. A new leadership is required to replace the class-collaborationist policies of the union bureaucrats with a policy of class struggle against the capitalists on the political, social, and economic fronts.

The political consciousness developed among Black workers in the fight for Black liberation in recent years will play a key part in forming a class-struggle left wing in the unions. Black people have already been in motion against the capitalists for over twenty years. Ideas of mass action, radicalism, and the need to find political solutions to problems working people face are more accepted among Black workers than among white workers.

Black workers, by the very nature of their oppression, tend to raise demands in their unions that go beyond the narrow bread-and-butter issues that dominate the thinking of the union functionaries.

Black workers have already brought into the unions methods of action and mobilization developed in the civil rights and Black power movements. These factors can be noted especially in newer public workers' unions such as the American Federation of State, County, and Municipal Employees (AFSCME), and the National Union of Hospital and Health Care Employees, District 1199, a mostly Black and Puerto Rican union. Reflecting their large Black composition, these unions have taken more progressive positions than most other unions in relation to Blacks, women, foreign-born workers, and the U.S. intervention in Indochina.

The 1974 sanitation workers' strike in Baltimore and a series of Black-led strikes in 1972 and 1973 in Atlanta are among the many labor battles where Blacks have used the same methods of organizing broad Black community support that were used in the civil rights movement. Often these struggles are seen as actions of both the trade unions and of the Black liberation movement.

Black workers will be in the forefront in the development of a class-struggle left wing because they are not part of the better-paid, relatively privileged labor aristocracy on which the bureaucrats are based. Victims of discrimination in the unions and the plants, and the hardest hit by inflation, layoffs, and bad working conditions, Black workers have nothing to lose and everything to gain from a shakeup of the union movement.

Blacks will also be an important link between the unions and the unemployed, and many of the organizers of a future unemployed movement will surely come from the ranks of Black workers.

An indispensable part of the program of a class-struggle leadership in the labor movement will be to break from dependence on the capitalist parties and launch a mass independent labor party based on the trade unions. Unions where Blacks are concentrated and left-wing currents are articulating the needs and outlook of Black workers will be at the center of any developments toward running independent labor candidates or forming a labor party.

Once formed, a labor party could rapidly become a political voice and center of attraction for the Black community as well as the labor movement. Black candidates running on a labor party ticket would be seen not only as trade union representatives but as candidates fighting for Black people.

It cannot be predicted whether the formation of an independent Black party will come before a labor party and give impetus to forming a labor party, or whether a Black party will be precluded by the emergence of a labor party in which Blacks are playing a leading role. Combined developments may take place in which candidates are jointly presented by labor unions and organizations of Black people.

The Black struggle and other radicalizing forces

The Black liberation movement draws strength from the colonial revolution and from the challenge to authority of other oppressed national minorities in the United States. In turn it provides inspiration for these similar movements of other exploited peoples. The civil rights movement of the 1950s and 1960s was in part a response to the collapse of colonialism in Africa and the Caribbean. And with the growth in power and self-confidence of American Blacks, their support for African liberation struggles can have an impact on the policies of the imperialist war-makers in Washington.

The Black movement has been greatly affected by the radicalization of other sectors of American society, particularly students and women. While the civil rights movement was an initial stimulus to the student movement, the student-based antiwar movement in turn helped generate a massive student radicalization that deeply influenced thousands of Black youth.

The example of the Black movement also influenced the development of the women's movement. In turn, the ideas and attitudes of the women's liberation movement have penetrated the Black community, radicalizing Black women and inspiring them with new confidence. This has strengthened the Black movement as a whole.

It has led to the formation of Black women's organizations to fight for the special needs of Black women. Black women have been deeply involved in the battle to prevent drastic cutbacks in child care. Important struggles such as the defense of Dr. Kenneth Edelin and Joanne Little illustrate the interrelationship between the interests and demands of the Black movement and the women's liberation movement. This is underlined further by the reactionary attacks of racists in Boston against women's rights as well as against Blacks.

The Black liberation movement also has had a strong effect on the radicalization of other oppressed minorities. The civil rights and Black power movements inspired Chicanos, Puerto Ricans, Native Americans, and others to fight for their rights. Similar modes of struggle and organization to those used by the Black movement have been adopted where similar problems are faced. All of the doubly oppressed and superexploited groups are natural allies to Blacks in their mutual fight for democratic rights and social liberation.

The Black movement has also had a pronounced impact in the armed forces. Inside the army and other services Black recruits rebelled against racist practices and spread opposition to the U.S. aggression in Indochina. Outside the military, the Black movement combined with the mass antiwar movement of the 1960s and early 1970s to promote radical new ideas that seeped into the armed forces.

Black GI groups and actions cropped up on military bases and ships in the United States, Indochina, and other parts of the world. This activity showed that radicalization of significant layers of the population cannot be quarantined from the military ranks, thus making it difficult for the imperialists to use the army in an unpopular war. The combination of Black dissidence and general antiwar sentiments among GIs contributed to forcing the U.S. out of Indochina.

With the formation of the volunteer army, an even larger percentage of the armed forces has become Black. Job discrimination and unemployment drive Afro-American youth to enlist. The problems this has presented to American imperialism have generated a debate among top military and government leaders on whether or not to limit Black recruitment.

Meanwhile there are also hundreds of thousands of Black Indochina veterans who returned to face unemployment and inadequate medical and educational benefits. This situation is worsened by the unfavorable stigma the employers put on veterans to try to create another outcast grouping in the working class.

The Black movement has also been a central factor in the numerous prison revolts in recent years. Once politically quiescent, the prisons, penitentiaries, and jails have become centers of discussion, political education, and anticapitalist radicalization. Prisoners, asserting their right to be treated as human beings, have launched actions to improve the conditions inside the prisons.

Large numbers of Black people have been put behind bars by racist cops and judges. In California, which has the most extensive system of public colleges and universities in the country, more Blacks are in prison than in the state college system.

Struggles by prisoners such as the 1971 Attica rebellion have received widespread support from the Black community and from other radicalizing layers.

Socialist Workers Party

Black liberation will be won through the coming American socialist revolution. Historical experience has shown that for the working class, Black people, and their allies to successfully carry through the revolution, a mass Leninist party must be constructed. In order to win against the centralized power of the ruling capitalist class, there must be a single combat party overwhelmingly proletarian, which is composed of cadres from every nationality that makes up this country, that can coordinate and lead the workers, the Black people, and all their allies in the struggle to wrest power from the hands of the exploiters and oppressors.

This mass Leninist party must have deep roots in the Black communities or it will surely fail.

The Socialist Workers Party is the nucleus of this future mass revolutionary socialist party. The SWP is the only party that understands the combined character of the coming revolution and has charted a program that links the immediate and day-to-day needs of Blacks and all the workers with the struggle for power. In order for the SWP to carry out its tasks, it must become more deeply rooted in the Black communities across the country.

New opportunities are opening up for the SWP to initiate and help build united actions by Blacks and their allies against the ruling class's racist offensive. The SWP enters this new stage with the most politically developed and capable Black cadre in its history. In this work, a key task is the winning of Blacks to the SWP and training these new recruits as revolutionary cadre. The party must turn to meet these new opportunities and carry through this task central to the success of the coming American socialist revolution.

Tony Thomas

Socialists and the Struggle Against Racism

This report on the resolution "The Fight for Black Liberation: The Current Stage and Its Tasks" was given to the August 1975 SWP convention in Ohio.

One way to view the situation facing Black people today is to contrast what President Ford said at the July 1975 NAACP convention in Washington, D.C., with the discussion at that convention. The discussion centered around how to respond to racist discrimination in employment, the schools, and housing, and how to fight back against economic cutbacks and the new racist attacks against the Black community.

Margaret Bush Wilson, chairwoman of the NAACP, gave a keynote speech in which she stressed the need for a new movement like the underground railroad organized by the abolitionist movement of the last century. She said this was needed to prevent the cutbacks and racist attacks from making the Black community a permanent "underclass" in this country.

President Ford, who personally addressed the convention, did not deny that Black people are hardest hit by the economic crisis. He even cited statistics showing how almost twice as many Blacks as whites are unemployed and how inflation hits Blacks the hardest. "An unstable economy is the enemy of equal opportunity," he said, adding, "While important advances can be made during economic good times, they can be quickly and cruelly erased during hard times."

But Ford had no response to the NAACP's demands for programs to meet these problems. He announced that there will be "no checklist of specific programs and promises for Blacks."

Summed up in the confrontation of views between the NAACP and Ford is a key aspect of the struggle between the capitalist class and the working class today: the struggle between Black groups such as the NAACP who are trying to advance Black rights and preserve social and economic gains won during the 1960s, and the American ruling class which is saying that in the new period of economic stagnation capitalism has entered these gains will have to be "quickly and cruelly erased."

Economic plight of Blacks

What Ford meant and what the NAACP was protesting can be seen when we examine the economic plight of the Black community in the current depression.

We have to remember that unlike most whites, Black people were unable to recover from the effects of the recession of 1969-71 before they were plunged into the depression of 1974-75.

Government figures claim that Black unemployment at the beginning of 1975 was about 14 percent. But the National Urban League recently released figures showing that real unemployment among Blacks, including discouraged workers, is actually twice that. In other words, at least one out of every four Black workers is out of a job.

In some industries the figures indicate an even more devastating picture. One such area is among government employees. The unemployment rate for Black local-level employees in January 1975 was six times the rate for whites.

We can see what Ford meant when we look at the statistic that 60 percent of Black youth looking for jobs are out of work, with some experts saying the percentage is actually higher.

To the attacks on jobs we can add the slashes in health, transportation, child care, education, housing, and similar social needs. Blacks, who are often dependent on these programs, are getting hit hardest by the cutbacks.

What Ford meant can be captured in the streets of Watts in Los Angeles, Bedford-Stuyvesant in Brooklyn, on Chicago's West Side, and in the Black communities of Detroit, Newark, and Baltimore. In some of these areas, Black unemployment is estimated at more than 50 percent.

We must understand that this desperate situation faced by many Blacks will not be limited to the current depression. The ruling class is openly projecting the maintenance of long-term higher levels of unemployment. The same thing is true of the cutbacks. The government is projecting deep cuts in social services which they hope to make permanent, well beyond the current downturn.

This means that a major feature of the new period we are entering will be one of singling out oppressed minorities for intensified oppression. There is going to be a continued widening of the economic gap between whites and Blacks, and more actions taken which will lead Blacks to lose hope in the ability of American capitalism to provide decent jobs, housing, education, and political and social equality.

Ruling class predicament

In order to understand the meaning of the attacks against Black people, and what we can do about them, it is useful to look back at how the struggle of Black people developed in the 1960s when we won many of the gains under attack today.

The massive radicalization and mobilizations of the Black community in the 1960s forced the capitalist class to make a number of major concessions. They abolished the legal structure of Southern Jim Crow segregation, they passed laws against discrimination in jobs and education, and created new openings for Blacks to go to college and to break into jobs previously denied them.

In addition, the Democratic and Republican parties were opened up to literally thousands of Black politicians in an effort to make it appear that participation in the capitalist two-party system would be a solution to the problems of the Black community.

All this was done to create a new image of the federal government as a fighter for Black people's rights. It was an attempt to quiet down the radicalization and channel the energies of Black people into electoral politics within the capitalist two-party framework. The extent to which the capitalists feel this policy was useful is reflected in the large number of Black Democratic mayors that now govern major cities such as Los Angeles, Detroit, Atlanta, Newark, and Gary.

The tactic of granting some concessions in the 1960s did not in any way represent a commitment on the part of the capitalists to ending the oppression of Blacks. On the contrary, it was an adjustment aimed at helping preserve their racist system. Racial oppression is intricately intertwined with the capitalist system and is of tremendous benefit to the capitalists. While they can be forced on occasion to give concessions, the ruling class recognizes that a real thrust toward equality for Blacks would threaten their interests in the most basic way. The vicious repression of Black activists, which went hand-in-hand with the concessions of the 1960s, is but one reflection of the ruling class's real attitude to the fight for Black liberation.

The capitalists are continually making tactical shifts in response to Black struggles, looking toward both repression and concessions, according to what they consider necessary for the protection of their profits. While on the one hand they pose as defenders of Black rights, they also try to keep the struggle for these rights from going "too far." When forced to abolish legal segregation, they support the maintenance of de facto segregation. They concede to Black equality in law, or in words, but refuse to fully implement these laws. They dare not denounce the gains of the 1960s or push them back completely for fear of a political explosion in the Black community. On the other hand they will do everything in their power to try to prevent the type of movement from developing that can maintain these gains, push them further, and link up with other oppressed and exploited forces.

The capitalists are not about to try to impose the program of bigots like George Wallace or Louise Day Hicks on a national level. At the same time they often look with favor on actions carried out by such racists which help push back the militancy and self-confidence of the Black community.

What this means is that the capitalists carry out a seemingly contradictory policy in areas like Boston where we see the strongest racist mobilizations.

Boston

Look at the situation in Boston. The ˉstruggle there, after all, started with a decision by the federal court—a ruling class institution—to implement limited desegregation in public education.

The decision by Judge Garrity to use busing was followed by racist mobilizations and threats of obstruction by Boston's school officials and sections of the city government. The terrorism they used against Black school children and the Black community in general was tolerated by the federal and local governments up to a point.

However, we should note that the federal government is neither able nor willing to simply support racist mob violence as it did in the South after Reconstruction—at least for the period we are in now when the ruling class is not prepared to opt for a fascist-like solution. They are under the pressure of Blacks and world public opinion and they have to maintain an image of supporting a modicum of protection for the Black community against the racists.

Thus, after the mobilizations of the Black community that led to the probusing march of 15,000 on May 17, the federal court again decided to maintain the busing plan and in fact to extend it through a second phase this fall.

While Ford and other Republican and Democratic leaders give encouragement to the racists by "sympathizing" with their opposition to busing, the government has not openly supported the racists' side.

The mentality that is being instilled in the white racists in Boston is one that says they can hold on to what they've got by pushing down Black people. It is an attempt to defend the relative privileges of some white workers and middle-class layers that are derived from de facto segregation.

The economic crisis and the growing series of battles around the struggle against de facto segregation has led to the growth of racist groups like ROAR, the Boston-based antibusing group that is moving out on a national level. We should also take note of how this provides the atmosphere for the growth of organizations like the Ku Klux Klan and even fascist sects.

The blows struck against Black people are spawning these reactionary forces, and developing recruits for them.

However, these forces do not set the tone nationally for the ruling powers. The ruling class needs a more flexible attitude toward Blacks than Louise Day Hicks—much less the Klan—can provide.

In fact, the revolt of the "new racism"—as it has been called— places the ruling class in a dilemma between their need to maintain a pretense of supporting Black rights and the necessity of nurturing the forces to block the drive to implement Black rights.

To fight back against the racist attacks we should understand how to take advantage of that dilemma. Particularly we must take advantage of the fact that Black struggles for equality in education and jobs have the law of the land behind them.

Racist pressures

We've seen how in various ways different tendencies on the left and within the Black movement have adapted to racist pressures and have shied away from taking firm positions in support of busing and against discriminatory layoffs.

Some have done this from a sectarian or "ultranationalist" viewpoint. Some Black students will tell you that we should pull back from supporting busing and other school desegregation battles by counterposing Black control of the schools to busing and similar desegregation plans. They claim that Black control of the schools is more "radical" or more "nationalist" than busing.

Some claim that the struggle can be ducked because the Black community really isn't for busing. This idea was a common rationalization for abstention from the struggle in Boston at its beginning, when the Black community faced huge intimidation from the racists. The same argument is being used today in places like Philadelphia and Detroit.

The issue involved is not an abstract discussion on how good particular busing plans are. The real issue is whether equal opportunities for Blacks to be educated are going to be implemented or not. It is the question of whether the buses are going to roll or whether they're going to be stopped by racist mobs.

When we look at this reality we understand why no one can be neutral or hesitant about throwing themselves into the fights that are going on around busing and school desegregation.

I want to say a few words about the demand for Black control of the schools in the Black community, which some falsely counterpose to busing.

Struggles around the issue of community control have taken place in New York, Philadelphia, Chicago, Newark, and other cities. Blacks and others fighting against inferior education and discrimination in the schools have wanted to take the schools in their own hands to get rid of the racism. We've been particularly involved in the community control struggle in New York's District One, where Black, Puerto Rican, and Chinese parents are fighting against racist education and administration.

Rather than being counterposed to busing or other forms of school desegregation, the demand for community control of the schools and bilingual-bicultural programs by oppressed minorities is part of the struggle for equal educational opportunities. It is one way that parents, depending on the particular circumstances they're in, have fought against discrimination in the schools.

Our position is for the elimination of Black oppression in the schools through community control, desegregation plans, and any other action that will move toward doing that job.

Long-term struggle

The struggle in Boston and other antiracist struggles are part of a long-term test of strength over the question of whether Blacks will be pushed back or move forward to eliminate racist oppression.

This fight against racism and to end the special oppression of Black people is crucial to the development of working class radicalization and in the class confrontations that we've talked about in our discussion of the political resolution, "Prospects for Socialism in America."

The deepening radicalization among Black workers will take a dual form, a struggle for equality and political power as a people, and a struggle against economic exploitation as a section of the working class.

We should also understand how important to the capitalist class's strategy is the development of racist attitudes among whites that can divert them from working class political consciousness. And the rulers also know that racism will be one of the key contributors to the reservoir from which the power of future right-wing movements can be built.

So in making a turn to the opportunities opened up by the beginning of a working class radicalization, socialists should put a special emphasis on the struggles of Black people against discrimination and oppression.

Another thing we have to take into consideration in charting a perspective for the struggle is the present level of organization and political consciousness of the Black community.

Given the weakening of the Black movement by co-optation and repression, and the disarray of the nationalist and civil rights groups that came out of the 1960s, there has not been an immediate political response from the Black community to the cutbacks and the racist attacks.

On a political level most Black people still look to the

Democratic Party and to the Black Democrats in particular for solutions.

Being hit by the new economic depression, being hit by the upsurge in racism in places like Boston, having to contend with the refusal of the union bureaucrats to break with a racist position on employment and the fact that nobody, including the Black Democrats, is charting a way out of this—all of these factors help to politically demobilize the Black community.

Some have given up hope that there is any course of action that can solve the problem. And a real snow job has been done by the Democrats in preaching that mass action is not the most effective way to struggle.

Like other workers, Blacks are also confronted with social and economic problems that are much harder to solve and require much bigger social forces to solve than some of the problems posed in the earlier fights. It takes greater power and a higher level of organization to mobilize the forces to come up with a solution for unemployment and inflation or to eliminate de facto segregation than it took to bring about the end of the Jim Crow system.

Big questions are being posed today, and big social forces will have to be put into motion to successfully defend the interests of the workers and oppressed nationalities. In fact, to fully defend these interests it will take nothing less than a socialist revolution.

Given this fact, many people are beginning to look to socialists for answers. It will be our job to provide such answers not only by getting out our socialist program, but also by projecting a strategy that will move the struggle of Black people forward. This requires actions in response to the racist offensive; actions that can renew confidence in the ability of the Black community to unite in struggle. A good example of the type of action that will help to do this was the May 17 demonstration in Boston.

Our orientation as a party must be to reach out to those layers of the Black community who are willing to move against the racist offensive, willing to take the initial steps that can chart the way toward mobilizing and educating the Black community.

The actions and educational work being carried out by the National Student Coalition Against Racism (NSCAR) are examples of the types of activities the party must throw itself into.

Our experiences of working with other activists in NSCAR have brought us into contact with workers, students, community activists, and organizations like the NAACP that are looking for a way to fight back.

The process that we've begun by working with NSCAR has to be extended to working with all types of organizations and movements within the Black community—community organizations, mass organizations, civil rights organizations, nationalist groups, trade unions, and trade union groups—the organizations to which Black people will turn for leadership in the fight against the economic cutbacks and racist attacks.

New tests

We also have to understand that there are new tests, new issues, and new opportunities arising today. Things will be different from what we would expect if we based ourselves on the immediate past.

Those of us who attended the NAACP convention in July were struck with how this organization, which was bypassed by many of the civil rights struggles and disliked by most Black nationalists, is meeting at least some of the tests posed by the current stage of the struggle.

We found ourselves working with the NAACP in building the May 17 action in Boston. Over the last weeks we've worked with them in responding to the racist violence at Boston's Carson Beach. We've worked with them around police brutality struggles, around defense cases like those of J. B. Johnson and Joanne Little. Also we take a similar position to theirs in the fight to defend preferential hiring plans and against discriminatory layoffs.

Some chapters of the NAACP seem more willing than used to be the case to engage in direct action. In Boston on May 17 and in the recent fight against racist violence they've gone into the streets with us and other forces.

We've also seen some changes in their formerly conservative attitude about working with radicals and revolutionary socialists.

The NAACP has broad contacts in Black communities across the country—with unionists and others. They now project extending their work among Black GIs, among Vietnam veterans, and in building chapters in the prisons.

The most important thing about the changes in the NAACP is their correct stand on some of the main questions before the Black community today.

They understand that the current economic crisis is producing an all-out attack on Black economic and social gains. They recognize that a fight has to be waged around questions like affirmative action and school desegregation that touch the general rights and problems of the broadest layers of the Black community.

Their insistence on a defense of equal rights led them to battle the heavy pressure put on their convention to drop their position against discriminatory layoffs. This was despite the fact that forces in the labor movement, the Democratic Party, and Social Democracy who are linked with the NAACP led the opposition. Right now in Detroit they're in a fight against Coleman Young because Young has come out against busing for Detroit.

The attitude of at least some of the leadership on the question of discriminatory layoffs, expressed by NAACP Labor Director Herbert Hill, was that the NAACP could not subordinate the interests of Black people to anybody, not to the labor leaders, not even to the idea of maintaining a "labor-liberal-Black coalition" in support of the Democrats. Hill said that if the NAACP couldn't take a strong stand against discriminatoy layoffs, they might as well go out of business.

Looking at these developments in the NAACP, we don't exclude the possibility that these types of changes will happen to other groups on a local or national scale. In fact we expect that there will be some surprising shakeups, shifts, and turnarounds in various groups and political currents in the Black community. The Nation of Islam, for example, is showing signs of going through some important changes. We should be very attentive to such developments and be open to working with and supporting Black groups that are getting involved in the new fights against racism and cutbacks.

We're going to be seeing a lot more antiracist struggles, local cutback fights, fights around housing, fights around Black control of the schools, lawsuits, and local job struggles.

We expect to see more frameups and police brutality struggles. The cops are bearing down on the Black community in a bigger way as the economic crisis of the Black community increases. We've seen this in the cop riot in Detriot a few weeks ago, in the cases of police brutality we're fighting in Cleveland and other cities, and in the cop murders in Elyria, Ohio, not far from here.

We've got to place a premium on responding to these types of local struggles and where possible publicize and build them nationally. Local conflicts can very quickly develop into national tests of strength, as has been the case with the Boston desegregation fight.

The case of Joanne Little was a good example of how a very localized issue became a case of national significance.

She quickly became a symbol to millions of Black people, and to millions of others, of the type of racist and sexist abuse Black women have faced since slavery. She became a symbol of the way Black youth are denied economic opportunities and then framed up by racist courts and brutalized by racist prisons.

The sentiment to defend Joanne Little was part of the insistence that this type of thing was not to be put up with any longer.

The Little defense effort was an important sign of the growing feminist consciousness, the growing self-confidence and militancy of Black women, which is going to continue to be a powerful revolutionary force.

The widespread solidarity she received has set an example of the type of unity and action that is needed within the Black movement on other fronts.

Our party was able to throw itself into this struggle and it is an example of the type of activity we're going to do more of in the future.

Black workers

When we look at what is happening at this initial stage of working class radicalization, we naturally stress the opportunities we're going to have to get involved in common action with, and to recruit, Black workers.

Trotsky pointed out how Black workers would be led to draw political conclusions quicker than other workers because the experience of national oppression would make them more used to looking at things in political terms.

We've already seen in strikes and other actions how Blacks have transferred the militant tactics and attitudes of the civil rights and nationalist movements into the labor movement.

We know that the union bureaucrats and layers of the more privileged white workers are going to play the ruling class game and try to push down Black workers, Chicano workers, women workers, and other specially oppressed workers, as the crisis continues. We know that by joining and helping to lead the struggle of the most oppressed sections of the working class in battles over questions like layoffs, job upgradings, and so on, we're going to be helping to chart the course for building a class-struggle left wing in the labor movement.

Job-trust unionism, whether it's practiced by the Shankers and Meanys or by self-proclaimed "socially conscious" liberals like Victor Gotbaum and Leonard Woodcock, is based on the idea of maintaining the bureaucracy first and foremost, and the privileged layer in the unions on which it rests, even though this means a decline in the membership and power of the unions they dominate.

This racist strategy of attempting to protect an ever-declining number of jobs at the expense of the most oppressed allows the capitalists not only to weaken the job positions of Blacks, but to weaken the forces at the disposal of the unions. It embitters Black workers toward the unions.

The labor movement is going to have to learn this lesson from experiences such as that of the United Federation of Teachers, where the racist policies of Albert Shanker have prevented the UFT from getting support from Blacks in many strike situations.

Unionists should also look at how Democratic politicians like Puerto Rican Congressman Herman Badillo have tried to use the racist policies of the unions to pit the nationally oppressed communities against the unions. In response to the crisis in New York, Badillo demanded cuts in city employee jobs and salaries to maintain community services.

We say that a fight has to be waged to transform the unions into weapons that can be used to advance the struggles of all the workers and their allies.

We have to enter the battle to get the unions to fight racism in hiring, promotions, upgrading, layoffs, and in representation of Blacks in union leaderships. We've got to get the unions to support Black struggles like the school desegregation fights, defense of framed-up Blacks like Joanne Little, and we've got to get them to enter the fight against cutbacks in social services that are needed by the Black community.

We noted in "The Fight for Black Liberation" how Black workers are concentrated in large numbers in some of the most important unions in this country. We've pointed to the importance of the growing number of Black union officials on a local and union-wide level, and we've noted the development of the Coalition of Black Trade Unionists.

While we take into consideration the racism of the union bureaucracy, we have to understand that one of the chief instruments Black workers will try to use in the antiracist struggles and in the class battles to come will be the trade unions. We've got to look to those unions, plants, and struggles in the labor movement where Black workers are concentrated.

We can expect that one of the vehicles for developing opposition to the bureaucrats will be all-Black or Black-based caucuses and human rights committees within the unions, fighting for Black rights.

We should also look for signs of resistance among the bulk of Black workers who are not in unions, and among the masses of Blacks who are unemployed.

Independent political action

The chief obstacle to the organization of Black people in a fight for their interests is the illusions that exist in the capitalist political parties.

While it has been possible through struggle to wrest some concessions from the ruling class under the present two-party system, there is no way any of the fundamental problems of working people are going to be solved without the creation of an independent party of the working class. To solve their problems, workers must themselves create a mass revolutionary workers' party that represents their interests and that is able to compete with the capitalist parties and take political power out of their hands.

As "The Fight for Black Liberation" states, we don't have a schematic view of how such a party will develop. The first thrust toward working class political independence may come in the form of a Black political party. Or it may take the form of a labor party. We don't know if a Black party will precede the labor party, or whether Black political independence might be expressed as part of a movement for a labor party.

Without making preconditions, we should advocate and educate about the need for both a Black party and a labor party, depending on the tactical circumstances. The creation of either a Black party or a labor party would represent a giant step forward for the working class and would create better objective conditions for building a mass revolutionary socialist party.

Although there are still deep illusions in the capitalist parties and no alternative to these parties for workers to look to, there are important signs of a deepening disillusionment in the Black community with capitalist politicians.

We can expect that as the confidence of the Black community increases and as it becomes more clear that the Black Democrats and the liberal capitalist politicians are not going to do anything to solve the mammoth problems of the Black community, the idea that Black people need to make a break from the capitalist parties will gain more adherence.

The racist attacks on the Black community and other effects of the growing crisis of capitalism will strengthen Black nationalism, that is, they will make Blacks even more conscious of their identity as an oppressed group which needs to organize as an independent political power.

Nationalist consciousness will not necessarily take the same forms as nationalist sentiment did in the 1960s, but it will continue to play a key role in the working class radicalization. It will give impetus, for example, to any moves toward independent political action on the part of Black people.

Building the revolutionary party

I would like to close with some points on building the Socialist Workers Party. When we talk about a working class radicalization and bigger opportunities for our party, we mean that broad sections of the masses are going to be looking for answers to big social and political questions.

More people, especially in the Black community, are going to be looking for ways to fight back, for ways to end national oppression and class exploitation. We can see this in the mushrooming interest in socialist ideas, in Marxism, and revolutionary strategy among Black radicals and activists. That's just a small harbinger of what's to come. Growing numbers of working people are going to be interested in socialist ideas and in our party.

One of our most important tasks is to show that it is the revolutionary socialists who have the answers. We've got to lay particular stress on the necessity of building the multinational revolutionary socialist party as the only realistic strategy for those who want to end the oppression of Black people.

When Leon Trotsky pointed out the vanguard role Blacks would play in the American revolution he linked this question to the crucial role of the revolutionary party. When he said that Blacks could stride toward the dictatorship of the proletariat in a couple of gigantic steps, ahead of the great block of white workers, he said this could happen only provided the revolutionary party "carries on an uncompromising merciless struggle not against the supposed national prepossessions of the Negroes but against the colossal prejudices of the white workers and gives it no concession whatsoever" [*Leon Trotsky on Black Nationalism and Self-Determination* (New York: Pathfinder Press, 1972), p. 18].

Later he said, "We must say to the conscious elements of the Negroes that they are convoked by the historic development to become a vanguard of the working class. What serves as the brake on the higher strata? It is the privileges, the comforts that hinder them from becoming revolutionists. It does not exist for the Negroes. . . .

"If it happens that we in the SWP are not able to find the road to this stratum, then we are not worthy at all. The permanent revolution and all the rest would be only a lie" [p. 43].

We stand on his words. Looking at our involvement in antiracist struggles—our response to the racist offensive, the growth we've had in Black membership, the political clarity on the Black struggle we maintain against all other tendencies—we see these things as crucial to whether or not our party is going to fulfill its historic responsibilities.

If we're going to make the turn proposed by "Prospects for Socialism in America" and "The Fight for Black Liberation," this means becoming known even more as the party of uncompromising, merciless struggle against racism. We're going to be known as the party that's going to be in the streets fighting for desegregation, in Boston and around the country, that will be fighting against police brutality, that supports workers' struggles, that supports the fight in District One, that defends Joanne Little and other framed-up Blacks, that is fighting alongside the SEEK students, the students at Brown University in Rhode Island, and all the other cutback fighters.

Our party is going to be on the front lines of the fight in the labor movement against the reactionary positions of the bureaucrats on discriminatory layoffs, fighting to make the labor movement see every struggle of Black people as its struggle.

Our party is going to be fighting alongside of groups like the NAACP and NSCAR to push back racism in the schools, housing, jobs, and to stop cutbacks and frameups.

The course we project in coming out of this convention is going to make us a party that not only supports these struggles but one whose members are more and more their leading fighters. We're finding more Black people who want to fight and are looking to us to provide a way to fight effectively. So, coming out of this convention we will be doing everything we can to build more branches of our party in Black communities, to bring larger numbers of Black militants into our party, and to deepen the involvement of our party in the Black liberation movement.

Barry Sheppard

To the Working Class!

This report was given to a plenum of the SWP National Committee in New York City on May 2, 1975.

The purpose of this report is to look at the present conjuncture and some of our tasks in light of the political resolution, "Prospects for Socialism in America."

I'd like to begin by repeating some of the conjunctural conclusions that we've already discussed under the point on the political resolution. In past resolutions at party conventions and National Committee plenums, we have discussed how the various movements of social protest that characterized the first stages of the radicalization had an impact on the working class. We also noted the offensive turn in capitalist policy with the announcement of the wage freeze in 1971 and what that would mean. We discussed the impact on the working class of inflation, the shortages, cutbacks in social services, and other economic shocks; of political shocks, like the developments around Watergate; and of the racist offensive on education, housing, and jobs against the minority sectors of the working class.

Now, with the impact of the depression, the development of the radicalization has reached a qualitatively new point in terms of the consciousness of the working class. Today growing numbers of American workers sense that they are faced, not just with a temporary conjunctural economic depression, but with a more enduring social crisis. And given the economic and political perspectives of American capitalism that were outlined in the political resolution, the layer that feels that way is going to grow.

It is one thing for workers to go through temporary adversity and feel, "Well, we may be in a depression now but it's all going to work out in the future and we'll be able to make up for it." It's another thing to begin to think, "No, I'm not sure at all about the future, or whether I can maintain my standard of living over the long run." That consciousness has begun to develop in layers of the American working class, on top of the deep distrust in the government that developed previously.

As workers begin to feel that the system cannot adequately deliver the goods, their fundamental outlook shifts. That is what we're beginning to see. So, we're at the beginning of a new stage in the development of political consciousness in the working class.

The resolution also points out that we're not yet at the stage where a class-struggle left wing has begun to be formed in the unions. That is, we do not yet have the leadership formation crystallizing in the unions that could chart a clear class-struggle course defending labor's gains, a course of labor leading social movements and breaking politically with the parties of the capitalist class. We're at the beginning of the radicalization of the working class. But it's a new beginning; it's not merely an extension of what we have talked about in past resolutions—of the impact on the workers' attitudes of the various social protests occurring in society—but a new and different stage that we've just begun to enter. And while we do not predict the tempo of the development of the radicalization of the working class, the clear direction is that it's going to get deeper.

The party has already begun to orient to the new tasks posed by this new stage. This can be seen in the work of the branches, although it's uneven between one branch and another, and in different aspects of work within any one branch. It is shown in the nature of some of the election campaign meetings we have had. Branches on the East Coast and some of the Midwest branches oriented toward the big action for jobs on April 26. There are a number of good examples of trade union fractions finding more opportunities for party work. And the desegregation struggle in Boston is one of the clearest reflections of the new openings that exist and the ability of the party to throw itself into the new tasks.

What we've got to do now is to consciously generalize what we have begun to do and to understand the turn we are making.

We are in the process of making a turn in party activities, in branch priorities, and in how we organize our work. In one way this turn will seem to be a continuation of the things that we have begun to do already. But it is correct to call it a turn because we are talking about consciously organizing this work in a new way and generalizing it to all the branches.

This turn is based on all the work we've done up till now. We're not saying we've made some big mistake that we have to correct. It's not that kind of turn. It's a turn toward new opportunities based on what we've done up to the present and what we can anticipate coming in the future. And it's only possible because of the cadres we've accumulated and trained through the work we have done in the first phases of the radicalization. They will be able to play a new role in the next stage as the working class begins to radicalize.

The key thing to be stressed is not how much we do right away between now and our August convention in implementing the turn, although there are going to be some adjustments. Our first task is to prepare the whole membership, through the preconvention discussion, so that we can come out of the convention as a united party that understands the new stage of the radicalization, understands the new tasks, and is ready to carry them out in the way we do everything, as a united campaign party.

What the turn is not

Maybe it would be best, in discussing what this turn is, to begin with what it is not. We're not proposing a colonization in the unions of the type that was carried out after the 1940 fight with the petty-bourgeois opposition [see *The Struggle for a Proletarian Party* by James P. Cannon (New York: Pathfinder Press, 1972)]. We have no internal problems such as exploded in the party at that time. As a matter of fact we have a rather healthy and united cadre.

Nor are we proposing some special, esoteric "tactic" for the next stage as workers begin to radicalize. We do not say that now we've got to sit down and think of some special gimmick, "tactic," or shortcut for building the party in the period ahead.

We're not saying that there is a big opening in any particular industry or union that we should throw ourselves into, at this point. We make no predictions about when or how fast such things will happen; when they do I think we'll know how to respond to them.

We are not proposing a narrow union orientation, turning our backs on the struggles of Blacks, women, or other layers, or concerning ourselves only with economic questions. On the contrary, as the political resolution points out, all of these struggles are essential aspects of the coming big battles of the working class.

What the new stage means is that we have increased opportunities to do political work, party building work, in wider sections of the working class, including the unions and the communities of the oppressed minorities. This is the opposite of economism or workerism. You know, one of the positive features of the way in which this radicalization has developed was reflected in the party. We were able to deal politically with workerism as a current before we reached this stage of the radicalization. That's valuable. If we hadn't we would be obliged to have a different kind of discussion here, one that would be much more confusing, and we wouldn't be able to concentrate and center our attention on the real opportunities and real tasks that we have before us. One thing that has been reflected at this plenum is basic agreement over the programmatic section of the political resolution, a very important section. So we have the advantage that workerism is not in our way now.

I want to read a paragraph from the political resolution that paraphrases the 1965 organization resolution on our proletarian orientation. It says, "The proletarian orientation means concerted, systematic work to root the party in all sectors of the mass movement and to recruit the most capable cadres to the party. It means work in labor organizations, in industry and among the unemployed, in the political organizations of the oppressed minorities, in the struggle for women's liberation, and in the student movement." Then the resolution points out that our work among students is carried out through collaboration with the YSA, and there is a continuing and deepening potential for the YSA among students.

The new stage of the radicalization means that the party has new opportunities to deepen its work in the much wider mass movements, among Blacks, Chicanos, Puerto Ricans, the unemployed, in the unions, in industries—in the whole working class. This means taking our general party work, the party campaigns as they develop out of the issues that are raised in the class struggle itself, into wider sectors of the mass movement.

Our work in the unions is going to help lay the programmatic foundations for the future development of a class-struggle left wing in the union movement. That is, our work to build a class-struggle left wing in the unions is at the stage of propaganda, not primarily agitation or organization. The work that we will be projecting will help step up that propaganda activity, make it more systematic, looking forward to the formation of a class-struggle left wing in the unions.

The campus and high school fractions are key to building the YSA. The YSA doesn't have a special "campus tactic" in its work. The campuses and high schools are the main arena of YSA work. That's the arena where the YSA is recruiting and carrying out its political campaigns; that's the milieu it's taking its campaigns into, and the means of doing that are its fractions on the campuses and high schools. To the extent that campus fractions can be built, the YSA's work in that milieu is strengthened and organized. In the same way, building party fractions in the unions, at places of work where we have comrades but there are no unions, in the Black and Chicano struggle, among women, in other mass struggles, will help the branches carry out the party campaigns in the coming period, and prepare us for bigger things to come.

There are many examples in the party of increased opportunities for political work in the unions in the recent period. For example, in Chicago we have a small fraction in an AFSCME local. Our comrades became known as builders of the union in some fights in the past period. These comrades helped organize a union committee to support the fight in Boston against the racists, and got a union bus to come to the December 14 demonstration; sold our press and subscriptions in that local, brought contacts to educational conferences, and won campaign supporters to Willie Mae Reid's mayoral campaign. They even took the initiative to organize an informal discussion for Willie Mae in the cafeteria where the workers eat.

We have another small group of AFSCME comrades in Philadelphia who were recently able to help organize union buses to go to the April 26 action. Our comrades on the job in other branches have been able to do similar kinds of things, taking aspects of the different campaigns the party is involved in—from selling of the press, to support for the Political Rights Defense Fund, to the desegregation fight, demonstrations for jobs, the election campaign, women's rights campaigns, recruitment—into their unions or to their places of work.

The branch organizers and executive committees should consider how they can help guide comrades seeking jobs into important unions and important industries in their cities. They have to think through the industries and union structures in their areas, and decide where we can do political work in the coming period. We have to pay close attention to this job. Where we have comrades in workplaces or unions we want to form fractions so they can meet and discuss what they can do, even if all they can do at first is sell the press.

They should meet and discuss how best to do that. It will lead to taking other campaigns of the party into their unions and workplaces.

Now, taking these organizational steps will not be of any value if the branch leaderships don't make an adjustment in their thinking and organization so that they pay political attention to the functioning of these fractions and help the trade union director. So we have to take some organizational steps, change some political priorities, and give greater attention to organizing the systematic political guidance of our work in the unions and at workplaces.

We don't project any great, spectacular leaps forward immediately in this kind of work. We'll make contacts, begin to recruit, and begin to develop our work. We're talking about the beginning of a turn that will develop further in the future. Remember, it takes the YSA a lot of time and hard work to build up its campus fractions. We don't rule out sudden explosions or new opportunities where we may be able to do more work in the unions. But it will take hard work and it will take time to build up these fractions and get them functioning more and more as party political fractions in the mass movement.

CLUW

We should see helping to build the Coalition of Labor Union Women from this vantage point. Several months ago Linda Jenness sent out a letter describing the character of CLUW in different cities. That evaluation of the general problems remains accurate. However, CLUW has continued to develop. It hasn't disappeared, and in fact in some cities it has made some leaps forward. It retains its importance, given everything we talked about in our political resolution, as a Coalition of Labor Union Women. It has big potential as a part of the developing radicalization. And we want to see it grow.

While we've got to pay attention to the city-wide meetings, CLUW will be built and will realize its potential to the extent it becomes a real organization in the unions themselves, and that's the direction of our work. CLUW will be built by reaching into the unions themselves and building a real base of women unionists. Sometimes this can mean trying to build a women's committee in a particular union situation, even if the city-wide CLUW is stagnant.

There was an example of this in Denver recently where one comrade in a teachers' union helped build a women's committee of about fifty or more. In that situation, where the city-wide CLUW is not the best, one comrade was still able to take this campaign of the party into her union.

Job protests

We've seen the first signs of reaction and action by workers to the shock of the depression. This has taken the form of various marches throughout the country, protests demanding that the government do something about jobs. Many of these have been rather small; some have been a little bigger. We have just heard the report of the demonstration of teachers in Texas which drew 25,000. And then, of course, the biggest was the April 26 AFL-CIO Washington, D.C., march, a very militant, spirited march that was the first action by large numbers of workers in reponse to the depression.

These marches do not signify a political break with the capitalist parties, nor do they signal the formation of a class-struggle left wing in the unions. But we do see signs of a new willingness to engage in action. They are indicative of the mood that's developing in wider sections of the working class, especially among those hardest hit, but not limited to them—that is, especially among Blacks, Chicanos, Puerto Ricans, other oppressed minorities, and women. Where these protests occur we want to be identified with them; we want to throw ourselves into them even when they are small, because we want to be known among whatever layers of workers are attracted to them, or think about them, as people who are for action, who want to do something about their situation. We want to reach with our program those workers who are the first to move around these questions.

We had a rather good response to our literature at the April 26 march. When workers are in a situation like that they are generally more responsive to listening to new ideas and to considering our ideas. One of the good things about that march is that all those tens of thousands of workers had to run the gauntlet of all the political tendencies and begin to think about the things the different tendencies were raising. We're not going to escape that, you know, as the workers begin to radicalize; we're not going to escape all our other opponents, from the Workers League all the way up to the Communist Party, from real screwballs up to the important opponents. People are going to take leaflets from them and are going to be interested in what they have got to say. We are going to be a part of that political discussion.

There are other developments in the unions that we want to keep an eye on, indications of changes from the past period. One example is the development in the miners' union where the entrenched, encrusted Boyle machine was overthrown by the reform-minded Miller leadership. This has had an impact among other workers who are interested in developments in the UMW, especially as it has raised social issues. UMW unionism is now a bit different from the unionism most workers are used to. The *Militant* has done a good job in covering this development and utilizing it for general educational purposes, like the article we had on the miners who ran independent of the Democrats for local office. That was a limited experience but we were able to use it to make general points, along with other articles we've had on developments in the UMW.

Another indicative thing was the Sadlowski victory last year as director of Steelworkers District 31 in the Chicago-Gary area. Although much more limited than the Miller victory, since it's in one local area, it's indicative of shifts in moods, things we should watch for.

Desegregation

In the past period we've made important steps forward in the Black movement largely through the desegregation struggle. This is a fundamental part of the turn we're talking about. This issue of de facto school segregation is a major social issue in the country. The fight is centered around busing. It is a national issue, on the agenda in many cities. At present, the chief battleground for this fight is Boston, but it will flare up in other cities. The potential exists in Milwaukee and Los Angeles, and in other places. Racists have been organizing around this question for some time, and not only in Boston. A concerted racist campaign in Detroit led to the 1974 Supreme Court decision that was a setback for Black rights.

The resolution points out that as the working class radicalizes, there is also going to be a class polarization. To a certain extent a polarization has already begun around the busing question. Some right-wing cadres are being organized in this fight. Against the racists, our line is the countermobilization of the Blacks and their allies. That is the basic line that we press.

Comrades in the discussion have mentioned some of the responses to this fight from the other radical tendencies. I'd just like to go over a couple of them, because every single one of our rivals has defaulted or capitulated to white racism to one degree or another on this question.

There is the outright capitulation of the Maoist Revolutionary Union which provides "socialist" cover for racism.

Recently there was an article in the New American Movement's publication that straddled the issue. It sat on the fence between the white racists and the Black community. They saw a "progressive thrust" to the demand of the South Boston community for control over its own schools—that's an anticapitalist struggle, they said.

The Communist Party has been less formally wrong on the question, but has backed away from the need for a countermobilization. At the founding conference of the National Student Coalition Against Racism (NSCAR) the CP demanded that April 4 had to be a key day of action. On April 4 they pulled back from the fight against racism, refused to join actions organized by the NAACP and NSCAR. They held their own sectarian demonstrations, in which the busing issue was absent, and which took up only the question of jobs. Of course, we are in favor of fighting for jobs; that's not the point. The point is that the YWLL and CP *substituted* the fight for jobs for the fight against racism in Boston.

Our participation has been very important in helping get a countermobilization going. If you look back to where we were in September and October when the racists attacked, you can see how far we have come. It took a little time and a lot of work. But we played an important part—from the December 14 demonstration and teach-in, the formation of the student committee, the conference of the student committee, to building for the May 17 march.

This struggle is going to heat up, in Boston and elsewhere, as the schools open in September.

Under the youth report point on the agenda we had a good discussion of the National Student Coalition. NSCAR is basically a student and youth group; that is, it is attracting nonstudent youth as well as students. Helping to build NSCAR is a major task for the YSA. But it is also a task for the party, because of the role this group is playing within the whole desegregation fight. It is the only group consistently projecting the proletarian line of mass mobilization. And the party's got to pay attention to it; we've got to help build it as a broad action coalition. That's part of the proletarian orientation we've been talking about. NSCAR can reach beyond its own forces to the NAACP, and other forces in the Black community especially.

This fight is the biggest single immediate opportunity for the party. In addition to the increased contacts we've made in the Black community through our participation in this fight, we've also greatly increased our potential recruits. As we recruit and get more and more involved in this fight, the composition of our movement will change, and the party will be seen more as a part of the Black community, as a leader in the fight for Black rights.

Abortion and the ERA

Concerning the women's liberation movement, I want to point to two things in addition to CLUW. First is the attempt by reactionary forces to try to roll back the abortion victory registered in the Supreme Court decision. The conviction of Dr. Edelin has been the most important of these attempts recently.

Another struggle developed in San Diego around this bishop who has excommunicated Catholic women who favored the right to abortion. One of the things we should note is that NOW is taking an interest in this, has organized some actions, and has at least talked about organizing some national actions around the abortion question—a step forward for NOW.

Another issue that some of the branches have been involved with is the struggle for the Equal Rights Amendment. And this has brought us into contact with a whole layer of women. The Atlanta branch has recruited out of work around the ERA in Georgia.

Part of our work has been the promotion of Evelyn Reed's new book and her speaking engagements. I understand that she is scheduled to take on the head of the anthropology department at UCLA soon in a major debate. Her tour next fall will not only be financially important and help push her book; it will help enhance the party's position among serious feminists.

Chicano and Puerto Rican struggles

The Chicano movement remains uneven in different parts of the country, and like the Black movement, suffers from a crisis of leadership. Raza Unida parties still exist and the strongest and most interesting developments are taking place in the Texas party.

And as in the Black movement, there is a growing interest among Chicano activists in socialism and Marxism. Again, as in the Black movement, some individuals and tendencies are confusing Maoism with Marxism. At this point these tendencies are not generally joining any of the established national Maoist groups. We can take part in this debate about socialism as we discussed under the Black report, discussing the relationship between the class and national struggles, and discrediting Maoism. The reports we have received indicate that we have opportunities for winning more Chicano recruits in the next period.

These same points about Maoism and Marxism, and growing interest in socialism, can also be made about Puerto Rican activists in this country. This is further influenced by the existence of the island-based Puerto Rican Socialist Party. Four struggles or events indicate the continued radicalization in the Puerto Rican community in the last year. One has been the continuation of the District One community control and bilingual education fight on Manhattan's Lower East Side; second has been the various Puerto Rican student struggles, at Brooklyn College and other places; third was the big Madison Square Garden proindependence rally, held in New York last fall, the largest Puerto Rican action ever held in the United States; and fourth, the demonstration against police brutality in Newark last fall. We've been involved in one way or another in such events and struggles, and in New York have recruited some Puerto Rican activists.

*   *   *

I want to say a word about the interrelation between some of these aspects of our work. One example is the fact that the rightist forces in Boston who have been behind the racist offensive on busing, have taken on other issues, like breaking up a pro-ERA meeting there. Our comrades are going to have to prepare a defense guard for the march this week in support of Dr.

Edelin because of these characters. But this has made it easier for women who are concerned about the abortion struggle to see the importance of also supporting the desegregation struggle and countering the racist thrust; they can see more easily that the racist offensive has a whole reactionary dynamic that spills over into other questions. It is also easier for Blacks to understand the importance of the abortion struggle. Defense of Dr. Edelin will undoubtedly be a feature of the May 17 march. Comrades report that the issue of the cutbacks will be part of this march. Another indication of growing awareness of the connections between these various fronts of the class struggle is the success of two buttons at the April 26 Washington, D.C., march for jobs. We sold 1,400 of the SWP's "Jobs for All, Not One Cent for War." That reflected the real mood in the crowd; it was an antiwar crowd. Second, NSCAR sold about 1,000 buttons advertising the May 17 march.

In all our arenas of work we have three basic educational tasks. We've talked about these before—the suit we have launched with the YSA against the government in defense of our democratic rights; the election campaign; and our press. I want to concentrate a bit on the suit, because this is a newer area and there are new developments in it that have increased its importance.

PRDF

The suit supported by the Political Rights Defense Fund is an important initiative in the context of the impact of Watergate, to expose the real Watergating that the capitalist government carries out against us, against the whole left, against the Black movement, against the labor movement. Of all the tendencies on the left, we've taken the lead in this situation. We saw the opportunity and took the initiative. This has already attracted people to us who see the party in the forefront of an important fight for democratic rights; it's a fight for everyone. And we've already had unprecedented results. Never before has the FBI been forced to turn over some of its files on what they do to socialist organizations. And in spite of the fact that the material is highly selected and censored, it is very damaging to the government.

More than that, this material shows what kind of party we are. That's one of the issues that naturally get raised in this case. The FBI admits it vamps on persons like Andrew Pulley. What kind of person is Andrew Pulley; what kind of people are in the Trotskyist movement? The FBI tries to get Fred Halstead beaten up in Saigon as our presidential candidate in 1968. What kind of person is Fred Halstead? In this week's *Militant* there is a story about Clifton DeBerry. The FBI thought they really had something when they attemped to smear Clarence Franklin when he ran for office in New York City. What did the FBI try to use? The fact that Franklin went to prison; he was a Black man who went to prison in this society. They don't want people like that running the government. [See *COINTELPRO: the FBI's Secret War on Political Freedom* (New York: Monad Press, 1975.]

The trial that will consider our suit is going to be of historic importance. For a long time the government utilized the Attorney General's list as their justification for victimizing our members and supporters. But in the aftermath of Watergate, they have officially abolished the Attorney General's list, and they have a problem in publicly stating why they deny us our democratic rights. This trial is going to force them to state publicly what they claim they can do to us and why. And they don't like to state things like that publicly; they don't like the books open on questions like that; they'd rather just do it and not have it come out publicly. The trial, just like the stories on the Cointelpro papers, will necessarily have to go into what the SWP is and what our ideas are. That's clearly going to be the thrust of the government's attack. The government's going to attack us for our internationalism, for example. Many of the same kinds of issues that were fought out in the Smith Act trial in 1941 where Franklin Roosevelt railroaded eighteen of our leaders to prison are going to be brought out in this one too. But this time we are suing the government. For the first time in history they are the defendants, not us. The trial is going to be important in helping to explain what the party is and what the party's program is, why the government is going after the SWP. It's going to show the party not only as a fighter for democratic rights, it is going to necessitate explaining our history and our program.

The 1976 presidential campaign

I think the response we're already getting to the presidential election campaign, the response Peter Camejo, Willie Mae Reid, Ed Heisler, and Linda Jenness have received, reflects the general radicalization and the beginning of the radicalization of the working class that we've been talking about. They are reaching wider audiences, finding a wider response at street rallies, at unemployment lines. We want to continue these sorts of campaign activities in addition to others, including plant gate meetings, speaking before union meetings, etc. We've already distributed campaign material rather widely, especially the "Bill of Rights for Working People." Our first printing of a quarter million is gone; most have been distributed to working people, and it has met with a good response.

Willie Mae Reid's campaign this spring for mayor of Chicago also indicated the potential and possibilities we have. This campaign was able to reach significantly more people on the streets, with sound trucks and other devices. I hope some of the Chicago people will discuss this because I think all the local campaigns can learn from the Chicago experiences.

The election campaign is one of our major tools to raise the program of the party before many, many more workers, Blacks, Chicanos, women, and students than we could otherwise do. We can't look at the campaign routinely and simply repeat how we've organized past campaigns. We have to meet the potential to reach out to wider audiences with this campaign, given the general situation we've been talking about. People brought around the campaign can be involved in campaign committees and campaign work.

The Militant

Our other weapon is our press. Through the sales campaigns we've made important progress in improving our sales to Blacks and other oppressed nationalities in the past period. The letters column also shows the continued impact the *Militant* has had in prisons as the process of the radicalization there continues, and among GIs. An area of improvement which we now have to pay serious attention to is the regularization of sales at workplaces and unemployment lines, in addition to keeping them up in the Black community and other places. This is something we must work on.

Through our sales campaigns we've made real gains in regularizing our sales and utilization of the press. But the branches should keep in mind the goal of these campaigns. The goal is not to see how many we can sell by stretching every single nerve and muscle of the comrades. The goal is to establish regular high levels of sales in each branch—but realistically set levels, taking into account total branch activity. Over and above such regular sales, of course, there will be times when we make special efforts around particular issues.

In addition to the *Militant* we have another important weekly weapon in our arsenal, and that's the weekly English- and Spanish-language magazine reflecting the views of the Fourth International, *Intercontinental Press*. Since it was established as part of the reunification of the world Trotskyist movement, *IP* has played a central role educating and building the international movement. We want to increase the circulation of *IP*. In the first place, *IP* represents one of the most important contributions that we are able to make in helping to build the world Trotskyist movement. Increasing the circulation will help to keep the costs within reason.

Second, it's important for our own party, for our own education and development. It can attract people on a level which is something different from the *Militant*'s. It adds the firepower of a weekly international newsmagazine to our arsenal. This is unique. There is no other radical organization in this country or internationally that has anything like it, anything near to its level. I'm sure comrades found it very useful in the past period of fast-breaking events in Vietnam, for example, to have both the *Militant* and the *IP* coming out weekly, a few days apart, to be able to help understand what was happening.

Right-wing attacks

Now I'd like to turn to some other tasks. In the recent period we have become the targets of some ultrarightists and small fascist organizations. We can expect that as our visibility grows and our activity increases we are going to draw more attention from these forces, especially as we become more and more identified as leaders in the fight for Black rights. That is a key question with the ultraright in the United States. The racist attacks provide fertile ground for some ultraright and outright fascist organizations to develop. They feel they have some wind in their sails, and some support behind them. They have begun to single us out.

One of these groups is the Nazis. We don't think the Nazis are the future of American fascism. American fascism is not going to be based on German nationalism; it'll be based on American nationalism. The serious American fascists won't be so thoughtful as to identify themselves so easily. Nevertheless, this group has developed in the past period in quite a number of cities and is trying to recruit on campuses. And it's dangerous, as the attack on our Los Angeles headquarters illustrates. We have to take effective steps against them and against the other rightist terrorists who have launched attacks on us or made threats against us in the past period. In addition to the Nazis, we've seen attacks by the gusanos and threats by the KKK.

We've got to mobilize the broadest possible defense against these attacks. Our ability to do this, again, helps project the party as a fighter for democratic rights. At this stage our central thrust is to mobilize support for our demand that the authorities put a stop to these criminal activities and attacks and threats. We can't allow this character in Los Angeles who calls himself a Nazi to openly brag that he can bomb the left all he wants and the cops aren't going to do anything about it. We've got to build the heat under Mayor Bradley and the other guardians of law-and-order in Los Angeles. We have to assure that statement proves to be false. We've got to do the same thing to them that we did to the Klan in Houston when they attacked us some years ago.

Our exposure of the complicity of the cops and the other agencies of the government in these right-wing attacks ties in with our suit. An example is the recent exposure of the ties of the police and army intelligence with the Chicago Legion of Justice which carried out a number of violent attacks against us in the past. The Chicago cops helped organize the Legion burglary of our headquarters; they sat across the street as lookouts and were ready to come to the Legion's aid if they ran into any trouble.

This defense work is important and must be pursued in a professional way, because we can't allow these groups to attack us with impunity, we must organize to put a stop to such criminal attacks.

Another important area of work is our efforts to help the United States Committee for Justice to Latin American Political Prisoners (USLA) defend Latin American political prisoners. The USLA tour of Juan Carlos Coral of the Socialist Workers Party of Argentina was quite successful. Especially in reaching out to Chicanos and Puerto Ricans and other people of Latin American descent. USLA hopes it can follow the Coral tour up and take advantage of some of these gains with a tour next fall by Hugo Blanco.

Opponents

Concerning our opponents, I just want to make a few brief remarks. The political report points out that the Social Democracy is split into two wings. Some years ago Social Democracy in this country was a pretty isolated current. But it has managed to expand its connection with the labor bureaucracy. The two wings of Social Democracy represent two wings in the labor bureaucracy. The Social Democrats USA (they're well named—they are the Social Democrats and of the United States of America) have become the political spokespeople for, speech-writers for, tacticians at Democratic Party conventions for, the Meany-Shanker wing of the bureaucracy. Their youth group YPSL anticipated our plenum by a couple of days and put out a leaflet in New York. They said the Socialist Workers Party is making a turn to the working class, but the SWP is no friend of labor. The proof is that the SWP is against the leaders of the American labor movement. The SWP opposed the strike by teachers at Oceanhill-Brownsville. (That's the 1968 racist strike that we did oppose and tried to smash.) The SWP isn't for Shanker. It supports the Por los Niños slate in the District One elections. Well, that's the Social Democrats USA.

The other Social Democratic grouping, headed by Michael Harrington, is allied with the Wurf-Gotbaum wing of the bureaucracy. We should note that the Democratic Socialist Organizing Committee has taken something of a friendly attitude to the May 17 demonstration and is less sectarian in regard to supporting things like PRDF and civil liberties issues we're involved in. The fact that both these groups have made this connection with the labor bureaucracy increases their importance. A debate was recently held between the two sides in the split, Harrington vs. Gus Tyler at AFSCME's District Council 37 headquarters. It was on what to do about the big economic problems of today, and several hundred workers attended. We can expect DSOC will be more attractive than the Social Democrats USA, because it is more open, and appears to be more left and more "socialist" than the other.

Our major opponent remains the Communist Party, which has deeper roots than we do in several sectors of the Black and labor movements. As we do more in these areas we can expect them to begin to squeal more, as they did around the party's work in the Boston desegregation struggle. We can expect that, and will be trying to find ways to take them on. They are going to grow in this next period, and their influence is going to grow. But we are in a good position to compete with them for radicalizing students and workers.

Just as the Soviet revolution retains an attractive power,

which newly radicalizing people can misidentify with Stalinism of the pro-Moscow variety, so the Chinese revolution is an attractive power which the Maoist Stalinists can capitalize on. The Maoists are not as organized as the Communist Party; they do not have its roots or money, but they are going to continue to attract, generally among the youth, maybe more so than the CP.

The preconvention discussion period

In the past few months the party has been engaged in a tremendous amount of activity. Every branch member, I'm sure, knows that. We've had national mobilizations coming to Boston. We've had a big mobilization of the East Coast and many of the Midwest branches coming to April 26. We had the Vietnam activity, big sales campaigns, many comrades had to be mobilized to help USLA in the defense of Coral; we launched the election campaign; we were immersed in all kinds of local campaigns of various types; we've mobilized to stop the right-wing attack in Los Angeles, and many other things. Plus all our regular activity, forums, etc. So we've been in a period of extremely intense activity which will culminate with the May 17 actions.

Now we are going into a different period in the rhythm of party life, a period of preconvention discussion. The party emphasis shifts now, and we *slow down* on activity and *step up* the important work of comrades reading and discussing in preparation for the convention. This is part of the process of consolidation of our cadre, and of course, in making the decisions that will guide our work after the convention. The discussion in the branches of the documents and the tasks and perspectives we are discussing at this plenum will be useful in the education of the party. In this regard comrades should consider discussing the resolution on the world political situation that's contained in the book *Dynamics of World Revolution* [New York: Pathfinder Press, 1974], whose general line we adopted at our December 1974 convention of the party. This resolution provides the framework for understanding "Prospects for Socialism in America"—the one flows from the other—that the National Committee adopted yesterday for submission to the party.

In the course of our activity few members have had the opportunity to study this world political resolution; and we can utilize this resolution for the eduction of us all. Many comrades have already made a point of how educational the discussion on the political resolution, "Prospects for Socialism in America," will be. We should think through the organization of the discussion with this educational purpose in mind.

With all these campaigns that the party is involved in, it can become difficult for some of the smaller branches to juggle them all and keep everything in the air at one time. From time to time smaller branches can't do it; they have to lay an egg down on the table before it falls and breaks. When this kind of adjustment is needed it should be made in consultation with the national office. That is, branches don't approach the national tasks that we have like a kind of smorgasbord where branch executive committees say, "Well, we like this campaign, and that one seems pretty good, but we're not interested in that one over there."

The branch executive committees are sometimes like short-order cooks, with a lot of things on different burners. This week we may have to concentrate on a tour, so we've got to put the tour up on a front burner and turn up the gas on it, and that means we have to shift sales back and turn down the gas there—but sometimes it is a little too much, and an adjustment has to be made in consultation with the national office. I hope you can keep all these metaphors straight about juggling the eggs and smorgasbord and cooking. Don't break the eggs; consult with the national office when there has to be a major adjustment on a national campaign, and we can come up with realistic ways to do that.

But I want to reemphasize that in the next three months, the activity slows down, the discussion steps up.

Geographical expansion and recruitment

Flowing from the political situation we have been discussing we can expect to find a favorable situation for the party in most cities in this country. Our general perspective as we move into this period is that we're going to be having smaller branches—we'll be dividing larger branches more, and we'll be building new branches in more cities around the country. The limits on our geographical expansion now are limits on our own ability to free up the members and resources necessary to move into new areas. Since the last convention, in December 1973, the Milwaukee branch has been chartered. There are four important cities where significant YSA expansion should be noted: Baltimore, San Jose,

San Antonio, and New Orleans. The first three are places where our rivals have a foothold, especially the CP. At this time we make no projections of where and when new branches should be built, but we will continue to help the YSA develop in these places and some others where the party can expand in the near future.

The steps we are discussing in consciously organizing and stepping up our political work in industry, in the unions, and among the oppressed nationalities, will have many facets and ramifications. One of these concerns recruitment. We're not yet at the stage where we can sign up workers and other new members easily. We're not yet at that stage in the development of the radicalization where recruitment is easy. We don't predict when that stage will be reached; it could be some time off. What we have seen in our campaign and other work this spring though (and it's one of the signs we've been watching) is that we have been generating more potential members from all areas of our work than we have in the recent past. This includes people who don't want to join the party but are good sympathizers, as well as others who would be recruits. Most of the branches report the same thing. There are new possibilities of bringing around more potential members from our work in the desegregation fights, from our work in the unions, and from our election campaigns.

Many of these sisters and brothers are YSA-age and attracted to the YSA. But a significant and growing number, though still a minority, relate more comfortably to the party directly. Some are in their late twenties and thirties. Some are younger workers who, given their life situation, are attracted more to the party than to a youth organization regardless of their age. A worker who is nineteen, has a family, has been working two years, and becomes interested in our movement through union activity won't necessarily join the YSA.

To take maximum advantage of these opportunities for recruitment we have to take steps in the branches to better organize our recruitment work. It takes time, and it takes effort, and it takes organization. It takes talking to people over a period of time to convince them and bring them in.

We don't want people coming around us to slip away because they felt we didn't take an interest in them, answer their questions, or give them something to do. So we must organize this work. The branches should establish recruitment directors or recruitment committees. The job of the recruitment director or committee is not merely to compile a list, although it is important to keep track of our friends. The work of the recruitment director or committee is also to organize the work of recruiting and winning sympathizers. Members have to be organized to talk with friends of the party. Thought has to be given to the kinds of discussions that are necessary for particular individuals, what political questions they do not yet understand or agree with us on. What activities should a particular person be urged to participate in? And so forth. There should be regular reports to the executive committees. We've got to discuss it. Members of the executive committees are going to have ideas, like what kind of class should be organized for a particular group of individuals. And there should be occasional reports to the branch meetings.

For the last fifteen years the majority of the recruitment to the party has been from members of the YSA. This aspect of our recruitment will continue to be important. When YSA members join the party we are recruiting people who have already decided they want to be professional revolutionists. They go through a process in the YSA that helps them make up their minds. They've learned something about the Trotskyist program, methods, and organization. It's going to be different as we begin to attract larger numbers of workers who are coming directly to the party. We should not succumb to the temptation to automatically think that all recruits to Trotskyism should join the YSA. Sometimes I think we've done that, precisely because it's a good training ground for revolutionists. What we have to begin to think about is that people we recruit directly to the party have not yet made the same kind of commitment, nor do they have the same kind of training as someone who has gone through the YSA. Recruiting comrades like this means that we have to offer that training and develop that commitment inside the party. That presents a different challenge, another organizational responsibility that we have to deal with. It means that when people join, special attention has to be paid in integrating them into party work, teaching them, and learning from their experiences in the class struggle.

We're a party of activists, and we want to build an activist party. Within that framework, we have to understand that recruiting from a wider layer is going to entail some adjustments. We have to be flexible and realize that different people have different personal obligations and can make different contributions to the party. The atmosphere we want to develop in the party is that all who want to pitch in and build the party are welcome and encouraged to join.

Flowing from this plenum the thing to remember is that the central immediate task in making the turn we are projecting is to discuss it thoroughly in the preconvention discussion that will prepare us to really move forward in the fall of 1975 and the spring of 1976. It would be wrong to think that the way to make this turn is to jump in the sailboat, grab the rudder, and yank like hell on it. You might find that the boat gives a violent lurch, the boom comes across, knocks you in the back of the head and into the water, leaving the boat to flounder around in the wind with no direction at all. What we want to do in making this turn smoothly is to take the whole boat with us.

So our key job is not so much what we can do immediately in implementing and generalizing the turn we have been discussing, but in absorbing it and discussing it. As the leadership of the party we must take the political discussions we have had here at the plenum to the entire membership and friends of the party, study the resolution, and thoroughly discuss exactly how to make this turn. We want to come out of the August 1975 convention as a really united team that understands the new situation, our new tasks, and is confidently prepared to carry them out in the fall.

Betsey Stone

What Socialists Should Do Now

This report on party tasks was given to the Twenty-seventh National Convention of the SWP, held in Ohio, August 17-21, 1975.

On a world scale, the capitalist system is entering into a new stage of crisis. We believe this to be a social crisis which is the counterpart, in the last quarter of this century, to the crisis of the 1930s.

At this convention we've discussed the many ways the U.S. is being profoundly affected by this crisis—about how, even with the so-called bottoming out of the present depression, we'll see continuing efforts by the ruling class to drive down our standard of living. We'll see continuing high unemployment, more inflation, more cutbacks, more attempts to make Black people bear the brunt of these attacks, more attempts to make women bear the brunt. We'll see more attempts to weaken, divide, and push back the labor movement. And, along with a growing class polarization, there will be a growing polarization of political views.

We can't predict the timing or duration of the crisis or all of the forms it will take. We can't predict the specific ups and downs of the economy. Nor can we predict the pace or all the forms of the countermobilization of the workers. What we do know is that we have passed from almost a quarter century of world capitalist development generally characterized by expansion to a stage characterized by relative stagnation and deepening crisis. And we do know that in such a period the capitalists cannot allow for raises in the standard of living of workers in the way they can when the economy is expanding. They will, no doubt, be compelled to give some concessions, but their options for doing this are becoming more limited.

Moreover, all the ills of capitalism which helped spark the

243

radicalization of the 1960s are exacerbated by this crisis. There is the continuing threat of war, the threat of nuclear annihilation, the continuing destruction of the environment, the further erosion of democratic rights, the whipping up of racist sentiment, and resistance to the extension of women's rights.

In such a period of crisis, all the rules begin to change. Politics change. The mood of the working class changes. The ruling class response to struggles of the workers changes. The union bureaucrats find they produce more defeats than gains for workers within the confines of their routine, class-collaborationist methods. And the opportunities for socialist workers to get a hearing increases.

If all this is true, if what we are saying about the change in the objective situation is correct, then what is required is a corresponding change in the functioning of the party. Our tasks change. Our priorities change. We make a turn.

Under this point on the agenda we'll be talking more concretely about this turn the party is making, about what the turn means in terms of the day-to-day activity of the party.

The best way to begin, I think, is to look at the changes the party has already gone through in response to the new situation. For already the party's activities have begun to look different from the way they did at the time of our convention two years ago. There are three things we can point to in particular which sum up the changes that are taking place.

The first is the fact that the party now has the opportunity to take part in broader working class struggles—in the union movement, in the fight against racism, in the Puerto Rican movement, in the Chicano movement, in the women's movement, and in a few instances among unemployed workers.

Second is the fact that we are finding a broader response among working people to our socialist ideas. Our election campaigns are taken more seriously by working people. And the program we are campaigning on, the solutions we raise, make more sense to more people.

And third is the recruitment of a small but growing number of workers directly to the party. That is, until recently almost all the party's recruits were youth who first joined the YSA and then the party. Now this is changing. More working people, in particular Blacks, Chicanos, Puerto Ricans, women, and young workers, are becoming sympathizers of our movement and are joining the SWP.

Participation in broader struggles

What are the new opportunities we have to participate in broader struggles of the working class? A good way to get a feel for this is simply to look through the pages of recent issues of the *Militant* and see the different kinds of actions we are involved in. It's quite striking to note all the pickets, rallies, strikes, protest meetings, campaigns, and various organizing efforts we've helped build in recent months.

Let me read you some of the recent headlines that have appeared in the *Militant:* "Boston commission hears testimony on racist violence," "L.A. coalition sets Aug. 26 women's rally," "J.B. Johnson released, thanks supporters," "Colorado teachers march for right to strike," "Texas farm worker drive draws new support," "Detroit pickets want killer's prosecution," "Atlanta public employees win dues checkoff," "Milwaukee pickets say, 'Free Ray Mendoza,'" "Minneapolis rally demands end to police brutality," "Rallies and pickets for Joanne Little from coast to coast," "15,000 in May 17 march on Boston," "Colorado women unite to defend the ERA," "Gay pride demonstrations draw thousands," "Oregon sit-in protests closing of Chicano school," "Racist threats won't stop abortion rally," "District 1 parents press Fuentes reinstatement," "Washington state students, teachers, parents united in fight to 'save our schools,'" and so on.

These are struggles we've participated in building and they're the types of struggles we can expect will continue. We will continue to look for openings to take part in growing numbers of such actions.

The fight against racist oppression will be at the center of much of our activity. In his report on "The Fight for Black Liberation," Tony Thomas pointed to the fact that there is disillusionment in the Black community because instead of making steady gains, Blacks are running into intensified economic problems and racist attacks. He also described the other side of this, the fact that along with disillusionment and the dashing of old hopes about what this system can give goes further radicalization. This is especially true given the rising expectations, confidence, and increased feeling of political strength in the Black community that developed during the radicalization of the 1960s.

More people are beginning to see that racism is more intrinsic to, more deeply embedded in this system, than they had realized.

And they see that a more deep-going struggle against it will be needed than they had once thought.

There are a growing number of Blacks—and also a growing number of Chicanos and Puerto Ricans—who want to fight back, who are looking for ways to unite with others in action, who believe, as one woman put it at the NAACP convention, that "We've got to get back into the streets." This means there are going to be more opportunities to unite with others in action against racist oppression, whether it be in support of desegregation of schools, or against police brutality or racist school books, or the fight to free the future Joanne Littles. And we can be sure that there will be more developments—like what's happening in Boston right now—which will make clearer the urgent need to mobilize the Black community and its allies.

There will also be more people who are going to be interested in our socialist view of the causes of racism and who are going to be looking for a political party that is challenging the whole capitalist system responsible for racism.

I also want to make a point about the National Student Coalition Against Racism. Building this coalition is not only a youth activity. It's an important activity of the party. The Student Coalition has already helped to unite broad forces in the fight against racism and we want to continue to help build it as a broad united-front coalition. We also want to work with and participate in building activities of other organizations fighting racism such as the NAACP. We should collaborate on common projects with various groups in the Black community that relate to antiracist struggles—all the way from organizations such as Operation PUSH, to the Coalition of Black Trade Unionists, to the Black churches and the Nation of Islam.

Trade union activity

An important aspect of the turn will be the strengthening of our trade union work and our trade union fractions. We have new opportunities to present clear revolutionary socialist ideas to members of the trade union movement. One of the best examples of the changing situation is the New York "budget crisis." We've had a lot of discussion on the New York situation, and this is good, since just as the strikes and other trade union developments in San Francisco and Atlanta helped prepare the party for new developments at an earlier stage, so understanding what is happening in New York can prepare us for what's ahead now.

The success of the employing class in making the cutbacks in New York will have repercussions nationally. Every city is going to see its version of Big Mac. Every public-employee union, teachers' union, transit union, every worker who is dependent on city services, is going to ·be under pressure to give concessions.

In New York we have had a situation where the public-employee union leadership totally capitulated to the city administration—fronting for the bankers and industrialists. Victor Gotbaum, the New York leader of the American Federation of State, County, and Municipal Employees (AFSCME), accepted the layoffs, covered up for Mayor Beame and Governor Carey when these two Democratic "friends of labor" tore up union contracts, accepted a wage freeze, and coupled this with a proposal that the jobs of civil service workers be saved by taking away jobs of the more oppressed workers in the federally financed Comprehensive Education and Training Act (CETA) program.

Within AFSCME, opposition to Gotbaum's policies had virtually no organized expression. In the delegate assemblies almost no voices except ours were raised with an alternative to these policies. And there were few civil service employees who didn't go along with the proposal to take away the jobs of the CETA workers. There was also, as one might expect, tremendous confusion within the union about what kind of effective action could be taken against the cutbacks.

Our response to this situation was twofold: First, we went on a big educational campaign, through our newpaper, through public meetings, through forums, through our election campaign, to clarify the issues. We put the blame where the blame belonged: on the Democratic Party, on Beame, on the banks, and on the crisis of an economic system whose logic is to drive down the living standards and job conditions of the workers, and deepen every division among them.

We put forward a program to reverse the cutbacks and layoffs, calling for a moratorium on interest payments to the rich, for an end to military spending and for using that money for massive public works, for a shorter workweek with no reduction in pay to share the work. And we educated about the need for working people to break from the present union policy of support to the Democrats and Republicans and called for the formation of an independent labor party based on the unions.

Second, we, along with other unionists, made a modest

proposal for action. We suggested simply that all those who were victimized by the cutbacks and layoffs should unite to fight back together. Such a theme of unity was a radical departure from the general response to the cutbacks. Frank Lovell told me there was even a story that circulated during the crisis that the union bureaucrats were wearing buttons with the acronym LOSE, which stood for "Lay Off Somebody Else."

The demonstration we helped build on June 28 was an attempt to begin the process of politically educating on the opposite approach. And in the course of building that action, despite its small size, we were able to discuss this important question of united action with many people and to make contacts in the union movement who will help us in the future.

One of our members commented that Gotbaum's strong opposition to the June 28 demonstration seemed somewhat like a giant going after a flea, given that there is as yet little significant organizational opposition to Gotbaum in the union. But his response was not totally irrational. That demonstration represented a challenge to his whole class-collaborationist approach, a challenge that he knows is in the interests of millions of rank-and-file American workers.

The general strategy of the Gotbaums and the Shankers in this period is to help elect capitalist politicians they think will be favorable to the unions, to give concessions where necessary, and *mainly* to hope and pray that the economy will get better—at least in "their" industry. The union bureaucrats don't face up to the fact that we have entered a general period of crisis for capitalism. They are not prepared for it. They are not confronting the problems; the problems are confronting them. This is still true also of the workers. But unlike the bureaucracy, experience can teach the workers otherwise.

What are the lessons of the New York experience? It shows, as other speakers have pointed out, the tremendous obstacle posed by the trade union bureaucracy. And it shows the correctness of our strategy of working toward building a clear, political alternative to the bureaucracy in the union movement, a left wing based on a class-struggle program. And we can see more clearly that the program of such a left wing, if it is to have real solutions to the problems of the working class, will represent a radical departure from the practices of the current trade union leaders.

The solutions and demands put forward by a class-struggle left wing must be tailored to deal with the problems stemming, not from a period of relative prosperity, but a period of crisis, when there is high unemployment, inflation, cutbacks, and exacerbation of racism and sexism. The program of such a left wing must challenge the present needs, prerogatives, and orientation of the employing class. It must view the labor movement as a social movement fighting for the toilers of this country and all the victims of capitalism's brutalities. And this left wing must break with the policy of subordinating the interests of labor to the Democratic and Republican parties. This is a tall order given the present state of the unions. It will take time and further changes in the objective situation in order to develop such a left wing, for what we are talking about is nothing less than breaking the working class from capitalist politics.

The events in New York and the modest challenge of some union militants to Gotbaum's sellout represent only a first round in a fight which will continue. It will be a protracted process, the workers will have to go through more experiences before they lose their illusions in class-collaborationist methods and the Democratic Party. But it is a process that has begun.

The significance of the New York experience and similar experiences around the country is that the conditions in the unions are becoming more favorable for explaining a genuine class-struggle political alternative to the course of the current union misleaders. Comrades report, for example, that it is a little easier now to talk with members of the United Federation of Teachers about the importance of supporting the parents in District One. Some teachers are now more nervous about the opposition of the Black and Puerto Rican communities in the event of a teacher strike. The teachers also have seen that it is those very same parents they've been fighting who came out on demonstrations with them to end the cutbacks and layoffs.

It is also a little easier now to explain to New Yorkers why Democrats such as Beame and Badillo and Carey should not be supported. Shanker and Gotbaum try to make out that Beame is not responsible for the cutbacks, that it is all the fault of the banks. But that raises the question of who runs the city anyway? Wasn't Beame elected? And if he's being victimized by the banks, why doesn't he fight back?

Once you grant the capitalists the right to make the workers pay for the crisis, there is no telling where it will end. As the experience with Big Mac in New York shows, once you give him a finger, he wants the whole hand. First it's a few layoffs of provisional workers, then it's civil service workers, then it's a wage freeze and "suspending" union contracts. Then Big Mac says he needs a higher subway fare. The question is, what do you gain by trying to pacify him? Where does it all stop?

Ultimately, as we have to explain to fellow unionists, it only stops when we create a government which is based on the interests of the workers. But the beginning of wisdom on the way to getting such a government is taking the stance that the employers, not the workers, must pay for every manifestation of the crisis.

In order to deal with the crisis created by their system, the ruling class is going to be compelled to make more and more direct attacks on the union movement. We cannot predict the speed with which these attacks will develop, but the trend will continue. And while we can't predict the pace of the response of the working class either, we can predict which sectors are going to be most militant. And we do know that given the contradiction between the relative wealth of this country and the high economic expectations of the masses of workers and the low level of political organization, that at a certain point the response can be quite explosive, involve rapid changes in consciousness, and readiness for independent political action.

The work we do now, much of it educational work, is preparation for the future. By proposing solutions and class-struggle approaches now in the unions, as we did in the New York crisis, we become known as people who tell the truth about what's going on and who know what to do about it. Everything from fighting within the Coalition of Labor Union Women for a proposal opposing discriminatory layoffs, to fighting for the right of teachers to strike in Michigan is groundwork for building an alternative to present union policies.

I have concentrated on New York, but there are other union activities around the country we have been involved in that can serve as examples of the type of opportunities we have. In Atlanta, for example, our members in AFSCME have been involved in a struggle to save their union from an effort on the part of the city administration to destroy it. We have won some victories in this fight. In the Twin Cities we are involved in an organizing drive to unionize workers at the University of Minnesota. In many areas we have helped win union support for the desegregation fight in Boston and for the ERA. And there are many other examples.

Every branch should become familiar with the union movement in its area, think out carefully where we want to have union fractions, and take deliberate steps to develop such fractions. Union fractions, along with our fractions in other mass organizations, are for the party what the campus base is for the YSA. If we have fractions in the unions, if we are getting to know people in various mass organizations, and getting to know people on the job, it helps us with all the various campaigns the party is building. And, of course, it is a milieu from which we win new members.

Our union work takes as its starting point the broad political questions of the day, outside the unions, which face the workers. We try to find ways to explain the need for the unions to act as potential political organizations, as potential leaders of broad social struggles.

One of the best examples of how union support can be gained for important national political struggles and issues was the National Education Association convention this summer. The NEA convention adopted a resolution supporting desegregation of Boston schools and urging teachers to attend the October convention of the National Student Coalition Against Racism. Another resolution was introduced and narrowly defeated on CLUW. A motion to support the Political Rights Defense Fund was introduced by fifty delegates and lost because of a maneuver against it on the floor, but in a news release at the time of the convention the executive secretary of the NEA condemned FBI harrassment of socialist teachers Evelyn Sell and Maude Wilkinson. Outside of the convention hall SWP election campaigners were highly visible, talking with hundreds of delegates. Willie Mae Reid spoke to the Texas teachers' delegation of 400.

Another point, something that was discussed in a number of contributions to the discussion bulletin, is the importance of talking on a day-to-day basis to co-workers we meet in our union activities or on the job; talking with them individually about various issues, about the union, about other struggles going on, as well as about socialism, and selling subscriptions to the *Militant.* As the radicalization deepens, we can expect to find more militant unionists who will begin to understand that it is not enough to be a union militant; if you really want to be effective in fighting for the needs of workers, you have to be in the socialist movement. We can also expect to find more unionists we can count among our sympathizers, who will work with us, who will support our campaigns, and be sympathetic to our proposals to democratize and revolutionize the unions so they can really fight for the workers.

The Coalition of Labor Union Women continues to be an important area of union work. We have been among the most consistent builders of CLUW since its founding and have played a not inconsiderable role in keeping many of the chapters going. Over the past year, as a result both of the destructive policies of the sectarians and ultralefts and the footdragging of the women union officials, some CLUW chapters have become narrow and relatively inactive. Nevertheless, CLUW as a whole is still alive and, if appropriate changes are made, represents a pole of attraction for union women.

CLUW is having its second national convention this December in Detroit and we can expect that the convention will attract some new members to CLUW. One of the things we want to do at this convention is to join with others in raising the need for CLUW to take a stand in opposition to discriminatory layoffs. The question of defending affirmative action and fighting for the right to equal employment for women goes right to the heart of what CLUW is all about. There are many women in CLUW who recognize this and who will join with us in an effort to educate on this question.

During the fall and at the convention we'll also want to participate in all the various activities that can help build CLUW. This means helping with the membership drive, getting CLUW involved in organizing union support for the campaign to pass the ERA, continuing to carry out educational activities on women's issues, and relating to issues of concern to women workers as they come up.

Women's liberation

Next I want to talk about an area we should give more attention to than we have recently—the women's liberation movement. There are new openings for action in support of women's liberation issues. In particular, the Equal Rights Amendment is something we should focus on, since a national battle is shaping up over this issue. The fight between the forces that support the ERA and the reactionaries that oppose it will determine whether the ERA is passed or defeated.

Already in some areas we have been active participants in the campaign to pass the ERA. In Atlanta we are helping to build a campaign where women in five states in the South that have not passed the ERA can combine their efforts. The YSA in Bloomington helped build an action of 500 Hoosiers in support of the ERA. In Utah, YSAers have been active in Utahans for the ERA. And in Colorado we're working to prevent the reactionaries from reversing the legislature's previous passage of the ERA. Another battle we will be part of is shaping up in New York, where an equal rights amendment to the state constitution will be on the ballot as a referendum in November.

In addition to participating in the fight around the ERA, we want to be involved with other issues such as the fight to defend the right to abortion and the defense of Doctors Edelin and Morgentaler, who are being victimized by antiabortion forces.

In most cities there continue to be quite large milieus of organized feminists. Some cities and campuses have women's centers. There are also Black women's groups, groups of Chicanas, gay women's groups, women's rights committees in unions, campus groups, various kinds of collectives and women's caucuses in broader organizations. The National Organization of Women (NOW) continues to be the largest feminist organization. Some of our members belong to NOW and we have found NOW to be an organization that often initiates actions for women's demands.

We should be familiar with the various women's groups in our areas. Some of them are groups we will want to build. Others we can work with in coalitions. It will differ from city to city.

Women's liberation sentiment continues to grow in this country. A recent poll reported that some 63 percent of all people now say they support the goals of the women's liberation movement. Along with this increased support for women's rights, there is also a growing interest among women's liberationists in socialism. The clearest example of this was the socialism and feminism conference held in Yellow Springs, Ohio, this summer which attracted some 1,600 women. There has also been the growth in some areas of socialist women's groups.

The relationship between socialism and feminism is something that we in the SWP are experts on. Since the beginning of the second wave of feminism the SWP has educated about the need for a socialist revolution if women's oppression is to be ended. And we have been the one socialist party which has consistently supported the building of broader feminist struggles.

Given the new interest in socialism and feminism, we should

make a real effort to get our ideas out, to get out our literature on this, to participate in study groups, to hold forums on women's liberation. In this regard, many branches report that their largest forums are often the ones scheduled on women's liberation topics. We should also take part in discussions sponsored by other groups.

If we do these things, we'll not only help to build the women's movement; we will also get in touch with more feminists who are interested in socialism, including those who don't even know about us now, but are looking for a movement such as ours to join.

Spreading socialist ideas

Next I want to take up another area where we have new opportunities. That's in getting out our socialist ideas through our election campaigns and our press.

In 1972 when we ran Linda Jenness for president and Andrew Pulley for vice-president, one of the points we made was that it was the biggest socialist campaign since Debs. In announcing the Camejo-Reid campaign last December in Saint Louis, we said this would be the biggest socialist campaign since Jenness and Pulley. And unquestionably it is. We are reaching more people with our ideas and we are being taken more seriously by those we reach as well as by the press.

The economic crisis has affected the way our campaigns are seen. People realize that during a period of economic difficulties, socialist parties tend to grow. And they recognize that there is now unprecedented disillusionment with the Republicans and Democrats. Many workers who were not interested in socialism at all a few years ago are now ready to give us a hearing.

One of the most encouraging signs of the openness to our ideas is the response we've gotten to the basic political program we're running on, the "Bill of Rights for Working People." This has struck a real chord. Already, 374,000 copies have been distributed, 30,910 of these in Spanish, and this is just at the beginning of the campaign. The response to the "Bill of Rights" is quite significant because it means that our basic ideas, the demands we are raising are making more sense to people in the context of the present situation.

The national campaign committee reports that we've gotten many requests from people who are not members of the YSA or

SWP to hand out the "Bill of Rights." We've also gotten many more letters in this campaign than the last from people asking how they can help with the campaign. In preparing this report, I picked out excerpts from a few of these letters to read to you to give you a feel for some of the people who are writing in.

For example, a person from Santa Maria, California, wrote: "Dear Camejo-Reid Supporters: The Socialist Workers Party is becoming quite attractive to me. I'm interested in supporting Mr. Camejo and Ms. Reid in their bid for office. Could you please send me several copies of literature, pamphlets, and even a few posters, buttons, and bumper stickers if you can spare any? I may be interested in opening a headquarters later on. Please send me information on how to do so. . . ."

A postal worker wrote: "I received the 'Bill of Rights' and your letter. I distributed most of them in about the first week. The types of people I distributed them to varied. Blacks, workers, and housewives mostly. Needless to say the response among Black people was excellent. . . . Also something of interest to you might be the fact that a postal employee has his own set of political restrictions. . . . What it boils down to is that I am not supposed to be passing out the Bill of Rights on or off my job. To me this is a violation of my rights. I am enclosing $20.00 as a contribution and $5.00 for another 165 Bill of Rights."

From Norfolk, Virginia, a group called People Incorporated wrote in. They said: "Dear comrades, We recently received a copy of 'A Bill of Rights for Working People' and find it an excellent publication and very timely. . . . Active in the struggle in the Tidewater area, we would like to have about 1,000 copies of this publication and would like to know the bulk order price."

A man wrote in from Shingle Springs, California. After listing a large order of literature, buttons, and posters, he asked, "Could you tell me how I can get personally and substantially involved in the Socialist movement?"

A school teacher wrote from San Antonio, Texas. He said: "When I attended a statewide teacher rally in Austin last month, I was handed a pamphlet, 'A Bill of Rights for Working People,' by some brave and heckled soul. . . . Presently, education in Texas in suffering severely due to manipulative underfunding. We teachers have worked very hard to implement fair funding for improved schools, but it seems our efforts are flatly in vain. Obviously, we have been defeated by manufacturing lobbyists. Today I walked into my classroom and saw 180 victims of state greed in my room alone. . . . Frankly I don't agree with many of the platforms outlined in the 'Bill of Rights' you propose, but I can no longer deny that our present system, dominated by capitalist interests, cannot guarantee basic rights. We've 'worked within the system' in Texas and it's failed. . . . I feel your answers come the closest to providing equitable solutions."

Another letter came from a woman in Union, Mississippi. She says, "After hearing of your party, and what it stands for, I would like very much to know more about it, and how I might become involved. . . . After thirty-six years of being under the leadership of the two major political parties, they have become reprehensible. The economic situation in this country is a disaster. I am convinced that socialism is the only answer to this economic disaster."

Another person writes from Green Bay, Wisconsin: "Dear Socialist Workers Party: Watching the TODAY show the other morning, I happened to see two of your people interviewed about government harassment of the party. I was much struck when one of them said that your party is distinguished by the fact that it puts human needs above profit. This seems to me something our country needs to do as a whole; therefore, I would appreciate receiving any information you have about the party and about membership."

And from Oklahoma City, Oklahoma, a woman writes: "Please send what information you offer on Peter Camejo. I will also post a sign on my front lawn which is near the downtown area, if you have them available. Also, can you inform me that I am correct that Houston is the nearest SWP and YSA headquarters, and that there are no socialist headquarters of any kind in Oklahoma."

One of the things you notice about these letters is that these people not only want to find out more about the campaign, they want to get involved. And this is a challenge we have in this campaign. How not only to reach people like this, but once we get in touch with them, how to involve them in the campaign and bring them into our party. It's the one they're looking for.

Already, we've taken a turn with our campaigns in terms of activities that can reach out to large numbers of working people. We are doing more street campaigning, distribution of literature at workplaces, setting up tables at shopping centers. We also are trying to take our campaign into the various neighborhoods of the cities where we live by setting up meetings in people's homes and speaking at community meetings.

Now we should take another step and think out how we can get those we meet in such work directly involved in campaign activity.

We need to ask members to help organize campaign volunteers. There should be one or two individuals on the campaign committee whose task should be to get in touch with and work on campaign projects with volunteers. We'll find that some volunteers will want to take considerable responsibility. They can organize coffee hours in their homes to meet the candidate, or help fix food for a campaign barbeque or fund-raiser, they can help canvass the neighborhood, sit at a literature table, petition to get on the ballot, or speak in behalf of the campaign. In short, they can do all the things SWP members do to help build the campaign.

Fred Halstead made a remark at this spring's National Committee plenum which I think captures what this work with the campaign should be. He said we should organize our campaign committee offices, and our campaign work, more like we do work in the mass movement. That is, we should work together with others who are not members of the party, making no big distinctions about who is a member or not, seeing ourselves as all the same thing—campaign supporters.

One thing that starts to happen when we do this is that these campaign supporters begin to consider themselves members of our party, just as someone who votes Democrat or works for the Democrats would consider themselves a member of the Democratic Party. And we want such supporters to join the party.

Another thing which relates to this is the question of our headquarters. These must be real campaign headquarters, places where campaign volunteers can work and where nonmembers feel at home. We can make these headquarters look more like what they are by putting up plenty of campaign posters. And we should make sure there is someone in the headquarters to greet people when they come in.

There is another side to making our party headquarters real campaign headquarters. And this has to do with the defense of the party. For, if the Klan threatens us, or when government agencies bug or spy on us, people see it as just that much more outrageous if this is done against the headquarters of a party which is contending in an election. It is part of deepening the contradiction they are in when on the one hand they admit we are a legal party and put us on the ballot, and on the other hand they spy on us as though we were illegal.

There has been a tendency in the party in recent years to move toward having much larger headquarters. This hasn't always been best suited to our needs. In many instances it's meant that in order to afford a large place, we've moved to a bad location, or in a dilapidated building. People judge our seriousness by the way our headquarters look, so we want our headquarters to be accessible and inviting to new people. We are now reversing that trend, moving toward more, smaller, and better-located headquarters.

The locale of the headquarters is important. In choosing locations for a headquarters we should consider the turn we are making, who we are trying to reach. For example, the Lower Manhattan branch found out through the experience of opening up a storefront campaign headquarters in the Lower East Side that by doing this, we were able to bring around many more people from that community. Our other headquarters was not that far away from the Lower East Side; just a few blocks, but the psychological distance was very great.

Ballot status is another way people measure how serious our campaigns are. In 1972 we were on the ballot in 23 states. The campaign committee tells me they think it's realistic this year to try to get on the ballot in 30 states.

We want to establish the SWP as a serious political contender in this country, and everything we do—all the way from ballot work, to the organization of volunteers, to the organization of poll watchers—should reflect the professionalism and approach of a party which intends to become a mass party.

One example of the approach we want to convey was the article which appeared on the front page of the *Hyde Park Herald,* a community newspaper in Chicago, announcing the setting up of a new SWP headquarters on Chicago's south side. This article, not written by us but by a young reporter, catches the spirit of what we are trying to convey:

"The Socialist Workers Party, heartened by the local showing of its candidate in April's mayoral election, will soon open a south side headquarters in Hyde Park.

"The headquarters, which will be located at 1754 East 55th Street, will serve as a radical bookstore, meeting hall, and storefront for upcoming political campaigns, according to party representatives.

"'Willie Reid, our candidate for mayor, did quite well on the south side, and particularly in Hyde Park,' said Suzanne Haig, a party spokesman. 'She won 5 percent of the vote in the black wards, and 15 percent in Hyde Park.

"'And in general, we've found an openness to socialist ideas in Hyde Park and the south side, so we felt it would be a good idea to have a headquarters down here.'

"Haig attributes the relative responsiveness of south siders to the Socialist Workers position to the fact that south siders feel the problems that plague society most acutely."

When we run for office, we're saying that working people have an alternative to the Republicans and Democrats. We want to do nothing less than replace the present rulers in this country. And if we do it right, not only with a political program that is correct, and that speaks to the needs of the great majority, but also with an organization of the campaign which is professional, we will convey our seriousness to increasing numbers of people. This is all the more true when workers see that we are not only building our election campaigns but that we are also active in broader movements such as the union movement, the women's movement, and struggles such as the one in Boston now; and when they also see that we have a strategy which can make these struggles effective.

The Militant

Along with our campaigns, we have another vehicle for reaching out to broad numbers of people and that's our socialist newsweekly. The *Militant* is gaining more of a reputation nationally as a paper that is a champion of the oppressed because of its truthful and consistent coverage of such things as the Boston desegregation fight, the Joanne Little trial, the frame-up of American Indian Movement activists, and the farm workers' struggle. More and more people are also looking to the *Militant* for answers to questions raised by the economic crisis, the attacks of the racists, the squeeze on the unions, and the continuing attacks on our democratic rights.

As part of our ongoing effort to get out the *Militant,* we are proposing a sales drive for the fall. Already in connection with our drives this past year we've had successful sales which go right along with the turn we're making. We've been selling at shopping centers, at workplaces, and in the Black community. In this fall campaign we want to continue these activities. In doing this we will try to make sales more integrated with the needs of our overall work.

In addition to the sales drive, we propose a subscription drive for the fall. We also want to make this drive fit in better with our day-to-day political needs. This means an emphasis on getting subscriptions on the campuses, where we work, in Black, Puerto Rican, and Chicano communities where we are active, and most important, through our day-to-day contact with people.

Another thing we want to do is make more use of the impressive international Trotskyist newsweekly, *Intercontinental Press*.

The fight for democratic rights

Mary-Alice Waters spoke yesterday about the importance of our suit against government harassment of our party, about how it represents an historic first. It is a first for us because we are going on the *offensive* against the government. By our action we are showing that it is the government—not us—which is undemocratic, which is violent, which is continually flouting the Bill of Rights.

There is no other party that understands the importance of defending democratic rights as we do and no other party with the tradition and know-how to fight back as effectively as we. In Los Angeles, for example, there are many groups which have been bombed by right-wing forces, but it is the SWP which is taking the initiative to unite the various victims to go on a campaign to put a stop to the bombing. And this example has been repeated many times. We are getting a reputation as a party that doesn't let people deny us our rights without a fight. And growing numbers of people are taking an interest in our suit and are beginning to realize that the outcome will affect the democratic rights of all those struggling to change this society.

Our suit demanding an end to government harassment of the SWP will probably come to trial in the next year and we can expect that at that time it will attract even more attention than it has up to now. It will most likely set precedents for others fighting for their needs. The central question posed by the trial will be, does the government have the right to harass us, to bug us, to victimize us, simply on the basis that they disagree with our political ideas? And in the course of this trial we will no doubt be discussing what are these ideas that they consider so dangerous.

Will we win this case? The answer is we've already won

victories. We've put the government on the defensive. One reflection of the position the government is now in was the announcement by the Attorney General several days ago that they are no longer going to use *agents provocateurs* in the radical movement, that is, provocateurs who urge people to commit crimes. We don't believe them when they say they'll cease doing this, but the fact that they had to admit that this was a general policy before is certainly of significance. Our legal offensive, our success in obtaining the release of incriminating documents, our campaign to get out the facts on what the repressive agencies of the government have done, has already helped push the government back and expose the truth about the government to millions of people. The COINTELPRO papers alone were a great contribution to the education of the American people. So our suit is to make the government retreat on this important question of democratic rights and in the process of doing this it is educating people about the real antidemocratic nature of this government.

Another area where the party has taken an initiative in the fight for democratic rights is through our fight to be exempted from the new election campaign laws, which demand that we turn over the names and addresses of everyone who makes a financial contribution to the campaign of an SWP candidate. This fight has not been an easy one, since these laws have been demagogically pushed by the ruling class as reforms. Nevertheless, it's an important fight because it has to do with the question of whether the capitalist parties will be able to maintain their political monopoly in this country. Contrary to what those who support these laws say, they are designed to keep any new parties, such as the Raza Unida parties, or a Black party, or labor party, or ourselves, from challenging the major parties. They are also designed to help minimize the role of the labor movement in the political arena.

The disclosure laws also legalize government snooping into people's individual political lives and are blatantly unconstitutional for this reason. We can expect that as the implications of this become better known, and as the disillusionment with the Republicans and Democrats deepens, more people will wake up to the threat these laws pose.

While I'm on the subject of democratic rights, I want to mention one new example of a denial of rights by the government. We have word that Kissinger is considering denying a visa to Peruvian peasant leader Hugo Blanco for his tour of the U.S.

in defense of Latin American political prisoners. According to the United States Committee for Justice to Latin American Political Prisoners, which is sponsoring the tour, they haven't gotten an official word on this from the government yet, but they believe that if a big enough hue and cry can be raised about the outrageous and undemocratic nature of this move by the government, that Hugo Blanco will be able to come. So this campaign of USLA's will be supported wholeheartedly by the SWP in the next month or so and we are sure that other supporters of USLA and many other groups and individuals will feel the same way we do and join in this effort.

Expansion

Next I want to take up an especially exciting part of the turn we're making, the expansion of the party into six new areas. This is part of an attempt to create more branches, smaller branches, and to extend the influence of the party into whole new regions so we can move further along the road of creating a truly national party. It's a move that is in consonance with our whole view of this period as a time when we're going to find more people from places like Shingle Springs, California, and Union, Mississippi, who are looking for the nearest SWP headquarters.

Going hand in hand with this expansion is the perspective of cutting down the size of some of the larger branches, so that members can be released to go pioneering in new areas—both in their cities and elsewhere. It's important to understand that these moves will benefit both the larger branches and the new areas.

The SWP constitution states that when a branch gets to be 50 members or more, it is supposed to divide into two or more branches. And we've learned of late that those who decided to write this into the constitution knew what they were talking about. When branches get too big, when they have 50, 60, 70 and more members, all kinds of problems arise. For one thing, it's impossible to organize a branch that size. There are too many people. And this problem becomes especially acute in a period such as we are going into now, where the kind of activity we'll be involved in—union work, participation in all kinds of mass struggles—will take close attention of the leadership.

Another problem of large branches is that it is simply harder for members to participate in the decision-making process of the branch. Branch meeting agendas become too long. And members begin to feel inhibited about raising ideas or questions, since they don't want to prolong an already lengthy meeting.

Still another problem is that it is harder in such branches for new members and less experienced comrades to take on responsibilities. There are always more experienced people around to do the job. So we aren't able to fully tap the talents and abilities of all the members. This is terrible, especially given the fact that the party is not big enough to take advantage of all the openings we have. We need to challenge all our members to contribute whatever they are able to give. And the more our opportunities increase, the more this will be the case.

So what we should look forward to in the future is more branches, smaller and better located branches, and more probes into new areas. There are many big important cities where the SWP doesn't have branches where we will want to expand in the future, cities like Kansas City, Cincinnati, Toledo, Phoenix, Birmingham, Dallas, and so on. To help lay the basis for this we want to keep reaching into such outlying regions with our election campaigns, and through the support we give to the YSA regional work. We want to continue working on projects such as the five-state ERA campaign, and we should help build chapters of the National Student Coalition Against Racism in the regions.

Our understanding of the growing social crisis of capitalism is what's behind our bold approach to the party's expansion. What we are saying is that we must prepare for the kind of period when opportunities will exist for our movement to grow rapidly. It's parallel in many ways to the prospects which existed for the growth of the small Communist Party at the beginning of the 1930s depression. It's not an exact parallel because this crisis is developing in a different way, and as has been pointed out, if we are looking for things to happen just as they did in the 1930s we will miss the reality of what's going on today.

We should think not just in terms of what new opportunities we'll see during the coming year, but of preparing ourselves for a whole new stage of the radicalization which will have quite different characteristics from the one we've just been through. It's quite apropos in this regard that Jim Cannon's new book, *The Socialist Workers Party in World War II,* is about the period 1940 to 1943, a time when the party was planning for new opportunities, which opened up at the end of the war and after. That book, along with Cannon's *Letters From Prison,* provides an example of how to prepare the party for new openings. They are sequels on the organizational level to what the *Transitional Program for Socialist Revolution* tells us about preparing the party politically.

Winning new members

Capping off the changes we are making with this turn will be a new attitude toward winning new members to our party. Over the past few months, recruitment to the party has begun to pick up and there is every reason to believe that this will not only continue, but will increase. Put very simply, we must make it easier for working people to join. Comrades may have noticed that on the volunteer card there was a place to check "I want to join the Socialist Workers Party." And when Jack Barnes welcomed people to this convention, he made a special welcome to all those who are here who don't belong to the party, and he said he hoped many of them will join. This is the approach we should take, to make it easier for people to see we want them to join and to remove any unnecessary barriers to this.

As this happens, we'll find that many of those joining will not have gone through the same political experiences as those who join from the YSA. They will have to get this experience inside the Socialist Workers Party. There are other experiences they will bring with them from their involvement in the mass movement, of course, that many YSA members have not yet had.

Along with the increasing numbers who will want to join our movement we can expect that there will also be more people who will become sympathetic with us, who will want to work with us on one or another activity, but who feel they would be better sympathizers than members. These people can be a big help in building our movement and in the various campaigns we're involved in.

Many of those who will want to join will be attracted to us because they are involved with us in mass struggles, because they see we are in the front lines of the fight against racism, because they see we are effective fighters for women's liberation and that we are the people that have a strategy for how to transform the union movement into an effective fighting force. These people will be interested in discussing with us our strategy for the various movements in which we are active. They will be interested in what we write, in "Prospects for Socialism in America," and in "The Fight for Black Liberation," and our earlier resolutions and articles on women's liberation. They will want to learn about our trade union policy. They will be interested, for example, in studying with us Farrell Dobbs's books on the Teamsters.

We approach our task of winning new members with the firm understanding that there is nothing more important than building our movement. We have to be constantly talking socialism with people. And we have to convey to prospective members what Jim Cannon always talked about, that is the importance of the contribution each individual can make to the struggle to change this society, a struggle that has become all the more urgent with the threats of the nuclear epoch.

In the coming months and years the party is going to be faced with new challenges. We go into this period with a cadre which has the political understanding and programmatic agreement that will allow us to take advantage of the new opportunities. The events of the past year have not surprised us or caught us off guard. They confirm the fundamental analysis of the radicalization we have hammered out.

We also go into this period with the knowledge that we still have much to learn. We have no detailed predictions to make about exactly how fast the crisis will unfold or what forms it will take. Nor do we have blueprints for what actions the party should make in response.

What we can do, and what we are doing with this turn, is to make adjustments in our functioning which will prepare us better for events as they unfold. And I want to end with a final point on this turn. I don't think we need to be afraid of being too adventuristic or of overdoing this turn. Our party is politically mature and there's not much danger that we'll go flying off the track. What we must do is be sure that we make the turn; that we make all the necessary adjustments in our functioning, so that we can be prepared for the new challenges we are going to see in the period ahead.

A Note on the Contributors

JACK BARNES was born in 1940 in Dayton, Ohio. He visited Cuba in 1960 and became a founder of the Fair Play for Cuba Committee. He joined the Young Socialist Alliance in 1961, and was elected its national chairman in 1965. He has served as national secretary of the Socialist Workers Party since 1972. He is a contributor to *Towards an American Socialist Revolution* (1971) and *A Revolutionary Strategy for the 70s* (1972).

MARY-ALICE WATERS was born in 1942 in the Philippines. She was national chairwoman of the Young Socialist Alliance in 1968 and has been editor of the socialist weekly the *Militant* since 1971. She edited the book *Rosa Luxemburg Speaks* (1970) and is the author of the pamphlets *GIs and the Fight Against War* (1967), *The Politics of Women's Liberation Today* (1970), and *Feminism and the Marxist Movement* (1972). Waters is currently a member of the Political Committee of the Socialist Workers Party.

TONY THOMAS was born in New York City in 1947. He has traveled widely in Europe and the Caribbean as a lecturer and staff writer for the *Militant,* for which he covered the 1970 Black rebellion in Trinidad. He is the editor of *Black Liberation and Socialism* (1974) and coauthor of *Angola: The Hidden History of Washington's War* (1976). He has contributed articles to the *Black Scholar, International Socialist Review,* and to the socialist press in Europe and the colonial world. He is a member of the Political Committee of the SWP.

BARRY SHEPPARD was born in 1937 in Morristown, New Jersey. He joined the Ban the Bomb movement as a student at MIT in the late 1950s, and was a founding member of the Young Socialist Alliance in 1960. Sheppard served as YSA national chairman, 1962-64. He later edited the *Militant* and accompanied Fred Halstead, the 1968 SWP presidential candidate, on a fact-finding trip to Europe and Asia. He is now the national organization secretary of the SWP.

BETSEY STONE was born in Cincinnati, Ohio, in 1939. She joined the Young Socialist Alliance in 1961 and was elected its national secretary in 1965. She is the author of the pamphlet *Sisterhood Is Powerful* (1970) and a contributor to the collection *Feminism and Socialism* (1972). She has been director of the SWP's women's liberation activities and a staff writer for the *Militant*; at present she is the national field secretary of the SWP and a member of its Political Committee.

Further Reading

For continuing news reports and analyses

THE MILITANT is a weekly socialist newspaper covering struggles against unemployment and inflation, racist discrimination, and the oppression of women, as well as international events. A unique source of news and opinions, the *Militant* has become the most widely read socialist newsweekly in the United States.

Subscription rates: Two months—$1. One year—$7.50. Address: The Militant, 14 Charles Lane, New York, N.Y. 10014.

INTERCONTINENTAL PRESS is an international Marxist newsweekly that specializes in political analysis and interpretation of events of particular interest to the labor, socialist, colonial independence, Black, and women's liberation movements.

Subscription rates: Six months—$12. One year—$24. Write for information about first class and airmail rates. Address: Intercontinental Press, P.O. Box 116, Village Station, New York, N.Y. 10014.

Books from PATHFINDER PRESS

America's Road to Socialism
  by James P. Cannon $1.95/£.80
Angola: The Hidden History of Washington's War
  by Ernest Harsch and Tony Thomas $2.45/£1.10
An Introduction to Marxist Economic Theory
  by Ernest Mandel $1.25/£.55
An Introduction to the Logic of Marxism
  by George Novack $1.95/£.80